Post-ecologist Politics

Since the late 1980s, ecological thought and the European eco-movement have gone through a phase of fundamental transformation which has been widely acknowledged, but not yet theorised in any satisfactory way. Numerous environmental sociologists have suggested that ecological thinking has come to maturity and that 'ecologism' has firmly established itself as an independent ideology. This book counters such assertions, controversially suggesting that, rather than being the vanguard of a future sustainable society, the eco-movement has become a rearguard battle defending modernist ideals which have largely lost their validity and attractiveness.

Challenging the increasing reliance on predominantly empirical and directly policy-oriented approaches, *Post-ecologist Politics* insists on the indispensability of theoretical models which may help us to interpret societal processes including environmental change and the multi-level discourse about it. Through the use of critical theory and systems theory (particularly the work of Luhmann), Blühdorn reinterprets the eco-movement and devises a theory of 'post-ecologism'. This book seeks to explain why radical ecological criticism has had so little impact on contemporary society. It offers a challenging theoretical critique of ecological thought itself.

Post-ecologist Politics is fascinating and thought-provoking reading for all students and scholars interested in the politics and philosophy of the eco-movement.

Ingolfur Blühdorn is a Lecturer in European Politics at the University of Bath. His previous publications include *The Green Agenda: Environmental Politics and Policy in Germany* (co-edited with Frank Krause and Tom Scharf).

Routledge Innovations in Political Theory

Post-ecologist Politics

Social theory and the abdication of the
ecologist paradigm

Ingolfur Blühdorn

London and New York

First published 2000
by Routledge
11 New Fetter Lane, London EC4P 4EE

Simultaneously published in the USA and Canada
by Routledge
29 West 35th Street, New York, NY 10001

Routledge is an imprint of the Taylor & Francis Group

© 2000 Ingolfur Blühdorn

Typeset in Baskerville by
M Rules
Printed and bound in Great Britain by
Biddles Ltd, Guildford and King's Lynn

British Library Cataloguing in Publication Data
A catalogue record for this book is available from the British Library

Library of Congress Cataloging in Publication Data
Blühdorn, Ingolfur.
    Post-ecologist politics: social theory and the abdication of the ecologist
    paradigm/Ingolfur Blühdorn.
        p. cm. – (Routledge innovations in political theory)
    Includes bibliographical references (p.).
    1. Green movement. 2. Environmental policy. I. Title. II. Series.
GE195 .B58 2000
363.7'0525–dc21   00-032173

ISBN 0–415–19203–X

For Annette

The environmental crisis is in crisis. Someday someone will attempt to establish a career by demonstrating that it only ever existed in people's heads.

(Ulrich Beck)

We here propose to do just what Copernicus did in attempting to explain the celestial movements. When he found that he could make no progress by assuming that all the heavenly bodies revolved round the spectator, he reversed the process, and tried the experiment of assuming that the spectator revolved, while the stars remained at rest.

(Immanuel Kant)

Contents

Acknowledgements

Some time in the mid-1980s, whilst reading the magazine of the German radical ecologist NGO *Robin Wood*, I came across a cartoon which showed a group of school kids visiting a highly secured *nature reserve* which was inhabited by a single tree bearing no more than a couple of leaves. Apart from the tree, there was only a thinly feathered (probably stuffed) bird, and the two exhibits were surrounded by a vast array of refreshment stalls and entertainment facilities. Under the supervision of their teacher, the kids – as a matter of routine all wearing gas masks – were bewilderedly gazing at *nature* with one of them bringing their experience to the point: 'Horrible such a tree, isn't it? Thank god there are no forests around these days!'

Retrospectively, I believe this was the starting point for the present book. A long time has elapsed since. Gradually, my initial gut-feelings about the cartoon evolved into more elaborate thinking. My first tentative theory went through several incarnations and reincarnations, and there were many wonderful friends and colleagues who helped me clarify my ideas. More than to anyone else I am indebted to Andrew Dobson, who has never believed much of what I wrote but whose critical comments and constructive encouragement have accompanied me ever since I came to the UK in 1991. Furthermore, there are Ted Benton, Ian Welsh, Arthur Mol, Frederick Buttel and a range of other members of the *Research Committee 24* of the International Sociological Association. In several different contexts and respects, they have provided me with the opportunity to present my ideas and have commented on my work. In 'my department' at the University of Bath I would like to thank, in particular, Mark Gilbert, Joseph Szarka and Axel Goodbody for their enormous personal and academic support over the past few years. Thanks are due to Milon Nagi at Routledge Publishers and to the staff at M Rules for their swift and professional co-operation.

And finally thanks are due to Annette Blühdorn to whom this book is dedicated in deep gratitude for the past 15 years. Needless to say, I alone am responsible for the strange ideas formulated in this book and for the remaining obscurities, which I now off-load onto the reader.

Preface

This book is an intellectual experiment designed to find out why, after several decades of environmental campaigning, the long-desired ecological U-turn has still not been achieved and does not seem to be imminent either. It is a political ecologist's exploration into social theory. It is the expression of a fundamental eco-ideological disorientation and the attempt to find some firm theoretical ground for the academic discipline of environmental sociology. The hypothesis the book examines is equally simple and – from an ecologist perspective – outrageous. It suggests that the so-called ecological problem was essentially a construction of specifically modernist patterns of perception which have meanwhile become obsolete so that the ecological problem has basically dissolved, with contemporary society being firmly – and happily – on its path into a future which ecologists would have described as socially and ecologically barbaric. This book does not aim, or claim, to reveal absolute truths about contemporary society or the state of its physical environment. It aims to contribute to the interpretation of the way in which contemporary societies construct and process their ecological issues. But contrary to much else that has been written about ecological issues, this book aims to be very clear about the unquestioned assumptions which are part of the set-up of its experiment and which qualify the validity of its results. The central hypotheses of this book, like the *abolition of nature*, the *end of ecologism*, and the *transition to a post-ecologist politics of nature*, are radically incompatible with the hopes and beliefs I myself cherish *as an ecologist*. They are likely to attract fierce criticism from at least three sides:

Firstly, the exclusive focus on the sphere of the *social* is likely to alienate all those participants in the ecological discourse who aim to replace, or at least complement, the dominant anthropocentric world-view with an eco-centric one. For radical and deep ecologists, accepting the thesis of the *abolition of nature* would mean giving up the centre-piece of their thinking, namely the theory of the *natural* being clearly distinct from the *social*, and the carrier of an intrinsic value. Their criticism is welcome, for the ecocentric and deep ecologist currents within the ecological discourse are the *purest* appearance of exactly those patterns of thought which this book wants to question.

Secondly, criticism is to be expected from those who are actively involved in environmental campaigning, social movement mobilisation and eco-political policy making. The thesis that substantial ecological progress has so far not been achieved and the idea that *nature has been abolished* seem to suggest that their long-standing and often self-sacrificing struggle for radical ecological change has always been in vain, and that instead of further campaigning, ecologists should rather indulge in mega-consumption until the not too distant day of the inescapable ecological collapse. This would be a rather pessimistic perspective. It would be quite incompatible with the currently dominant optimistic views of the increasingly successful *ecological modernisation* of contemporary society and its passage into what is expected to become the *century of the environment*. However, although this study calls for considerable modesty regarding the ecological achievements so far and the further political potential of the eco-movement, it neither wants to deny that *some* progress has been made, nor does it aim to disseminate any gloomy pessimism. On the contrary, the idea of the abolition of nature implies that there will never be the kind of *ecocalypse* the fear of which has fuelled environmental campaigning over the past 30 years. This message may be regarded as a source of optimism – admittedly, in a rather dubious sense that remains to be explored. Furthermore, the abolition of nature must not be confused with the end of the politics of nature. In the *post-natural* condition, so I will argue, the political struggle regarding nature and the environment retains its importance. Traditional ecological campaigning will continue to make sense, in an unexpected – literal – way, though. So this book does not aim to discourage environmental activists, nor does it intend to belittle or even deny the societal changes they have already achieved. It merely wants to encourage ecologists to take a somewhat more critical attitude towards their own thinking and activity. I am, of course, painfully aware that too much critical enquiry – and here we are faced with a serious dilemma – might easily destroy the basis of ecological committedness and activism.

Thirdly, this study is likely to provoke protest from those contributors to the ecological debate who insist and focus on empirical work, be it in the field of environmental management, economics, technology, or within the social sciences. This book has been written, and will be read, in an academic and societal climate which is fundamentally sceptical *vis-à-vis* theoretical and cultural studies approaches. There is a general lack of trust in the capabilities and necessity of theory formation and philosophy. Given the almost exclusive reliance on, and preoccupation with, empirical approaches, critics will undoubtedly not just complain about the lack of empirical evidence for the abolition of nature, the end of the ecologist movement and the emergence of a *post-ecologist* paradigm, but they will immediately provide data themselves, proving that these ideas are all ill-conceived. But surely any such empirical evidence will remain relative to the conditions of its generation and interpretation. In both these dimensions empiricists necessarily rely on a set of theoretical and cultural assumptions about nature and ecology which are by no means unquestionable and which are, indeed, the very focus of this book. I am, therefore, not afraid of their criticism. Whilst the theory this book develops can certainly be expected to be able to handle the full spectrum of empirical observations about nature, ecology, the eco-movement and contemporary society's ecological discourse, its own architecture can be measured only against the criteria of theoretical consistency and plausibility – but not against any allegedly more irrefutable *empirical* evidence.

These three anticipated sources of criticism already give a first indication about the place this study assumes within the wider ecological debate. Firstly, it takes an anthropocentric rather than an ecocentric approach – although I will argue that neither of these concepts is really appropriate. Secondly, it is sympathetic to the eco-movement and the ecological cause, but critical regarding the understanding ecological thinkers, activists and policy makers have of their own aims and capabilities. Thirdly, this study takes a predominantly theoretical approach. Rather than generating new empirical data, it seeks to provide an analytical framework for the reinterpretation of established ecological certainties and already existing knowledge about ecological issues. Despite this preoccupation with theory, however, and despite its *post-ecologist* theses – this must be emphasised once again – this book is meant to be a political ecologist's enquiry into social theory rather than a social theorist's encounter with ecology. It has been inspired by several years of eco-movement activism which has always been accompanied by fundamental doubts about the aims, the self-understanding and the usefulness of such activism. It is against this eco-movement background that in this book I turn to the work of major contemporary social theorists, hoping to gain a better understanding of what ecologists actually aim to prevent or achieve, what societal impact they can realistically hope to make, why substantial ecological progress seems so difficult to achieve, and what significance nature and ecology have for late modern societies.

Moving on from this initial self-location, the position of this study within the ever-swelling ocean of academic literature on ecological issues may be further clarified by defining three main points of orientation which provide the framework for the following enquiry. The first is the assumption that the whole of the ecological discourse, in both its political as well as its academic dimensions, is characterised by a profound deficit regarding its theoretical foundations. The second one is the thesis that around the turn from the 1980s to the 1990s, the European eco-movement and ecological thought went through a phase of fundamental crisis or transformation which has not yet been conceptualised in any satisfactory way. And the third is the hypothesis that following this shift of paradigm, contemporary societies are rapidly adopting a style of ecological policy making which can suitably be referred to as *post-ecologist politics* – a concept which I first introduced in an article published in 1997. These assumptions immediately imply the three main objectives of my projected journey into social theory: (a) to highlight the weak spots of ecological theory which have so far obstructed the success of the ecologist project; (b) to conceptualise the crisis of the ecological discourse and explore its full dimensions and implications; and (c) to devise a *theory of post-ecologist politics* on the basis of which we may interpret contemporary eco-rhetoric and action, and predict how the transformed environmental issue might continue to exert its influence on future politics. It goes without saying that in order to achieve these objectives, it is necessary to transcend ecological thought in the narrow, that is ecologically committed, sense. Ecologists themselves are bad analysts of their own aims, strategies and actions. Their theoretical grasp of their own cognitive, normative and strategic limitations is (inevitably) restricted. Their particular self-understanding, social discourse and relationship towards late modern society needs interpreting from an outside, that is a non-ecologist, perspective.

In the three preliminary chapters which constitute Part I of this book, I will undertake an introductory discussion of each one of my three pivotal suggestions. This will clarify my point of departure and sharpen the awareness of the problems that will be discussed in Parts II and III drawing on the conceptual assistance of *critical theory* and *systems theory* respectively. In Part II the first point of reference will be *early* critical theory (Chapter 4), or more precisely, the work of Max Horkheimer and Theodor W. Adorno, the founders of the Frankfurt School of critical theory. What I am hoping to find in their work is, in particular, clarification about the deeper meaning of nature, and advice on the interpretation of human concern for nature. Of course, Horkheimer and Adorno were not writing about environmental problems in today's sense. Nevertheless, the concept of nature plays a major role in their philosophy, and like that of modern ecologists, Horkheimer and Adorno's thinking was clearly inspired by the experience of alienation from nature, and the strongly felt desire for reconciliation with it. I therefore want to explore in some detail how early critical theory's *pre-ecological* concept of, and concern for, nature may help us to achieve a more comprehensive theoretical explanation of specifically ecologist concerns.

In the second half of Part II (Chapter 5) I will then turn to Ulrich Beck, who clearly continues the tradition of *critical* sociology, but tries to update earlier critical theory. In Beck's thinking specifically ecological issues assume a central position. His theory of the *risk society* is a direct response to the unprecedented temporal and spatial dimensions ecological threats and destructions have acquired in advanced modern societies. From my particular perspective in this study, Beck's work is especially interesting because it tries to take *the abolition of nature*, which Horkheimer and Adorno only described as a possibility and threat, as its point of departure. Beck's theory of the risk society also introduces a number of postmodernist elements into critical thinking. It replaces the older model of linear (simple) modernisation by the notion of *reflexive modernisation*. The analysis of Beck's model will reconfirm that critical theory can provide significant help with trying to explain ecological concerns and to understand the ecological critique as they were formulated in the 1970s and 1980s. However, both its early as well as its updated versions get caught up in theoretical inconsistencies. When it comes to conceptualising the way in which contemporary societies, at the beginning of the new millenium, frame and handle their ecological problems, critical theory proves inappropriate. For this reason I will finally abandon the critical paradigm and turn to the fundamentally different thinking of *systems theory*.

Part III continues the project of theorising contemporary ecological concerns and the societal debate about them on the basis of the work of Niklas Luhmann, an eminent social theorist whose overwhelmingly comprehensive and systematic model of contemporary society has – outside his home country – so far been largely neglected. Luhmann's model of contemporary society is, arguably, significantly more powerful than the ones suggested by the host of sociologists continuing, *mutatis mutandis*, the critical tradition. It is, however, fundamentally incompatible with ecologist thinking, which is probably why ecological theorists and environmental sociologists, in particular, have so far refused to engage in a serious exploration of this work. Chapter 6 provides a brief outline of Luhmann's sociological thinking and terminology. Chapter 7 then turns back to specifically ecological issues and undertakes a detailed analysis of Luhmann's work on the eco-movement and ecological communication. The discussion of the systems-theoretical approach leads to a much more comprehensive understanding of the principles, difficulties and the relative failure of ecologist thought than could be achieved on the basis of critical theory. But at the same time, Luhmann's perspective implies the complete deconstruction of the ecologist paradigm. Adorno's modernist *linearity* and Beck's semi-postmodernist *reflexivity* are replaced by the truly non-modernist principle of *self-referentiality*. This destroys the normative basis for any ecological critique of contemporary society, but at the same time it provides central cues for a *theory of post-ecologist politics*.

After the systems theoretical deconstruction of ecologism, Part IV is devoted to the elaboration of this *theory of post-ecologist politics*. This theory aims to fill in evident gaps in Luhmann's treatment of ecological questions and iron out some obvious inconsistencies. It shares neither the pessimism of early critical theory nor the optimism displayed by Beck, Giddens and the host of other neo-modernist thinkers in the critical Enlightenment tradition. Without wanting to be ideologically prescriptive, it tries to reinterpret the contemporary ecological discourse and policy. Beyond this, it seeks to make hypotheses about the future political potential of the ecological issue. Chapter 8 tries to define post-ecologism and distinguish it from its ecologist counterpart. Chapter 9 discusses the most obvious objections ecologists will probably want to raise against post-ecologist thinking. Chapter 10 finally provides a post-ecologist reinterpretation of the currently fashionable and dominant societal discourse and policy of *ecological modernisation*. Like any theoretical model, the *theory of post-ecologist politics* relies on a set of normative assumptions which may be contested. What makes it even more contestable is that it seems to lend itself to being instrumentalised by ideological interests that radically contradict the ecologist beliefs which provided the starting point of this study. But being aware of these dangers, I still want to make the experiment of taking a primarily observing position, and try to devise a theoretical framework for the meta-critique of the ecologist critique. If environmental sociology is not prepared to question even the most sacred constituents of ecologist thinking, it loses its status as an academic discipline.

Part I
Preliminaries

1 Ecological concern and theoretical enquiry

The proposition that after three decades of ecological critique, the environmental discourse is still characterised by striking theoretical deficits does not, of course, mean to say that there is no ecological theory at all. Particularly in the English-speaking world, ecologically committed scholars have generated a plethora of books aiming to establish *ecologism* as an independent political ideology, or at least to provide a solid theoretical basis for the ecological restructuring of contemporary society (e.g. Atkinson 1991; Mathews 1991; Eckersley 1992; Goodin 1992; Pepper 1993; Martell 1994; Dobson 1995; Hayward 1995; Barry 1999). In recent years, these *ecologically committed* studies have been complemented by a whole series of volumes approaching the ecological issue from a more *sociological* perspective (e.g. Beck 1992, 1997a; Dickens 1992; Giddens 1994; Redclift and Benton 1994; Hajer 1995; Hannigan 1995; Goldblatt 1996; Lash, Szerszynski and Wynne 1996; Jagtenberg and McKie 1997; Murphy 1997; Macnaghten and Urry 1998). Although it conspicuously lacks a lasting institutional basis in universities and other centres of academic research, environmental sociology seems – for the time being – to have established itself as an independent sociological sub-discipline, and its theoretical strands are trying to compensate for the 'thin record of environmental concerns in the mainstream sociological theory of the early and mid-twentieth centuries' (Goldblatt 1996: 5). So the problem is not that there are no ecological theorists at all, but rather that their questioning is not sufficiently radical. As Hayward correctly remarks, they often prefer 'intuitive responses' which 'have not always been brought under adequate concepts' (1995: 1). For reasons that remain to be explored, political and intellectual radicalism do not seem to be readily compatible. What I describe as the theoretical deficits of the ecological discourse concerns, in particular, the *sociological* and *philosophical foundations* of all ecological diagnoses and remedial imperatives. As I will elaborate below, these deficits may originate from a kind of fundamental incompatibility between ecological thinking and theoretical enquiry. But if we want to understand what the ecological discourse is all about and why ecological progress is so difficult to achieve, *empirical* approaches have a rather limited explanatory capacity: a *theoretical* consolidation of the eco-debate is the only promising way ahead.

1.1   Sociological and philosophical abstinence

It has correctly been pointed out that as yet, 'the obstacles to radical green change have not been properly identified' (Dobson 1995: 23). These obstacles, in particular, are what I am interested in in this book. Ecological theorists still tend to find comfort in the belief that the lack of ecological progress is the fault of irresponsible decision makers, egoistic consumers and profit-oriented businesses who all stubbornly refuse to listen to the ecological truth. Without wanting to deny that there is some truth in this belief, I suspect that major obstacles are also located on the side of ecological thought itself. A good deal of intellectual energy has been invested in constructing ecological theories as if we were living in a cultural vacuum and did not have to take into account that whatever diagnoses and recommendations ecologists may come up with are both defined and restricted by complex constellations of social, economic, political and other conditions which are inherited, and which leave little scope for implementing – and perhaps even thinking – the radically different. Rudolf Bahro's (1986) often quoted idea of ecologising society by reorganising it into 'basic communes' of around 3,000 people, which would constitute 'liberated zones' determining autonomously their modes of production and consumption, is a prominent (though now dated) example that in much of ecological thinking, 'the social and political context receives no attention at all' (Dobson 1995: 61).

In recent years ecological theory has been trying hard to get more real and realistic, but in more moderate shades, this preference for building castles in the air permeates even contemporary green thought (e.g. Hayward 1995; Barry 1999). Correctly, Michael Jacobs points out that even after the advent of *sustainable development*, which in his view 'has done much to bring the green movement back into the realms of feasibility', the ecological discourse remains 'deeply idealistic in tone'. It is 'based on unashamedly value-laden statements about how the world should be organised' and appears sometimes 'entirely oblivious to the world as it actually *is*' (Jacobs 1997: 5). On the one hand, contemporary ecological theory still displays striking *sociological* weaknesses: in the same sense that the social sciences and social theory may be said to be 'predicated on the forgetting of ecology', ecological thought 'is guilty of forgetting about society' (Beck 1995a: 40). On the other hand, contemporary ecological thought displays significant *philosophical* weaknesses: it is strikingly uncritical concerning the validity of its analytical and prescriptive judgements.

The theoretical deficits of *ecologically committed* thinkers are largely caused by their commendable desire to solve the ecological problem. They quickly proceed to formulating prescriptions for what needs to be done in order to avoid the ecological collapse and pave the way towards a greener future. But they pay little attention to the rules and mechanisms which factually determine the development of late modern societies and which 'seem in almost every case to be working *against*' ecological ideals (Jacobs 1997a: 5). Compared to these ecologically committed thinkers, environmental sociologists seem to be much better positioned for the distanced analysis of the preconditions of ecological thought and action. By the very nature of their subject they pay closer attention to structures and mechanisms that control the development of contemporary societies. Rather than making ecological prescriptions, they primarily attempt to describe and conceptualise how contemporary societies and their political institutions factually respond to ecological problems and crises. Only in a second step do they also try to make pragmatic recommendations about how to respond more effectively. Much like the eco-ideologically committed theorists, however, environmental sociologists normally fail to reflect on the *philosophical* assumptions they are making when they talk about environmental problems, crises, necessities and solutions. What are the normative criteria defining these concepts? In what respects – and for whom – is the ecological problem actually problematic? What exactly is environmental concern concerned about? What – if anything – makes ecological necessities inescapable? The answers to these questions seem so obvious that the questions are hardly ever seriously posed. But these are crucially important issues. They touch upon complex *philosophical* problems which ecological thought, if it wants to be taken seriously, cannot afford to ignore. In the same way that ideologically committed eco-theorists have to strengthen their *sociological* credentials, environmental sociologists therefore have to enhance their *philosophical* foundations.

Contemporary ecological thought may thus be said to be still strongly committed to the Marxian belief that the project of changing the world should take priority over interpreting it. Whilst ecologists have traditionally been quick and strong in the field of ideological prescription, they have been much weaker in the field of analysis and description. The demand that ecological theorists should try to re-acquire something of the pre-Marxian modesty will of course immediately raise the old criticism – which had already been raised against Hegel – of political quietism. Nevertheless, there might be some wisdom in Hegel's suggestion that human rationality is more suitable for interpreting *that which is* than for issuing instructions on how the world *ought to be*. Trying to shift the emphasis – at least temporarily – back to analysis and interpretation may perhaps help us to understand where ecologists themselves went wrong, and where ecological thought helped to obscure rather than clear the obstacles to radical green change. If ecologists really want 'to make the transition soon' and to 'persuade the intransigent, the selfish, the powerful and the uninterested' (Goldblatt 1996: 203), it would seem essential that they become much more self-critical. More specifically, it would seem essential that they get a clearer understanding of the *problem* their ecological strategies are supposed to remedy. This improved understanding of the problem – and not, for example, the moderation of overly radical ecologist demands (e.g. Barry 1999) – has to be the point of departure for the project of consolidating ecological theory.

1.2   The non-negotiability of nature

Yet, since the inception of the ecological debate, there has always been a range of arguments sweeping theoretical approaches from the table. Up to the present there is the notion that 'the optimism of action is better than the pessimism of thought' (slogan on a recent Greenpeace mailshot). It was not just that the environmental crisis appeared so evident and imminent that it seemed neither necessary nor advisable to waste any time on theoretical investigations into its nature. Ecological theorising also tended to remain committed to ideological traditions (at both ends of the ideological spectrum) which were not particularly conducive to the mobilisation of ecological mass support, and which tended to undermine the green claim that ecologism goes beyond left and right. Furthermore, ecological progress and success strongly depended on the co-operation of the media and the general public, and it therefore seemed not just convenient but structurally necessary to avoid too much theoretical complexity. But underneath such rather superficial explanations, there is arguably a much more profound reason for the anti-theoretical stance of the ecological discourse. My investigations throughout this book are driven by the suspicion that the simplifications ecologists offer are not necessitated by external factors like the ones mentioned above, but rather by the fact that ecological concerns and theoretical enquiry are fundamentally incompatible. I will argue below that despite the ecologist insistence on rational justification and transparency, no ecologist ideology will ever stand firm in the storm of rational debate and theoretical enquiry.

Of course, any participant in the ecological discourse will try to produce rational arguments in support of their demands. In secular liberal democratic societies rational discourse is the entry ticket to the arena of public opinion formation and democratic policy making – even though it is, of course, well known that electoral choices, political decisions and consumer preferences are influenced by a whole range of non-rational criteria. Rational arguments may not be sufficient on their own, but they are certainly indispensable if people are to be persuaded to change their beliefs and behaviour, or to cast their vote for ecological programmes. Unsurprisingly, the project of establishing an ecological rationality has, therefore, for a long time been a focal point of interest for ecological theorists (e.g. Dryzek 1987, 1990, 1997; Murphy 1994; Hayward 1995; Mol 1995; Eder 1996a, 1996b; Spaargaren 1997; Barry 1999). However, when pursuing the source of environmental concern and the motivation for ecological activism, any ecological discourse will soon reach the point where it can only refer to the phenomena of existential *Angst* and *fundamentalism*. At the end of a series of *why*-questions, one will invariably arrive at the statement: *because I am afraid*, or: *because this is my irreducible belief*. This is most obvious in the case of radical- and deep-ecologist discourses whose major point of reference is the ecological collapse or the intrinsic value of nature. But, as I will demonstrate at a later stage (see Chapter 7), even for more moderate and reformist eco-discourses whose main point of reference is *sustainability* or the *quality of life*, the ultimate justification will always be *Angst* or irreducible (fundamentalist) beliefs. What *Angst* and *fundamentalism* have in common is that they are pointing towards the limits of reason and rationality – and beyond. Their central role for the eco-movement and in the eco-debate reveals the close connection between ecology and the *non-rational*, that is the counterpart of rationality (which must not be confused with the *irrational*).

In the ecological context, *Angst* arises when human rationality seems no longer capable of controlling the development of the civilisatory process which it initiated itself, and which it keeps promoting. One might say *Angst* emerges where human rationality generates more risk and contingency than reassurance and certainty. Given the ever-increasing difficulties with managing the intended and unintended (material and non-material) effects of progress and rationalisation, nature and the natural – at one stage the threatening enemy of human civilisation – suddenly appear as the comforting and reassuring antidote to rationality, as the cure for *Angst*. They are the guidelines for a less frightening course of civilisation; the sign-post towards *re-embedding* what modernisation and rationalisation have *disembedded*. As Ulrich Beck puts it, 'nature appears as a passageway to *consecrated* self-evident truths; as an endangered treasure[1] of unbreakable rules to be discovered, guarded and cultivated' (Beck 1995a: 53). The attempt to use *nature* where rationality fails to provide a point of orientation is the essence of ecological *fundamentalism*. As Beck phrases it, nature 'is a kind of anchor by whose means the ship of civilization, drifting in[2] the open sea, conjures up, cultivates, its contrary: dry land, the harbour' (Beck 1995a: 39).

Ecological fundamentalism, and fundamentalism in general, is a reaction to the modernist practice of subjecting every established truth and certainty to rational doubt and enquiry. Although well intended, the modernist attempt to base society on scientific knowledge and rational discourse, rather than vague beliefs and superstition, leads to the irreplaceable loss of substantive values. Despite its indisputable achievements, modernisation also leads to the experience of new uncertainties and spiritual disenchantment. As I will argue in the following chapters, this is because the modernist practice unconsciously substitutes *form* for *content*. At an advanced stage, the destructive insistence on rational discourse can trigger 'a refusal of dialogue', that is fundamentalism. As Giddens describes it, fundamentalism 'is a rejection of a model of truth linked to the dialogic engagement of ideas in a public space' (1994: 6). Fundamentalism reinstalls basic values which are deliberately pre-rational, that is not open to rational debate. Beck (1997a) uses the term 'constructed certitude' to capture this more or less conscious decision to safeguard specific certainties by not allowing any questions. In the case of ecological fundamentalism, this basic value is the non-negotiable, intrinsic value of nature and the natural. Ecological fundamentalism does not have, as John Ferris suggests, 'a *large element* of non-negotiability' built into it (Wiesenthal 1993: 4, my emphasis), but non-negotiability is the main gesture and attitude with which it confronts the disintegrating, destructive and dissolving forces of scientific rationality. In the eco-theoretical literature it has become common practice to make a sharp distinction between fundamentalist deep-ecologists and those who do not subscribe to the idea of nature as an intrinsic value. Aiming to strengthen the ecological cause and

---

1 The official translation suggests 'store' for German '*Schatz*'. Unfortunately, the translations of many texts used in this book are rather faulty. Also, English editions of foreign books are often revised versions of the original text. Wherever it seems appropriate I will offer amended translations, referring to the official version in the footnote.

2 Official translation: 'sailing over'.

protect it against anti-fundamentalist attacks and criticism, most ecological thinkers are now very keen to distance themselves from any kind of ecological fundamentalism (e.g. Barry 1999). But the case I want to argue in this book is that, ultimately, the so-called eco-realists are not that far away from their fundamentalist counterparts: far beyond what is commonly referred to as the radical- or deep-ecologist currents within the eco-movement, any statement of ecological problems and imperatives is ultimately based on the non-negotiability of nature and the natural.

At a later stage (Chapters 4 and 7), the issues of *Angst* and fundamentalism will be discussed in more detail. I will want to explore precisely what relevance and function they have within the ecological discourse. In order to get a full understanding of their implications for ecological thought, we need to unpack what the above quotations by Beck and Giddens only tentatively indicate. However, already these preliminary thoughts disclose to what extent the ecological debate, however rational it might try and pretend to be, is involved with the counterpart of rationality. Beyond all *post hoc* rationalisations, its motivation and legitimation ultimately refer to the pre-rational (not the irrational). Its focus of interest, nature, is the *Other of rationality* which is not – and *must not be* – accessible to reason. Nature precedes and transcends all rational analysis. To the extent that the question of what environmental concern is ultimately concerned about, or what the term nature actually signifies, is not accessible to rational enquiry and debate, the whole of environmental discourse may be referred to as a mass-monologue. It is prevented from becoming dialogical or discursive by the tacitly accepted rule that what it is talking about, nature, was given to humanity and was around first. As a *datum*, it is the non-negotiable starting-point. The question of what it actually means *cannot* and *must not be asked*. This is what is meant by the statement above that environmental concern and theoretical analysis are ultimately incompatible.

In as much as theoretical analysis is unable fully to conceptualise the ecological problem, ecological thought is overburdened with the task of sketching out appropriate solutions. Coming back to the issue of pre-Marxian modesty, ecological theory might therefore be well advised to place much more emphasis on exploring its own foundations and limitations. Any attempt to consolidate the theoretical basis of the ecological discourse will have to clarify why exactly such conceptualisations and solutions are not possible. Any critique of ecological theory will entail exploring the incompatibility between rational thinking as the *means* and the non-rational as the *subject* of ecological thought. It will have to investigate how ecological thought seeks to encircle a topic which it cannot reach. How do ecologists legitimate their judgements concerning the unknown? Is not the idea of an ecological rationality a contradiction in terms, and politically a stillborn child? The critique of ecological thought thus merges into the larger project of the critique of reason. But there is no guarantee that this kind of theoretical consolidation can really strengthen the ecological case. It may well be that ecology's 'intuitively' negative attitude towards theoretical enquiry is a kind of self-protection. Hayward may be far too optimistic when he (intuitively) suggests that better theory could initiate the 'ecological renewal of the enlightenment project' (1995: 7), and break the 'resistance to ecological thinking' which 'has remained too easy' (ibid.: 1) so far.

1.3   The false promise of empiricism

Particularly if there are concerns that further theoretical investigation might weaken rather than strengthen the ecological case, the question arises why one should pursue this project at all. The risk of being criticised as anti-ecological or of falling into the hands of those who have vested interests in silencing ecological criticism is very obvious. And even if such allegations can successfully be warded off, there is still the danger of being seen to argue at a rarefied level of theoretical abstraction which is both unable and unwilling to engage with the empirical reality of ecological problems and politics. Against this background it seems appropriate to ask once again whether it would not make more sense to intensify *empirical* rather than *theoretical* research into the ecological crisis, possible strategies for its solution and the obstacles to their implementation.

Of course, the proponents of further empirical research into the causes of and possible remedies for ecological problems are fully right. Empirical research is the indispensable source of our knowledge about the physical environment, the basis of concrete environmental policy making and a main strategy for the analysis of policy failure. Nevertheless, some fundamental scepticism seems appropriate. The exclusive reliance on, and confidence in, empirical approaches is symptomatic of the present era which desperately fights against the label (and reproach) of postmodernism and seeks to defend (or reconstruct) its status as modernist. In their pursuit of certainty, knowledge and truth, the sciences apply ever more sophisticated methods and employ ever more sensitive instruments to generate ever more comprehensive data collections, and ever more detailed descriptions of the world. They hope and believe that the increasing quality and quantity of empirical observations will gradually reduce the necessity of interpretation until eventually, the data will *speak for themselves*. Interpretation is to be avoided. It is the gateway for error and ambiguity. It is a dubious business because it involves the application of pre-existing normative categories. In contrast, the accumulation of empirical data which *are not* interpreted and do not seem to *require* interpretation (i.e. which are taken for the whole truth) claims to provide protection against wrong beliefs and ideological distortion. Empiricism supposedly provides hard facts against postmodernist arbitrariness.

After the collapse of the so-called grand narratives of modernity, the strong orientation towards empirical research is fully understandable. In a way, it can also be regarded as a form of post-ideological modesty. But in actual fact, the positivist rejection of interpretation, which leaves the data in their isolation and refuses to construct a systematic coherence that makes them meaningful, promotes exactly what empiricists are fighting against: it is itself ideological and generates the unconnected plurality, contingency and uncertainty of postmodernism. Furthermore, the empiricist sciences are actually far from being purely descriptive without subjecting their material to any preconceived normative criteria. To a significant extent, so-called empirical research is about constructing a *scientific* case for preconceived assumptions. Consciously or unconsciously, the sciences always make a whole range of normative assumptions without which useful empirical data could not be generated in the first place. Empirical data can never be intrinsically meaningful. Where they seem to be speaking for themselves, they merely reflect the parameters of their generation. The ideal of pure description and the claim of ideological neutrality is itself ideological. This insight is not particularly new, but it obviously has to be repeated much more regularly. The discourses of *sustainability* and *ecological modernisation*, for example, are prominent examples of this truism being notoriously forgotten.

The belief that any knowledge is based on a layer of *ideology* which can perhaps not be removed, but which at least has to be made visible, is the very essence of the modernist belief in *enlightenment*. To the extent that this book aims to achieve such enlightenment about our ecological knowledge and certainties, its approach is – despite its postmodernist appearance – deeply modernist. Any attempt, however, to throw light on the unreflected normative framework for the generation and further processing of empirical data has to confront serious obstacles: such critical analyses can themselves never transcend the societal context and cultural foundations which they seek to conceptualise. A detached outside perspective onto society and the cognitive and cultural conditions of its (ecological) knowledge and certainties is not available. For this reason (ecological) enlightenment in the above sense can never reveal any absolute truths, but has to restrict itself to more or less convincing speculations (philosophical theories). Societal reality, however, has become so complex and the amount of information and knowledge so immense that it seems impossible to bring them into a systematic order and construct a meaningful (meaning-generating) coherence. Philosophers are confronted with a fundamental crisis in their discipline. Empirical plurality seems increasingly incompatible with systematic integration. Philosophical thinking capitulates *vis-à-vis* the chaos. It leaves the terrain to patchwork theorising – which once again opens the door to postmodernist arbitrariness.

All this seems to reconfirm that further theoretical investigations into the obstacles to radical ecological change are really futile and that there is no viable alternative to empirical approaches. But as I pointed out before, one of the main obstacles to radical green change is probably that we have an insufficient understanding of the ecological problem. As if it was aiming to avoid the philosophical complexities outlined above, the whole of the eco-debate keeps reproducing the dogma that 'there need be little serious disagreement about *identifying* what are the problems' because they are evident 'in a fairly straightforward sense' (Hayward 1995: 89). This assumption is most certainly wrong. But a deeper understanding of the ecological problem cannot be achieved by double-checking, for example, whether or not oil spills really kill sea-birds, or whether civilisatory progress really diminishes biodiversity. The important question is rather for what reasons and to what extent such empirically measurable phenomena and developments can be conceptualised as problems and crises. This, however, is clearly not an empirical question. The conditions and reasons why individuals and communities interpret certain empirical phenomena as problems and crises are not really accessible to empirical research. We can only hypothesise about them on the basis of comprehensive philosophical models whose validity, however, can neither be confirmed nor denied by empirical investigations. For this reason, theory formation and systematic thinking remain indispensable, even though they have to cope with the fundamental difficulties outlined above.

At least some environmental sociologists are well aware that empirical approaches – important as they undoubtedly are – invariably remain highly restricted (e.g. Macnaghten and Urry 1998). So far, however, they have been rather undecided as to how to handle this problem. Surveys, questionnaires, opinion polls, focus group analyses and so-called in-depth interviews all provide very limited information about environmental concerns and consciousness. Whatever questions pollsters may ask are simplistic. They can never reflect the complexity of concrete life-world situations. The way in which they reduce this complexity always predefines the range of possible answers. Also, interviewees can give very limited information about their own decision-making structures. Firstly, they always rely on multiple rationalities, and secondly, conscious rational criteria are always complemented by a whole range of momentary and subconscious parameters. So empirical sociological research generally reveals very little about the life-world relevance of environmental concerns and their influence on concrete actions. Yet it reveals particularly little about the *constitutive parameters* and *internal structure* of environmental problems, concerns and consciousness. Hence empirical sociology is ultimately incapable of identifying the obstacles to radical green change and of devising more appropriate environmental strategies. This underlines the indispensability of a theoretical approach.

This brief analysis of the false promises of empiricism picks up arguments which have been rehearsed for several decades. Already in the 1960s, Adorno, Habermas, Dahrendorf, Popper and others were engaged in the so-called *positivism controversy* (Adorno et al. 1969). Until today this debate has lost very little of its topicality. For my eco-theoretical argument in the following chapters, these considerations lead to two conclusions: Firstly, acknowledging the good intentions and practical indispensability of ecological imperatives, I will try to shift my own focus of attention from ecological *prescription* to the analysis of the normative *foundations* of such prescriptions. Secondly, acknowledging the important contribution empirical research has made and will continue to make, the focus of my own research will be on sketching and testing comprehensive theoretical frameworks for the *reinterpretation* of already available information rather than on *generating* more empirical data. Particularly since environmental sociology has established itself as an independent academic sub-discipline, it should be possible to make a clearer distinction between ideological prescription and sociological description, and also between data generation and data interpretation. For the theoretical consolidation of the ecological discourse, the immediate level of reference is obviously not the empirically describable world of the natural sciences but the environmental discourse itself, that is the societal communication *about* this empirical world, by means of which problems are discursively constructed and politically negotiated (see Chapter 3). It is very important to keep in mind that the primary aim of theoretical consolidation is not to establish new societal practices or patterns of behaviour, but to find an explanation – to construct an interpretative framework –

for already existing patterns of ecological discourse and (non-)behaviour. This discourse and (non-)behaviour, however, is very real in the empirical world, and it would therefore be absurd to criticise my approach in this book for refusing or failing to engage with real life and concrete politics. Beyond this, one may of course also hope that, as a welcome side-effect, closer reflection on the unquestioned assumptions underlying our analytical and prescriptive judgements about the environment will make the political recommendations of ecological theorists and environmental sociologists more relevant and effective.

2 Ecology in crisis

Traditionally, the so-called *ecological crisis* was assumed to be a condition of the physical natural environment. Towards the end of the 1980s, however, this crisis in the material world was complemented by a crisis of the discourse which had framed this physical crisis and tried to tackle it. Although the condition of the physical environment and the prospects for its further development had not changed in any substantial way, public environmental interest and concern suddenly began to wane. Concerns about employment, economic growth, crime, drugs and the like, once again took the top places on political agendas. As Macnaghten and Urry note, green voting in Europe peaked in 1989, and green consumerism and environmental activism shortly before the Rio summit (1998: 79ff.). For the better part of the 1990s, however, the environment seemed to be 'marginal' politically, and 'failed to excite conflict between major political parties', with genuinely ecological parties being 'tiny and barely relevant' (Jacobs 1997: 5). Having taken 'a crash course in environmentally friendly rhetoric', the major political parties have 'returned to politics as usual' (Carter 1997: 192). Weidner and Jänicke note that due to 'insufficient will and skill' the considerable *eco-political capacities* built up over the 1970s and 1980s are not being used, and that 'in certain areas there is even a loss of eco-political capacities' (1998: 202). Paul Lucardie suggests that in the 1990s, ecological ideas 'withered away like autumn leaves' (1997: 183). And, finally, Detlef Jahn predicts that in the near future 'the environment does not look like becoming a major issue again' (1997: 181). Such comments, which originally referred to the situation in particular European countries, may well be generalised.

Thus, the ecological discourse itself – in both its theoretical as well as practical dimensions – may be described as in a state of crisis which has neither been properly conceptualised nor, of course, resolved. But like any crisis, this crisis, too, offers a unique opportunity for rethinking and reshuffling the very basic parameters of established patterns of eco-political thought and action. This fundamental review takes place within the wider context of the contemporary quest for social change and societal transformation in a much more comprehensive sense. At the beginning of the twenty-first century there is widespread agreement that modern society has entered a categorically new stage, but that we are still trying 'to comprehend the ambiguous interregnum between late modernity and the early postmodern period by invoking ways of thinking which belong to the modern world we are leaving' (Gray 1997: 156). In ecological terms, the ideal starting point for such a review of the basic conceptual parameters is the notion of the *environmental crisis* itself. As indicated by the quotations at the very beginning of this book, I want to use this concept in a different, but perhaps more legitimate way.

My reinterpretation of the so-called environmental crisis is, firstly, based on the assumption that a crisis is necessarily temporary, that is it cannot last forever. It denotes a state of instability occurring because a previously stable system is temporarily destabilised by internal or external factors before it restores stability by eliminating the source of disturbance or by adapting to the new conditions. So the concept of crisis implies either the return to the former state of normality or the transition to a new state of stability. But in the case of the natural environment and the societal relationship towards it, there is neither return nor stability. Particularly in a context where change, innovation and flexibility have been installed as the highest values to strive for, the term *environmental crisis* and its implications have become anachronistic. Collapse and reorganisation are not a temporary phenomenon, but a permanent condition. The restoration of earlier states of the environment or the society–environment relationship is neither possible in itself and nor would social élites, locally or globally, have any interest in such restoration. Most of the rainforest, for example, is gone, and it is barely conceivable that anyone should seriously attempt to recreate its state of only ten years ago. Anyway, the natural environment has never been a stable system, but has always been subject to processes of constant transformation. Politically, such observations are, of course, rather dangerous. But this must not conceal the fact that the concept of the environmental *crisis* is dubious. Consciously or unconsciously this expression makes assumptions and raises hopes which are known to be unfounded.

Secondly, and more importantly, my suggested reinterpretation of the so-called environmental crisis is based on the assumption that, as a matter of principle, crises are never empirically measurable phenomena occurring in the material world, but subjective conditions which are related to individual and social patterns of perception and consciousness. The constant human and non-human-induced transformation of the natural environment (evolution) implies that our subjective world-view, the patterns of consciousness we employ to process the phenomena we observe, also require regular adaptation. If this process of adaptation does not keep pace with the changes occurring in the empirical world, or to be more precise, if there is a subjective sense that such a discrepancy has occurred, this results in the perception of a crisis. Phrased differently, a crisis is a perceived mismatch between *incoming data* and available mechanisms for their processing. Hence a crisis is a subjective experience rather than a specific constellation of external, physical conditions.

This subjectiveness of crises becomes even more comprehensible if we remind ourselves of the Kantian difference between *phenomena* and *noumena*, that is between our (human) perceptions (constructions) of the external world and its *a priori* reality. Against the background of this certainly valid distinction, the so-called environmental crisis can be conceptualised as a mismatch, not between incoming data and our capacity for processing them, but between *self-generated images* and our capacity of processing them. In other words, the so-called environmental crisis is a (temporary) incompatibility between two subjective capabilities (perception and further processing), and thus an entirely *internal* rather than external phenomenon. Such an experimental redefinition of the environmental crisis places the human consciousness rather than the physical environment at the centre of the environmental debate. It is the eco-theoretical equivalent to Kant's demand for a Copernican revolution in epistemology (Kant 1787/1934: 12). Ulrich Beck would certainly reject any such reconceptualisation of the environmental crisis, but the polemical statement quoted in the epigraph to this study (Beck 1998a: 154) clearly demonstrates that he is aware of both the *crisis in the ecological discourse* as well as the potential of what most ecologists would reject as *ecological idealism*.

However, if crises in general, and the environmental crisis in particular, are conceptualised in this somewhat heretical way, there emerge new perspectives for their resolution which are crucial to what I want to describe as *post-ecologism*. To be more explicit: neither human perception nor the way in which perceptions are processed follow unchangeable patterns or mechanisms. Both are based on culturally mediated norms. The most efficient way of confronting the so-called environmental crisis might therefore be to adapt the established norms of perception and social processing of perceptions in such a way that the mismatch is removed, or at least no longer perceived. For (eco-)political or ethical reasons, one may be inclined furiously to reject such strategies. One may be disgusted by the demand even to consider their possibility. But as I indicated above, I do not want to let eco-ethical beliefs and the pressure for *ecological correctness* distort my analysis. After all, the continuous change of norms of perception and perception processing is an historical normality without which ecologist norms themselves could never have emerged. And it is blatantly evident that – consciously or unconsciously – modern societies are currently redefining a whole range of other basic concepts (e.g. equality, social justice, welfare, democracy, inclusion, work, health) – perhaps mainly to ensure that they do not have to be abandoned wholesale. So the same probably applies to concepts like nature, the environment and the environmental problem. And if such changes in the established parameters of the ecological discourse occur, it needs to be explored which parameters were constitutive for the established patterns of perception and consciousness, how and for what reasons they had originally emerged, and under what conditions they may be modified or replaced. Such a (non-ecologist) analysis will undoubtedly make its own unavoidable normative assumptions, but it might at least succeed in trying to avoid being *ecologically* normative. However unwelcome for political ecologists, adapting the respective social norms seems to be significantly more tempting and feasible (pragmatic) than bringing about substantial changes in society or the constellation of physical conditions. For environmental sociologists, it would therefore be serious negligence not to explore the flexibility (adaptability) of individual and societal patterns of perception.

At a later stage these introductory reflections on the concept of crisis and the various possibilities of crisis management will be elaborated in more detail. For now I want to return to the idea that the whole of the ecological discourse is currently going through a phase of crisis or transformation. I want to distinguish three dimensions of this crisis. The first one concerns the ecological ideology: arguably, the idea and project of an independent ecological ideology has failed and lost its theoretical credibility and political relevance. Secondly, there is the crisis of the eco-movement: it is uncertain whether the movement is in decline or just in a phase of reorganisation, but it is evident that since the late 1980s it has been undergoing a significant transformation. And the third point I want to raise is a crisis in social movement theory: the existing interpretations of the eco-movement do not convincingly capture the current state of the societal debate on the environment.

In all three respects I want to make an important strategic simplification: Strictly speaking, it is of course not possible to speak of *the* ecological discourse, *the* eco-movement, or eco-movement theory in the singular, that is as if they were homogenous and clearly discernible entities. Such concepts (or entities) are academic constructions (simplifications) which seek to forge a coherent identity from a diversity of more or less overlapping strands. And in the same sense that it is dubious to speak of *the* ecological discourse or *the* eco-movement, it is of course also dubious to speak of a crisis in *the* eco-movement or ecological theory as a whole. Nevertheless, for the purposes of my argument this simplification is still useful and legitimate. In the section on *the non-negotiability of nature* (Section 1.2) I have already indicated why the ecological discourse, despite its manifold currents, may be considered as a 'mass-monologue'. In the course of the following chapters I will provide more evidence that in certain respects, *the various ecological currents all rely on shared foundations*. It is specifically these shared foundations which provide the basis for my own distinction between an *ecologist* and a *post-ecologist* paradigm. The turn towards post-ecologist thinking and politics implies the undermining and dissolution of characteristics which are most visible in radical- or deep-*ecologist* thinking in the narrow sense, but which are, arguably, *common to most or even all of the multiple currents* which environmental sociologists normally prefer to keep separate from each other. In order to extrapolate these common foundations and their decline, it seems not only legitimate but actually very helpful to take a macro- rather than a micro-perspective.

What I want to say about the crisis of ecological ideology formation, the eco-movement and eco-movement theory is neither radically new, nor in every detail essential for my argument in the following chapters. Given that the thesis of this crisis or transformation is one of the central assumptions in this book, it seemed appropriate that as part of these preliminary investigations I should outline where and how it actually surfaces. Strictly speaking, however, *the general fact* of this crisis or transformation (which became fully visible in the first half of the 1990s) is much more important than *the details of its appearance*. Readers who are prepared to accept this general fact – even if they might disagree on parts of my description – may therefore wish to proceed from here directly to Section 2.3 (or even the next chapter) where I will try to establish a platform from where the ecologist paradigm may be transcended towards *post-ecologist* thinking and politics.

2.1   An ecological ideology?

Ever since the emergence of the ecological debate and the claim that greens are neither right nor left but 'ahead', there has been uncertainty to what extent – or whether at all – green thinking qualifies as an ideology in its own right. As Petra Kelly once pointed out, greens do not intend to offer a 'ready-made ideology' because 'all too often in the past, we have seen the ways in which ready-made ideologies have led to destruction and aggression' (1984: 22). Indeed, most Green Parties and environmental NGOs have studiously been trying to adopt a non-ideological stance because this was – and still is – widely regarded as 'almost certainly the only way to wield any influence at all' (Jacobs 1997a: 15). Nevertheless, in order to give the ecological movement and the ecological restructuring of society coherence, orientation, motivation and endurance, a solid ideological basis seemed to be indispensable.

According to Dobson, the precondition for such an ecological ideology to emerge is the availability of three basic ingredients: first, 'an analytical description of society', that is a diagnosis providing the background against which political prescriptions may be formulated; second, a vision, a social utopia 'employing beliefs about the human condition that sustain and reproduce views about the nature of the prescribed society'; and third, 'a programme for political action' showing 'how to get from the society we presently inhabit to the one prescribed by the ideology in question' (Dobson 1995: 2). At one stage, all three of these ingredients seemed to be readily available, and as the existing socialist and capitalist systems appeared to be equally destructive to the environment, *ecologism* was hailed as the ideology of the future. Andy Dobson's *Green Political Thought*, which is certainly one of the most widely read texts on the issue, therefore presents ecologism as a 'political ideology in its own right' (1995: 9). In a similar vein, Klaus Eder, for example, enthusiastically suggests that the ideology of ecologism will, 'for the first time in modern history' fill an as yet 'open position in the field of ideological currents' (1996b: 208). Dobson, Eder and most other ecological theorists (e.g. Goodin 1992; Hayward 1995) concede that ecologism might not yet have come to full maturity, but the fundamental belief in its theoretical possibility and ecological necessity is widely shared among contemporary ecological thinkers.

For some reason, however, ecologism never managed to gain much political influence. Contrary to the ecologist prophecies, the western-style combination of liberal democracy and socially cushioned capitalism proved remarkably stable, and there is little indication of its being seriously challenged by ecological dangers or ecologist revolutions. But how is it possible that a problem as existential and globally relevant as the one identified by ecologists triggers no more than a few environmentalist reforms? Why is it that ecologist ideas had so little political impact? The explanation I want to try out in this book is that none of Dobson's ingredients were really available: arguably, (a) the ecologist diagnosis was wrong or at least misleading; (b) their utopia too vague or too unattractive; and (c) the suggested strategies were never sociologically convincing. At the beginning of the twenty-first century, ecologists have to acknowledge that there is little hope for a consistent ideology that could integrate the eco-movement and give a direction to the ecological restructuring of late modern societies. With some degree of desperation, Jonathon Porritt, for example, still urges ecologists that 'if we are to ensure that the environment movement does not *lose its soul*', then 'its values need to be brought to the forefront of its work rather than allowed to languish in obscurity' (1997: 71). But it may well be too late for this. Ecologist theory formation has hit a state of fundamental crisis.

(a)   With regard to the first of Dobson's ingredients, that is the ecologist diagnosis, the dilemma can be demonstrated with a brief look at four central beliefs which were constitutive for the project of an ecologist ideology: first, the belief in indisputable environmental *degradation*; second, the idea of the *finiteness of resources* and the *limits to growth*; third, the assumption that the *continuation of current economic practices* will, before long, lead to an *ecological collapse*; and fourth, the idea of *global affectedness*, which implies that humanity as a whole will be hit by the eco-catastrophe. Over the past few decades, all of these basic constituents of ecologism's 'analytical description of society' turned out to be significantly more contentious than ecologists would want to admit. In the case of the normative concept of *degradation*, ecologists had to admit that, empirically, there is no evidence of it. Natural scientists may be able to measure *change* in the physical environment, and social scientists may record *concern* about this change, but the category of environmental degradation remains problematic. As I have indicated in the previous sections, it makes reference to flexible social norms, and is hence a rather unreliable constituent of the ecological diagnosis.

The idea of the *finiteness of resources* was first weakened by the discovery of larger resource deposits than were known in the early 1970s, when the *limits to growth* appeared at the horizon. But, probably more important, was the realisation that the concept of the *resource* allows for a lot of flexibility. A resource becomes a resource through its connection to human purposes for which it can function as a means. Human purposes, however, as well as the means of achieving them, change over time. New technologies and patterns of consumption render materials which were once required in large quantities less important, whilst others which were once unknown or not usable suddenly become vital. In the process of modernisation finite resources can become replaceable by less finite or renewable ones. The introduction and normalisation of new patterns of social distribution can help where scarce resources cannot easily be replaced (e.g. drinking water). There are, of course, physical and cultural limits to both resource substitutability and distributive reorganisation (e.g. Daly 1995; Holland 1997; Dobson 1998, 1999), but it is obvious that the threats of finiteness are considerably less concrete and urgent than ecologists erstwhile assumed. And as regards the *limits to growth*, the current debate on *ecological modernisation* (see Chapter 10) seems to suggest that ecological necessities may well trigger new rounds of economic growth rather than establish its limits.

From these considerations it also becomes apparent why the warning that the *continuation of current economic practices* will soon lead to *ecological collapse* has lost much of its mobilising force. This warning does not take into account that the process of modernisation is reflexive, that is that it is both a fault-creating as well as a self-correcting mechanism (see Chapter 5). It may be true that, ultimately, modern society will not be capable of managing the side-effects of its development, but there is undoubtedly considerable potential for at least delaying the disaster. Anyway, the notions of collapse and disaster are themselves rather dubious because the latter is clearly a normative concept, whilst the former merely implies (partial) structural reorganisation, but not necessarily total apocalypse. This realisation that environmental change tends to cause local crises rather than global collapses also meant that the idea(l) of global affectedness had to be given up. The vision of a global ecological apocalypse affecting, without difference, the whole of humanity is simply inappropriate. And even in those cases where one might still concede global affectedness, accessibility to the means of removing or controlling unfavourable conditions is very diverse. In the recent literature, questions of distribution and social justice have therefore become a focal point of attention (e.g. Pepper 1993; Martell 1994; Hayward 1995; Lafferty and Meadowcroft 1996; Mathews 1996; Dobson 1998, 1999).

So, much of what ecologists had suggested in terms of their diagnosis eventually had to be revised. Obviously, this cannot mean to say that all is well and that there is no reason for concern. Human-induced changes in the physical environment are real, and natural scientists produce ever more empirical evidence for them! People are affected by these changes! Resources are scarce and render certain practices unsustainable! But the ecologist reading of these facts made a range of assumptions which were more contestable than it had been assumed. Over the years, these assumptions have become more visible and increasingly controversial. In other words, although empirically measurable developments in the physical environment continued largely unchanged, the simplicity and self-evidence of the ecological diagnosis had to be given up.

(b) With regard to Dobson's second ingredient, that is ecological utopia, the situation is not significantly different. As Hayward suggests, 'there are certain fairly common features' in what theorists present as their ecological utopia. He believes that particularly with regard to 'questions of political organization there is something approaching consensus' (1995: 188). Depending on the formulation of the problem, the ecological vision is humanity's *reconciliation* with nature, the *liberation* of nature, the restoration of the lost *equilibrium*, the achievement of environmental *sustainability*, and so on. What these different versions of the ecological utopia all have in common is that they are so abstract that they are close to being meaningless. The positive side of this level of abstraction is the integrative capacity of such ecological utopias. The evident drawback, however, is that the consensus disintegrates as soon as the abstract ideals are to be filled with concrete meaning. Hayward's structural principles are a good case in point: the idea that an ecological order 'would have to be non-hierarchical and decentralized' (ibid.) seems 'an ideal worth striving for' as long as we are discussing 'broad principles' (ibid.: 190). But this may easily change if we leave the level of 'broad principles'.

Picking up an idea that Goodin (1992) brought into the discussion, I will argue in Chapter 7 (particularly Section 7.5) that the underlying value of all ecological utopias is the norm of *naturalness*. Traditionally, nature, to which this norm obviously refers, was assumed to be *out there* and one and the same for everybody. Common sense therefore suggested that nature and naturalness genuinely qualify as a truly common good. But the idea of a singular nature that is distinct from society is rapidly giving way to that of multiple contested natures (see Chapter 3), and therefore the meaning of *naturalness* suddenly becomes open to debate. What emerges may suitably be described as a *post-natural* (Giddens 1994) condition in which a once seemingly homogeneous ecological utopia diversifies into multiple and incompatible belief systems defending very different ideals of *naturalness*, which may even be quite unrelated to the *green nature out there*. Ecologists have tried to escape this dilemma by focusing on the ideal of sustainability, which does not seem to make reference to nature or naturalness. But for sustainability to become politically meaningful, ecological theorists still need to clarify *what* is to be sustained, and *why*. As I will argue in Chapter 7, this reintroduces both the ideal of naturalness and the related difficulties through the back door. In the recent ecological literature there is probably no other concept that has been as severely flogged as sustainability (see, e.g., Baker 1997; Dobson 1998), but all this has contributed very little to providing the ecological discourse with a new focus and protecting it against the forces of paralysis and disintegration.

(c)   Finally, Dobson's third ingredient, that is the programme for social change, needs addressing. In the early 1970s, when the environmental crisis was first identified and publicised, there did not seem to be any need for a specific strategy for reversing modern society's course towards ecological collapse. Then it was assumed that information alone would mean 'the initiation of new forms of thinking', leading 'to a fundamental revision of human behaviour and, by implication, of the entire fabric of present-day society' (Meadows et al. 1974: 190). Up to the present, the belief has survived that such revolutionary change in our patterns of thinking and behaviour are simply common sense and in the enlightened self-interest of each individual and of humanity at large (e.g. Hayward 1995). Admittedly, individual preferences and short-term interests tend to get in the way of this common good and interest, but there is still a lot of confidence that rational discourse can, and will, resolve these superficial conflicts, and that once the pressure becomes sufficiently serious, ecological common sense – and eco-rational choice – will eventually prevail. Accordingly, ecologists are still firmly convinced that public information and education are the central means of promoting the ecological U-turn (e.g. Macnaghten and Urry 1998). However, as there seem to be considerable weaknesses in the chain leading from *degradation* via *information*, *concern* and *action* to *restoration* or *sustainability*, additional supportive strategies for the ecologisation of society seem to be urgently required. Here ecological theorists have always been confronted with three fundamental problems: (i) How can their ecological prescriptions be legitimated? (ii) What incentives or motivation would there be for ecologically more benign behaviour? (iii) Who would begin with the

implementation of ecological change, that is who would be the most suitable social agent?

The first of these problems could never be resolved because of the irreducible plurality of social values. Given the post-Habermasian consensus that after the abdication of metaphysics, normative standards can only be established discursively through social negotiation, ecological theorists have recently emphasised the ecological significance of communicative or dialogic patterns of politics (e.g. Dryzek 1987, 1995, 1996; Giddens 1994; Hayward 1995; Beck 1997a; Jacobs 1997). 'Deliberative democracy' has become an ecological buzz-word. However, so far ecologists have not produced any evidence for an intrinsic link between ecology and democracy. Practical experience suggests that public deliberation and participation are more likely to obstruct than promote ecological progress. They introduce even more interests and beliefs into the political arena and further dilute the ecological content and efficiency of any compromise that may be achieved. From a theoretical point of view, it may be added that the belief in deliberative democracy actually presupposes much of the consensus it only wants to establish. It involves 'a commitment to discursive democratic procedures which itself is non-negotiable' (Hayward 1995: 205). This commitment implies the unquestioned assumption of both the theoretical possibility of, and the practical will for, a consensus.

Given the level of differentiation and complexity of contemporary societies, the plurality of competing interests and the abdication of metaphysical truths, it is hardly surprising that the debate has actually shifted away from specifically ecological issues and turned towards the more general question whether and how social cohesion and consensus might be rebuilt. The social economy, civic culture, the third sector, the regeneration of social capital, a resuscitation of local democracy and the project of a global civil society have moved into the centre of interest. For the successful negotiation and legitimation of any political goal and prescription – including ecological ones – the availability of such social cohesion is surely a central precondition. Yet so far, it has proven very difficult to disperse the suspicion that the new emphasis on – or rhetoric of – local communities and social capital can really be more than the attempt to provide coping strategies for individuals and local communities which are left with problems caused (more or less deliberately) at societal levels beyond their influence and control. Local trust and cohesion may well help to make the life-world consequences of global developments more bearable, but they will probably not reverse the processes of individualisation, differentiation and globalisation, and provide the basis of a bottom-up process of ecological consensus formation, eco-political legitimation and the effective ecological restructuring of contemporary society.

The question of the motivation for ecologically benign behaviour has so far not been answered because for most people, the allegedly superficial pleasures and satisfaction granted by material consumption remained much more tangible and attractive than the *real and lasting fulfilment* promised by ecologists. As an incentive, the unspecific promise of *ecological happiness* could, to some extent, be supplemented by the fear (*Angst*) of potential personal harm caused by environmental hazards or catastrophes. Yet in most concrete situations, the risks seemed comparatively small and the catastrophes merely a possibility in the distant future. Also, there was little evidence that individual action or self-restriction would really contribute much to their prevention. Hence it seemed prudent to postpone drastic changes in personal behaviour and lifestyles until such time that general participation could be guaranteed. Given the pressures of the established socio-political structures, even a semi-religious eco-ethics could not provide a lasting source of motivation. But beyond these rather inefficient incentives ecologists have so far not suggested any more efficient way of mobilising the masses. Undoubtedly, the discovery that it might be possible to make pollution prevention pay has turned a new leaf, but any such approach would surely have to be entered into the account of reformist environmentalism rather than that of radical ecologism.

As regards the agent of ecological change, ecologists have nominated a number of potential candidates, the most promising ones being Green Parties, environmental NGOs and the so-called post-industrial service proletariat. Green Parties, however, seem to become increasingly reformist once they are involved in parliamentary politics and the struggle for votes (Raschke 1993; Richardson and Rootes 1995; O'Neill 1997). Social movements and their organisations (e.g. Dalton 1994; Princen and Finger 1994; Blühdorn 1995; Hjelmar 1996; Rawcliffe 1998) are highly dependent on media attention and a large fee-paying membership. Rather than sticking to uncompromisable ecological principles, they therefore have to respond to changing social perceptions of what is natural and worth preserving. For reasons of customer orientation and public accountability, their 'movement identity', which 'aims at challenging the political order', gradually gives way to a 'pressure group identity', which 'accepts the political order' and seeks influence 'through conventional channels' (Hjelmar 1996: 2). And the so-called 'post-industrial proletariat' (Gorz 1994) does not really qualify as an agent for ecological change either, because it is wrong to equate being set free by industrial society with being in opposition to it, or even working towards an ecologically more sustainable alternative. The post-industrial service proletariat is not exempt from increasing differentiation and individualisation. There is no reason to assume that they should suddenly be able to establish lasting common interests and class ties, least of all ecological ones.

Admittedly, this is a very brief and superficial review, but it should have made sufficiently clear where I see the crisis of ecological theory. Dobson's three ingredients for an ecologist ideology once seemed to be readily available, but it gradually transpired that ecologists cannot offer a solid diagnosis of the illness they want to cure, their social utopia loses its attractiveness as soon as it is spelt out in concrete terms, and their strategies for the transition from the current condition to the desired one are, from a sociological point of view, simply implausible. Even if we accept Eder's thesis that at the end of the twentieth century ecology has established itself as 'a new ideological masterframe' (1996a, 1996b), and that we have achieved a 'new consensus' about 'ecology as non-controversial collective concern' (1996a: 183), this does not contribute much to the project of an ecologist ideology. For as Hajer correctly points out, we still have to confront the 'new environmental conflict', which 'no longer focuses on the question of *whether there is* an environmental crisis' (1995: 13; my emphasis), but is a 'complex and continuous struggle' over its 'definition and meaning' (ibid.: 15). In the process of this continuous struggle the ecological issue and discourse gradually loses rather than establishes its independent identity. Increasingly, ecological questions are being reframed as economic questions, legal questions, welfare questions, security questions, and so on, and are being dealt with in the respective academic and societal discourses. In a way, this permeation of all societal contexts had, of course, always been the final goal of ecological thinking. But the idea had been that all aspects of society should be reorganised in accordance with ecological principles, and not that ecological issues be reframed in accordance with the established principles of the various societal contexts. One may therefore say that the apparent success of ecologism coincides with its complete failure: ecologism has *lost its soul*, there are no values left to be brought *to the forefront*.

Of course, the decline of ecologism has to be seen in the context of the decline of all ideologies of the nineteenth century. Much of what was said above about ecologism applies, *mutatis mutandis*, to political ideologies in general. The failure of ecologism is particularly hard to admit because it comes at a time when huge progress in the fields of the human Genome project, cloning technologies, biotech-food, and the like, seem to render an ecological ideology more necessary than ever. But in the absence, or after the abdication, of an ecologist ideology that could provide guidance, these issues will now (have to) be decided in a *post*-ecologist way. What that means remains to be seen. Ecologists themselves have, of course, recognised their dilemma and have looked for possible escape routes. *Nolens volens*, they have departed from the idea of radical ecological change and have finally embraced reformist incrementalism. They have paired the seemingly least troublesome utopia, sustainability, with a similarly 'uncontentious' strategy: ecological modernisation. This means that at least the problems of the agent of change and its motivation have been resolved. The normative problem, however, has simply been placed into the hands of the *polling culture*. Market research and opinion surveys are trying to detect the remains of social (ecological) values, which might still be sufficiently strong to fill the normative vacuum and provide the guidance that ideologies and their institutions no longer provide. But unsurprisingly, the record of success is rather modest. Nevertheless, incremental reforms are arguably better than none at all. If nothing else, they reassure us that *something* is being done. What exactly this implies remains to be seen. Chapters 8 and 10, in particular, will explore in more detail what this *post*-ecologist politics achieves.

2.2   The eco-movement in transformation

Like in the case of ecological theory, one might say that for the eco-movement(s), too, the fundamental crisis occurs in the moment of absolute success. In the industrialised countries, and far beyond, environmental organisations have mobilised unprecedented support for their cause(s) (e.g. O'Neill 1997; Rootes 1999). While political parties, trade unions, churches, and so on, are all confronted with an exodus of their established membership, green pressure groups boast an ever increasing mass of supporters (e.g. Dalton 1994; Blühdorn 1995; Rawcliffe 1998; Macnaghten and Urry 1998). Examples of these groups exerting considerable influence on national and international political and economic decisions have become plentiful. General information about environmental threats and the under-standing of complex ecological relations has reached an unprecedented level. In many countries environmental education now starts at pre-school age. There is no such thing any longer as being anti-environmentalist. In less than three decades the eco-movement has managed to generate large-scale agreement between green campaigners, governments, opposition parties, academics, business leaders and the general public on the absolute necessity of tackling environmental problems quickly and effectively. Given this overwhelming success, the suggestion that the eco-movement is in decline or that it is in a state of severe crisis does not sound par-ticularly convincing.

Nevertheless, there can be no doubt that since the late 1980s, the eco-movement has been subject to a fundamental transformation which can only superficially be described with widely used concepts like institutionalisation, professionalisation and internationalisation (e.g. Roth 1994; Blühdorn 1995; Rucht et al. 1997; Brand 1999a, 1999b; Rootes 1999). The more participants got involved in the ecological discourse and contributed to the shaping of ecological ideas, the more questionable it became whether those – actors and ideas – who originally started this discourse would be able to 'survive in this market place of communication on the environ-ment' (Eder 1996b: 203). Jamison diagnoses 'an interesting transformation of the original environmentalist message', which affects 'the nature of the problems as well as the proposed solutions', and changes the movement 'into something quite different than it was originally' (1996: 226). Andrew Rowell provides evidence for a global *Green Backlash* (1996). Jonathon Porritt notes that 'we are moving into new territory', whereby it is as yet uncertain 'what the contours of that territory will turn out to be' (1997: 62). Jagtenberg and McKie (1997) seek to conceptualise the ongoing transformation as a 'change of paradigm' towards the 'greening of post-modernity'. And along the lines of Hajer's 'new environmental conflict', Macnaghten and Urry suggest that after the 1992 Rio Summit – which in their view represented 'the pinnacle of international environmentalism' – there was 'the beginning of a new phase of uncertainty', in which environmental groups are struggling 'to redefine their role in a world in which environmental discourses are now accepted as a legitimate part of a new world order' (1998: 61f.).

So there is wide agreement that in the 1990s the eco-movement entered a rad-ically new phase, yet it remains uncertain exactly what this implies, and how these changes may be conceptualised and explained. In particular, scholars are un-decided whether we are confronted with the eco-movement's decline, or whether phenomena like Britain's new road protests, Germany's new anti-nuclear protests, international animal rights activism, worldwide protests against GM-foods, and the like, might indicate the movement's rejuvenation and new radicalisation (e.g. Doherty 1999). Anna Bramwell suggested at a fairly early stage that we are confronted with *The Fading of the Greens* (1994). Porritt believes that the environmental movement is currently just 'going through one of its periodic bouts of repositioning' (1997: 62). Christopher Rootes, too, believes in bottom-up democratic renewal and thinks that we are witnessing the 'iron law of democracy' according to which, 'cumbersome bureaucratic organizations are sooner or later – or perennially – challenged by new, uninstitutionalized forms of collective action' (Rootes 1997: 328f). But Roland Roth notes that in the *movement society*, an ever increasing number of protest events with ever smaller numbers of participants fails to attract much public attention and trigger any significant political effects. As regards the issue of democratic renewal, he points out that the 'policing of protests often replaces the discourse about their substance'. Looking beyond the horizon of the ecology movement in the narrow sense, Roth notes that if 'democracy was the topic of the new social movements, there is nothing but the conclusion that is so typical of social movements: A historical mission unfulfilled' (1999: 59).

This ambiguous current state and uncertain future of the eco-movement warrants further investigation. The most obvious symptom of the ongoing transformation is probably that economic neo-liberalism and new pressures for competitiveness in the globalised market place have focused public attention once again on issues of economic growth, employment, law and order, and material welfare. For both governments and local populations, the possible aggravation of ecological problems is less concrete and threatening than the immediately tangible effects of economic crises and the pauperisation of certain sectors of society. This *rematerialisation of post-materialist politics* dramatically changes the current situation and future prospects for the eco-movement (Blühdorn 2001). A second symptom is the fate of Green Parties throughout Europe. In the 1999 European elections the Green Group in the European Parliament (GGEP) achieved their biggest ever number of MEPs, and in various EU countries Green Parties are involved in coalition governments. Yet what appears as a green success is actually the result of rather discouraging developments: wherever election results look positive, they reflect extremely low electoral turnouts, the disastrous shape of the competing parties and/or the abandonment of green demands for radical change in favour of market-friendly eco-policies. Even the German prototype of European Green Parties now fails to attract young voters and has to struggle against the decline of its membership. In 1998, two decades after their first foundation, the German Greens finally became the junior partner in the country's coalition government. But as they had reached this position of potential influence, they suddenly had to realise that, under contemporary conditions, the classical green views and projects find less public support than ever. Even a moderate ecological tax reform or the very gradual phasing out of nuclear energy were almost impossible to implement. After 18 months in government the coherence and profile of the party had eroded to such an extent that only exceptional external and internal circumstances (Kosovo war, Kohl's party finances) and the charismatic Green foreign minister, Joschka Fischer, could secure their survival on the political stage (Blühdorn 2001).

A third symptom of change in the environmental movement is the shift from personal involvement and responsibility to representative protest by professional campaigners (e.g. Blühdorn 1995). Whilst in the 1970s and 1980s the ecology movement had carried forth the ideal of the grass-roots taking the ecological and political fate of society into their own hands, grass-roots involvement has now become largely symbolic, rarely transcending bottle recycling and a half-hearted commitment to green consumerism. The ubiquitous rhetoric of local empower-ment, horizontal networking and democratic renewal can hardly conceal that the primary aim of getting local people involved is now to devise individual-centred coping strategies and establish self-help groups rather than to achieve bottom-up changes in politics and society at large. The trend towards professional, efficient, representative – yet one might say *post-democratic* – environmental campaigning to some extent mirrors a general shift towards managerial and media-oriented styles of politics as practised, in an exemplary way, by the UK government under Tony Blair. Admittedly, marginal groups of animal rights activists, anti-road protesters, anti-nuclear campaigners, and the like, have in recent years engaged in new forms of *guerrilla protest* which has attracted a fair amount of media attention. But rather than 'creating affective nodes for activists to engage in *facework* activities' (Welsh 1999: 79), such forms of direct ecological action are at best smiled on benevolently, but more often rejected as anti-innovative or even criminal.

And as a fourth obvious indicator of fundamental change in the eco-movement, one may also point to the fact that the doom and gloom scenarios of the 1970s and 1980s have been superseded by a significant *Eco-Optimism* (Maxeiner and Miersch 1996). Although it will probably be difficult to provide evidence of any improve-ment in the overall ecological state of the globe, there is suddenly a lot of scepticism about ecological *Scare Stories* (BBC series broadcast at the time of the Kyoto climate conference, December 1997) and growing support for views along the lines of those promoted by the American *Wise Use Movement* (e.g. McCarthy 1998). Probably on the basis of a modernised understanding of the idea of *har-mony*, considerable confidence has emerged that 'already in the near future, we all will live in harmony with nature' (Maxeiner and Miersch 1996). And for those who feel less attached to the traditional idea of harmony or reconciliation with nature (see Chapter 4), there is a new brand of anti-romantic 'realism' which claims that nature has been irretrievably lost, and that this does not really matter because nature and the natural have always been fundamentally deficient and in desperate need of technological improvement, anyway: 'nature is dying, long live technology!' (Bohnke 1997: Part I).

All these are evident symptoms of the transformation of the eco-movement, yet they do not tell us much about the deeper causes of these shifts. For a more com-prehensive understanding, it is useful not to focus too narrowly on the eco-movement itself, but to look at the whole of the movement and protest culture which provides its ideological and infrastructural context. Since the late 1980s, social movements in general have undergone most profound changes. Mass move-ments bridging all lines of social division, and demonstrations of solidarity across the most diverse parts of society, still take place – yet it seems that it is less often the environmental issue which catalyses such overarching social consensus. Also, com-pared to their predecessors from the 1970s and 1980s, the character of contemporary mass movements is radically different (e.g. Baringhorst 1996, 1997). Events like the *Brent Spar* affair in 1995, the BSE crisis in the second half of the 1990s, the Berlin *Love Parades* throughout the 1990s, the unprecedented Diana-Movement in the latter half of 1997, or the various aid-campaigns to alleviate the consequences of the series of *century-catastrophes* in the late 1990s, all display very different features of contemporary mass movements, and represent very different kinds of public self-expression, yet they all provide evidence of a paradigm shift in the social movement sector. With a view to the discussions in the following chapters, I want to describe this shift with three broad theses:

(a) In a process of *radical temporalisation* political *campaigns* are taking the place of the traditional social *movements*. These campaigns are increasingly adopting the character of social *eruptions*.
(b) In a process of *individualisation* social movements are turning into virtual communities of individualised activists and followers. Aspects of *self*-construction and *self*-expression are becoming the focal point of the movement experience.
(c) In a process of *aestheticisation* symbolic action and radical emotionalisation are assuming the position formerly held by rational discourse and argument. They are becoming the dominant means of internal integration and external demarcation.

The gradual transition from social *movements* to political *campaigns* and on to social *eruptions* firstly implies that public moods and interests are articulated in ever shorter waves of activity. Secondly, it implies a programmatic contraction. Whilst the social movements of the 1970s and 1980s explicitly demanded large-scale political changes, campaigns like the *Brent Spar* affair tend to have a much narrower single-issue focus. Eruptions like the Diana-Movement do not formulate any explicit political demands at all, but still undoubtedly have a political dimension and can trigger political reforms (e.g. reforms to the British monarchy). Thirdly, the *temporalisation* of social movements implies that the formerly future-oriented and proactive social movements have become predominantly present-oriented and reactive. Contemporary mass movements respond to catastrophic events or high-profile issues which raise short-term concern, but are not seen in a wider context or from a long-term perspective. Such isolated events or issues trigger short waves of intense activism, sympathy or help. However, the instant collective reaction, mobilised, co-ordinated and integrated by the mass media, wears off as quickly as it is whipped up. Given the multiplicity of issues one could (or should) get concerned about, lasting commitment is neither intended nor possible. Due to the fierce competition for the finite resources of media attention and individual responsiveness, instant support by means of telephone and credit-card is the kind of public involvement campaigners are primarily trying to mobilise.

A further factor restricting the life expectancy of contemporary movements is certainly the absence of non-controversial political enemies. On the one hand, this is an immediate effect of the general depoliticisation and de-ideologisation of the mass movements. On the other hand, the lack of clear-cut enemy images is due to the high level of complexity achieved in late modern societies. The diversification of social values and individual lifestyles constantly increases the number of legitimate viewpoints and interests, and renders the resulting social conflicts ever more complex and irresolvable (*democratic sclerosis*). As a precondition for effective mass mobilisation, political campaigns have radically to reduce the complexity of political issues and interest constellations. By this strategy they manage to synthesise and cultivate the enemy images on which social movements vitally depend for their internal integration. Yet, in the public discourse, these simplifications cannot stand. In highly complex late modern societies, simple explanations and remedies are in themselves suspicious. The weaknesses and inconsistencies of any campaign are quickly exposed. Enemy images therefore need to be permanently reconstructed and redefined, with the strategic coalitions between political actors being based on *weak ties* allowing for constant reshuffling.

The second of the above-mentioned trends, that is the *individualisation* of social movements, does not merely mean that in the age of instant global communication a handful of individuals are enough to mobilise hundreds of thousands of supporters (donators), and that the latter increasingly operate – as individuals – from their private TV-set, telephone, or home computer. Beyond this, the individualisation of social movements implies a shift of focus from altruistic aims and values towards the individual *Self*. Whilst, for the new social movements of the 1970s and 1980s, the emphasis clearly seemed to be on the political dimension and the implementation of *common* interests, with personal aspects playing a subordinate, merely instrumental role, contemporary mass movements are crucially a forum of *Self*-construction, *Self*-experience and *Self*-expression in the movement community. Undoubtedly, these *Self*-centred aspects have always been part of the social movement experience (Touraine 1995; Hellmann 1996b; Melucci 1996), but as *common* goods and interests are ever more difficult to identify, and problem constellations have become too complex for individual activity to have any noticeable political effect, the *Self* is, in comparison to the community, gaining in relative importance. With the decline of *objective* (common) values and truths, *subjective* perceptions and concerns are moving into the centre. And with the range of available options becoming ever wider, the focus shifts from changing and shaping the menu (the external conditions) to picking and choosing already existing building blocks for the personal identity – or image (Schulze 1993). Questions of *reorganising the empirical world* thus turn into questions of *constructing new subjectively meaningful perspectives*. But whilst, on the one hand, the new *Self*-centredness of social movements emerges *by default* through the decline of common goods and interests, it may, on the other, also be seen as a reaction of *Self*-defence against the decline of the individual which – as a long sociological tradition in Europe has always emphasised – has come under existential threat in modern mass society (Maffesoli 1995).

Closely connected to the issue of *Self*-construction and *Self*-defence is what my third thesis describes as the *aestheticisation* of social movements. One function of social movements has always been to provide the indispensable larger context which alone can infuse the Self and its activity with meaning. However, what changed in the 1990s is the way in which this larger context is defined and sustained, and how the reassuring feeling of individual meaningfulness is generated. The movements' traditional emphasis on rational and argumentative discourse is gradually giving way to openly non-rational forms of integration and communication. The cohesion of movements is no longer (if it ever really was) based on shared rational convictions and political aims, but primarily on participation in ritual and symbolic actions. In other words, meaning no longer has its foundation in rationality, but rather emerges from symbols and rituals. At the same time, argumentative discourse is replaced by predominantly emotional and aesthetic modes of communication. In a context where social movements emerge and decline largely in accordance with the rules dictated by the mass media, symbols and images become much more powerful than empirical facts and rational arguments. Whilst, for the social movements of the 1970s and 1980s, the goal was to enlighten and convince the public, which implied the dissemination of information and the offer of argumentative assistance, contemporary mass movements increasingly rely on emotionalising the public. As confidence in the *objectively better argument* declines, the earlier orientation towards conflict and rational debate – not just with the political enemy, but particularly within the movement itself – is superseded by the construction and celebration of emotional unity. The experience of emotional coherence and inclusion – even if they lack any lasting foundation – represents the urgently required antidote to societal complexity and fragmentation. In this way, the traditional *movement* experience gradually turns into a *moving* experience (emotional and ego-oriented) which grants compensation for the deficits of contemporary societies.

With these three broad theses about the change of the social movement culture, I am of course almost asking for criticism. The complex changes which distinguish contemporary social movements from those of the 1970s and 1980s are difficult to capture in a few catchy formulae, and any attempt to do so will invariably be accused of making sweeping generalisations and being strongly reductionist. Also, there is the danger of a retrospective glorification of the social movements during the 1970s and 1980s. But even though I cannot do justice here to the full diversity and complexity of the social movement sector, the discussion of my three theses will be enough to illustrate the main point which is under discussion in this section: that contemporary social movements are fundamentally different from their predecessors in the 1970s and 1980s. And the ecology movement, which has always been only one player in the wider movement context, has not remained unaffected by these changes. In the following chapters the issues of temporisation, individualisation and aestheticisation will re-emerge at several points. What seems immediately evident is that these trends undermine rather than strengthen the striking power of the eco-movement. Although the exploitation of natural resources, the destruction of biodiversity, the increase of global population, and so on all continue in a largely unchanged manner and pace, the eco-movement seems to lose its specific and clearly distinguishable identity. Ecological voices are becoming ever more polyphonic, and their message becomes ever less precise. Alternatively, one might, of course, say that the ecological message becomes ever less simplistic, and that the eco-movement becomes ever more aware of its earlier illusions and simplifications.

It might seem somewhat provocative and premature to announce the end of the traditional eco-movement, but there can be no doubt that the movement has failed to reach its central aim of changing the most fundamental principles of the capitalist growth economy and the industrial consumer society. Rather than bringing about the envisaged revolutionary change in society, it has itself undergone fundamental change, and adapted in its structures, strategies and demands to a new *Zeitgeist* and the principles of late modern society. Arguably, the environmental movement merges into the fun and entertainment culture or dissolves into interest groups for consumer protection, national heritage, healthy eating, and the like. This process of transformation and reorientation is what I described as the crisis of the eco-movement. It is a shift which is an essential ingredient of the assumed paradigm change towards *post-ecologism*. How exactly this shift affects the political potential of the ecological issue remains to be explored.

2.3　A rearguard battle?

Among social theorists, however, it is still the dominant view that the new social movements, most notably the eco-movement, are the pioneers of a general departure towards new forms of social and economic organisation. Even though the ideological foundation for the ecological alternative is obviously much less solid than is often assumed, and the contemporary eco-movement does not appear to have retained much revolutionary energy, there is still the widespread assumption that ecologists represent the vanguard of an emerging ecological society. In the most recent literature, this optimistic sense of departure also materialises in the surprising confidence in a new cosmopolitan republicanism and an emerging transnational – or even global – civil society which is supposedly pioneered, in particular, by environmental NGOs (e.g. Princen and Finger 1994; Beck 1997b, 1998b, 2000b; Habermas 1998). In the light of the above observations, however, it seems necessary to revise the existing interpretations of social movements, including the ecology movement (overviews: e.g. Frankland and Schoonmaker 1992; Martell 1994; Rucht 1994; Hannigan 1995; Richardson and Rootes 1995; Rootes 1997). In the context of this study a brief review of the existing theories firstly sheds light onto the third dimension of my topic *ecology and crisis*, namely, the *crisis of social movement theory*. Secondly, it can draw attention to the fact that the different theories make very different suggestions of what the ecological discourse is all about. And thirdly, it is interesting to see what – if anything – these theories tell us about the contemporary transformation and future potential of the eco-movement.

The most obvious, and most traditional, explanation for the emergence of the eco-movement is that it simply reflects the factual deterioration of the natural environment and the emergence of increasingly urgent environmental problems. This *reflection hypothesis* (Hannigan 1995) suggests that environmental discourse is about environmental problems which exist independent of the societal debate about them. It assumes that objectively existing problems necessarily raise concern, and that this concern more or less automatically translates into protest and the desire for political change. Factual information is seen as the crucial link between objectively existing problems and social movement activity. But as I indicated in the previous sections, the connection between environmental change, problems, concern, activism and improvement is actually very loose, and significantly more complex than the reflection hypothesis assumes. Also, the reflection hypothesis would seem to suggest that the environmental movement will continue to grow as long as environmental degradation grows, and as long as the availability of information about this degradation increases. But this is obviously not the case. Although contemporary societies by and large continue to consume and destroy the natural environment in an unabated fashion, and although ever more information about these processes of change and deterioration becomes generally available, this does not translate into constantly rising levels of ecological concern, protest and activity. On the contrary, the eco-movement seems to be running out of steam, although today ecological protest might seem more justified and necessary than ever. Hence the reflection hypothesis is evidently somewhat simplistic.

Secondly, there is Inglehart's theory of *post-materialism* (1977, 1990, 1997), which suggests that the environmental movement was not so much triggered by an increasingly deteriorated physical environment, but primarily by the satisfaction of material needs and the related emergence of post-materialist values. According to Inglehart, 'the goals of both individuals and societies are changing as a result of the diminishing marginal utility of economic growth' (1997: 237). What is interesting about this theory is that subjective values and preferences, rather than objective conditions in the physical environment, become the decisive criterion. *Security*, *emancipation* and *autonomy* are key concepts in Inglehart's analysis, and as Inglehart points out, it is 'not one's economic level *per se*' which provides the central stimulus, but 'one's *subjective* sense of security' (1997: 34). This shift of emphasis towards individual values and perceptions is fundamentally important. Also, Inglehart's theory groups environmental concerns together with a whole range of other post-materialist concerns like peace, democratisation, gender equality, and so on. In other words, the relative importance of environmental concerns in the narrow sense is further decreased. According to Inglehart, the *environmental* cause only emerged as 'the symbolic centre' of a 'broad cultural emancipation movement' because many of the other post-materialist causes 'tend to be divisive', whereas 'practically everyone likes clean air and green trees' (1997: 244).

This explanation of the eco-movement takes account of the fact that a whole range of not directly environment-related issues has, indeed, always been an essential constituent of *green* protest and politics, even though social theorists have so far largely failed to explain their intrinsic connection to each other. Yet, as has often been pointed out, Inglehart's theory relies on a dubious categorisation and hierarchy of needs. Secondly, it does not reflect that much of the environmental movement – especially in its younger currents – is actually about very material issues. Thirdly, although Inglehart concedes that a 'collapse of security' may result in a 'gradual shift back toward materialist priorities' (1997: 35), his model does not offer a convincing explanation for the obvious resurgence of material values after the allegedly post-material years of the 1970s and 1980s. Fourthly, the thesis of post-materialism would suggest that the steady increase of social wealth translates into a steady increase of environmental concern. This suggestion, however, can hardly be sustained; and as the analysis in the previous sections indicates, the major reasons for the recent decline in ecological concern and activism are probably located in value shifts which are quite unrelated to changing levels of material provision. To some extent, this is also acknowledged by Inglehart's recent shift from the conceptual pair *materialism–post-materialism* towards *modernisation–postmodernisation*. So the theory of post-materialism leaves a number of questions unresolved. It is probably safe to say that in the 1970s, the unprecedented level of material wealth provided favourable conditions for the emergence of the new eco-movement, but this is not a sufficient explanation for the phenomenon of ecological concern and its changing political impact. In particular, it does not explain how exactly the connection between material saturation and ecological concern is supposed to work.

Two theories which place the emphasis neither on the state of the natural environment nor on a theory of individual needs are the *new middle class* thesis and the attempt to explain the eco-movement as a *reaction against political closure*. In both these models structural features of late modern societies are the crucial criterion. The first one suggests that the eco-movement and green politics are essentially a middle-class phenomenon which is particularly strong in countries with a significant well-educated and high-earning post-industrial service sector. This approach regards environmentalism basically as a specific class interest. Such class based theories, however, are incompatible with the ecologist claim that the green issue transcends all lines of social division. Also, environmental protest is by no means restricted to rich post-industrial societies where the middle class flourishes. And beyond this, the theory fails to explain why, since the early 1990s, the European middle class has obviously lost a lot of interest in environmental matters. The second structural explanation suggests that ecological movements and Green Parties become particularly strong where the established political system fails to accommodate new social interests, and excludes significant parts of society from social opportunities and the process of democratic decision making. According to this theory, the marginalised minorities get frustrated with the established system, unite, and begin to carve out social spaces for their self-realisation. In other words, according to this theory, the main thrust of green politics is not about the natural environment, and not about post-material values, but about the emancipation of social minorities, that is effectively about questions of inclusion and exclusion. But the obvious drawback of this theory is that it does not differentiate between different social movements and says very little about specifically green concerns. Secondly, in times of economic globalisation political closure and social exclusion are certainly on the rise, but the same does not seem to be true for social movements, including the ecology movement.

The last two theories I briefly want to address are, firstly, the attempt to explain the eco-movement largely as the *construct of moral entrepreneurs* and, secondly, the suggestion that social movements – including the ecology movement – have to be seen as a *response to cultural alienation*. Both these approaches are very important for my argument in this book. Their constituents will be discussed in some detail in the following chapters (particularly Chapters 3 and 4). The first one seems particularly applicable to environmentalism since the early 1980s, when environmental pressure groups like Greenpeace, as well as the media, began to play a major role in the eco-movement. It takes account of the fact that without these social actors, it would not have been possible to reach a mass audience, achieve large-scale ecological mobilisation, and construct a political case for the environment. But quite unacceptably for ecologists, this theory also seems to suggest that the eco-movement is to a large extent based on the social construction of modern myths and a public hysteria whipped up by dubious scaremongers. What this theory does not explain is why, despite the increasing professionalisation of these moral entrepreneurs, the mobilisation of eco-activists and supporters is becoming increasingly difficult. Also, this model does not really say what motivates the moral entrepreneurs and the people who respond to their campaigns. At least for this latter question, the cultural alienation thesis seems to offer a plausible answer. It might be the subjugation of all spheres of life under the imperatives of strategic thinking and economic rationality which triggers the protest against the established socio-economic structures. But, firstly, this is a rather general approach which does not analyse specifically green concerns and, secondly, it again cannot explain why the opposition against the established structures appears to be in decline although, in the context of globalisation, instrumental rationality and economic thinking have certainly become more rather than less important. Obviously, the suffering from alienation and the corresponding desire for reconciliation are not as strong as they used to be.

What these different theories demonstrate is, firstly, that there is considerable uncertainty regarding the questions about what exactly triggers ecological protest and what ecological politics is really all about. The so-called environmental problem is obviously considerably more complex and less closely related to the physical environment than it is generally assumed. Secondly, it seems evident that whilst all of these theories may contribute to an explanation of the eco-movement during the 1970s and 1980s, none of them is able to explain its transformation or decline since the 1990s. Consequently, none of them provides a suitable basis for predictions regarding the development and relevance of the ecological issue and the eco-movement in the new millennium. In order to get out of this explanatory dilemma we evidently need a new theory. Developing aspects of both the constructionist and the cultural alienation approach, I therefore want to try out the idea that the eco-movement is a transitionary phenomenon that emerged at the passage between classical modernity and its successor, and which disappears as soon as this transition has been completed. In other words, what I want to explore in this book is whether social movements, and particularly the ecology movement, can be interpreted as a *rearguard battle* defending the unfulfilled promises of modernity at a point of time when these promises are becoming both increasingly unfulfillable and unattractive.

The suggested reinterpretation of the eco-movement as a *rearguard battle* is in line with Joachim Raschke's suggestion that, in contemporary society, the function of social movements has fundamentally changed. Given the ever-accelerating pace and depth of seemingly unstoppable and uncontrollable social change; that is under the conditions of the *political economy of uncertainty*, the former pioneers of a general departure towards a radically different society have transformed into an essentially conservative force: they 'normatively demand a restriction of change', but no longer 'proactively intervene into determining change' (Raschke 1999: 78). This reinterpretation of the eco-movement is also in line with John Gray's description of the eco-movement and ecological thinking as an *endgame*. According to Gray, ecological thinking is deeply indebted and committed to the old traditions of Enlightenment humanism, and is, exactly for this reason, 'peculiarly ill-suited to the realities and dilemmas of the emerging postmodern age' (1997: 159). 'In all its standard varieties', Gray believes, 'Green theory remains a pot-pourri of Enlightenment hopes and Romantic nostalgias' and is 'far away from the time of endings and beginnings in which we live' (1997: 161).

In two respects the view of the eco-movement as a rearguard battle can be described as *post-ecologist*: firstly, it no longer interprets the eco-movement and ecological discourse as centring around the preservation of nature and ecology in the natural science sense. Concern for certain aspects of the physical environment is merely a surface phenomenon, but the real issue is the preservation of modernity. Secondly, it suggests that the eco-movement is not the spearhead of a new revolutionary set of values and social order, but the rearguard of a dying modernist culture. It is, however, crucial to understand that I do not suggest that the eco-movement and ecological thinking are in any way reactionary. The suggestion that they are struggling to defend a set of ideas which are rapidly being phased out does not mean to say that they are defending the social or political *status quo* or something that has ever been part of societal reality. As I indicated above, they are defending ideals and promises of modernity *which have never been fulfilled*. The eco-movement is a social institution that processes and digests the decline and disappointments of modernity. Without being aware of it, it thereby secures and smoothes the transition to new – *post-ecologist* – patterns of thinking and social organisation which ecologists themselves would strictly reject.

3   Towards post-ecologism

In the last chapter I demonstrated how the crisis of ecologist theory formation, the crisis of the eco-movement, and the crisis of eco-movement theory all point towards an end of the ecologist paradigm. Environmental issues, however, are undoubtedly still very high on contemporary political agendas. But the ecologist patterns of framing the problems and devising solutions have lost much of their political influence and theoretical credibility. The reasons for the emergence of *post-ecologist* patterns of discourse and policy making, and their significant social and political implications, cannot be spelt out with the conceptual tools provided by traditional ecologist thought. For this purpose we require a *theory of post-ecologist politics*.

Of course, the arrival of yet another *post* will be greeted with scepticism. Why should we need a theory of post-ecologist politics, when we have not even managed to sketch out the ground rules of ecologist politics, let alone implemented them? Arguably, the arrival of post-feminism has not contributed anything really new to the feminist debate; why should this be any different with post-ecologism? Since the advent of postmodernism we have been confronted with a plethora of *posts*, most of them being vaguely defined, hardly understood and very short-lived, almost immediately making room for their successors, the *post-posts*. Given the inflationary use of *posts*, the emergence of post-ecologism was perhaps almost inevitable, but one may wonder how many post- and post-post-ecologisms we are to expect – after all, the eco-movement is anything but homogeneous and has generated a whole range of different ecologisms. Indeed, the first of these ecological *posts* seems to have arrived quite some time ago, when John Young published his book *Post Environmentalism* (1990). A few years later Klaus Eder picked up the concept and announced that 'the age of environmentalism' as the age of 'collective mobilization' is over (1996a: 191) and superseded by the age of post-environmentalism, which begins, as I quoted earlier, 'where ecology is established as a masterframe' (ibid.), a 'non-controversial collective concern' (ibid.: 183). However, neither Young nor Eder devise any ecological theory that really goes beyond ecologist thinking. Their shared belief that 'the environment is the issue that brings collective rationality back into the theory and practice of modern societies' (Eder 1996b: 205), the conviction that contemporary societies have achieved a 'collective consensus on a green agenda' (ibid.: 180), and the above-mentioned confidence in ecologism as a powerful contemporary ideology, all provide evidence that both Young and Eder hold fast to the most crucial characteristic of ecologist thinking, which is the principle of *unity*, as opposed to *plurality*.

As I indicated in the section on *the non-negotiability of nature* (Section 1.2), the thinking and ideology of ecologism is – despite its multiple currents and appearances – not pluralistic. It is based on the modernist assumption that there is only one nature, one global ecological equilibrium, one human interest of survival, one intrinsic value of nature and one human rationality which has to be – and eventually will be – able to convince everybody that it is in humankind's best interest to act rationally, that is to respect the integrity of nature and organise society in accordance with ecological principles. Irrespective of the fact that ecologists are talking a lot about pluralisation and democracy, ecological thought has so far been firmly based on this principle of unity, which is actually the core principle of all *modernist* thinking. This belief in the principle of unity is not specific to ecologism, but represents the shared foundation of conservationism, environmentalism, ecologism, ecological modernisation and all other *modernist* varieties of ecological thought. In the sense that this ecologist (modernist) principle can only once be replaced by the principle of plurality, we can assume that there is no more than one transition to post-ecologism, which may, of course, be theorised in different ways, but which will not be followed by any *post-posts*. And the categorical difference between the principle of unity and that of plurality ensures that post-ecologism is indeed something radically new which is categorically different not just from ecologism, but also from its less radical or comprehensive green competitors.

In the field of ecological thought the condition of postmodern plurality arrives in the form of the *abolition of nature* – or to be more precise, its pluralisation and democratisation. It is because the theory of ecologism is essentially modernist that the theory of post-ecologist politics becomes necessary. The affinity of post-ecologist thinking to postmodernist thinking will, of course, not help the post-ecologist case. Postmodernist approaches do not enjoy a favourable reputation. As I outlined in Section 1.3, contemporary society is desperately trying to understand itself as modernist. The ubiquitous talk of *third ways*, the inclusive society, social capital, cosmopolitan republicanism, and so on, indicate that in the contemporary literature *neo-modernist* theories (Giddens 1998; Habermas 1996, 1998; Beck 1997b, 2000b) have once again taken the lead over postmodernist approaches. In ecological thought and environmental sociology, however, postmodernist approaches have so far been explored only in rather superficial ways. And modernist ecologist thinking has become inadequate because it can neither conceptualise *the fact* of nature's pluralisation and democratisation, nor understand that (and why) the modernist unity and cohesion are simply *no longer required*. Furthermore, the modernist framework seems fundamentally inadequate for the conceptualisation and interpretation of an environmental politics after the abolition of nature. Even if it were just for the sake of the experiment, it is therefore very useful to explore how ecological issues can be reinterpreted in a postmodernist – better still: non-modernist – conceptual framework. As a preliminary exercise on the way towards a comprehensive theory of post-ecologist politics, I want to devote some thought to the idea of the abolition of nature and reflect on its consequences for environmental sociology.

3.1   The abolition of nature

One of the most often quoted *topoi* of the environmental debate is the idea that the collapse of nature is imminent, and that radical – and probably uncomfortable – measures for nature's protection have to be taken immediately. However, it is hard to believe that the disastrous catastrophe environmentalists have been awaiting for several decades – especially if earlier waves of environmental concern (around the turn of the twentieth century) are taken into account – is any closer today than it was at any other point in time. It also seems unlikely that civilisatory progress should have left nature so powerful that humans are exposed to its revenge without any protection. Having said this, it is, however, equally hard to imagine that environmentalists have always been wrong and worrying about nothing. In this book I want to take their fears as very real and legitimate. But contrary to the common belief that the catastrophe is still to come, I want to try out the thesis that it has already happened. Although the *abolition of nature* is a catastrophe of unimaginable magnitude, it has, paradoxically, arrived largely unnoticed, for it has inbuilt mechanisms which protect it from being recognised and conceptualised. In line with my above-mentioned assumption that the environmental crisis is first and foremost a crisis of consciousness, I would suggest the abolition of nature has intellectual rather than physical reality and significance. This, however, neither precludes its having a physical appearance nor does it in any way make its effects less serious.

The idea of the abolition of nature is anything but new. Already Marx had pointed out that 'nature, the nature that preceded human history . . . today no longer exists anywhere (except perhaps on a few Australian coral island of recent origin)' (1977: 175). In the early 1960s the idea was implicit in Rachel Carson's *Silent Spring* (1962), which is widely considered as the starting point of the contemporary ecological debate. In the literature of the environmental movement since the 1970s the idea is known, for example, through Edward Goldsmith, who was concerned that a 'surrogate world' would gradually replace the 'real' one. It was 'the technosphere or world of material goods and technological devices' (1988: 185; originally published in 1977) which Goldsmith called the surrogate world, and for him 'the process of building (it) up' implied the 'contraction and deterioration of the real one' (ibid.: 187). In his simple model, the artificial world was pushing the other back spatially. Yet the real world, nature, would always be 'more real' than the surrogate world, and although this would have followed logically, it was inconceivable to Goldsmith that it might lose its reality and be entirely replaced by the surrogate world.

In 1980 Carolyn Merchant announced *The Death of Nature*. Merchant tells the story of modern (male) science and its tool, instrumental reason, which subjugates nature and denies the existence of alternative forms of rationality. By and large, she reiterates the criticism voiced so powerfully in Horkheimer and Adorno's *Dialectic of Enlightenment* (1944/1972), which will be discussed in some detail in the next chapter. While Merchant only pointed towards the possibility and danger of the future abolition of nature, Bill McKibben, in *The End of Nature* (1990), tried to take its historical reality as the starting point for his considerations. Acid rain and human-induced climatic change, McKibben argued, have converted every spot of pristine nature into human environment. The planet we are inhabiting is therefore a 'post-natural world' (p. 55), and his book is supposed to be written from a post-natural perspective. McKibben was terrified by the idea that mankind has taken on the task of global management – not just because he believed that human managerial competence and strategies will never become sufficiently sophisticated to match the complexity of the task. For him, an equally significant dimension of the catastrophe was that after the end of nature, 'there is nothing but us' (p. 55). Living in a 'post-natural' world means that 'we can no longer imagine that we are part of something larger than ourselves' (p.78). What he referred to is the cultural significance of nature as the paragon of the good, true and beautiful which he believed to be indispensable as the ultimate source of human values and the meaning of human life. Here, McKibben touched upon a fundamental point, yet he did not spell out its implications. Irrespective of his own diagnosis, according to which the patient was already dead, McKibben still thought it useful to devise a therapy. From the post-natural world he fell back into the appellative mode known from the earlier literature and continued the tradition of formulating imperatives to secure nature's survival. It would never have occurred to McKibben (nor to Goldsmith or Merchant) that the abolition of nature might also have positive implications. Historical fact or still to take place, it was an entirely and exclusively negative caesura.

Not until the 1990s did this pessimistic, loss-oriented view begin to turn into the positive. In particular, Ulrich Beck, whose thinking is the focal point of Chapter 5, strikes an entirely different chord. Beck tries to differentiate between the two dimensions of nature which McKibben confused, but it is evident that one can hardly be thought without the other. In a seemingly conventional way Beck argues that 'the process of interaction with nature has consumed it, abolished it, and transformed it into a civilisatory[1] meta-reality that can no longer rid itself of the attributes of human (co-) creation' (Beck 1995a: 37). In this quote Beck seems to be referring to material nature, to 'that world entirely independent of us which was there before we arrived and which encircled and supported our human society' (McKibben 1990: 82). But for Beck the other dimension of nature, that is its function as a metaphysical source of meaning and a normative standard which is accredited to it exactly because it 'was there before we arrived', is at least equally significant. And the abolition of nature in this sense – with the concomitant invalidation of all nature-derived ethical and political imperatives – is, in Beck's view, a positive development because, as he argues, whatever we call natural tends to be the product of naturalisation: 'after all, we decide who and what is nature, by means of science if need be' (Beck 1997a: 86). Beck urges us to acknowledge the 'irreversible artificiality of nature' (1995a: 37). He is concerned about the ideological potential of the issue of nature which he regards as a 'political chameleon'

---

1   Official translation: 'civilizing'.

(1998a: 161). In a cultural context where reliable social values and binding ethical guidelines are high in demand but chronically low in supply, nature and the natural may serve as political justification for all kinds of ideological currents.

Arguing along very similar lines, Gernot Böhme suggests that 'the contemporary invocation of nature as a value proves ideological because it makes reference to the conception of nature as something unchanging just at the point of time when – historically probably irreversibly – it is disintegrating' (1992: 115). As Böhme points out, 'making reference to nature as it is in itself', and 'making reference to nature as a norm . . . is an illusion', and in order to prevent any possible anti-democratic and anti-modernist twist of ecological concerns, he is 'sympathetic to the demand to abandon the concept of nature altogether' (ibid.: 22). In order to avoid nature being instrumentalised for any ideological purposes, both Böhme and Beck demand 'to make nature itself political, that is to negotiate politically which nature we want at all' (ibid.: 24). The old backward-oriented project of saving nature is wiped out by two fundamental insights: 'Firstly there is no movement seeking to protect the *Other* of society; secondly, there is no natural nature' (Beck 1995a: 182). The old *conservationist* project is replaced by the future-oriented project of democratically negotiating nature: 'nature becomes a societal project, a utopia' (Beck 1997a: 114). In actual fact, the abolition of nature becomes a political demand, an essential prerequisite for a genuinely democratic politics 'which may control the anti-modern, dictatorial potential' of the ecological issue (Beck 1995a: 191).

The abolition of nature implies that ecological thought, rather than trying to enhance its ecocentric credentials, has to become fully anthropocentric and turn into social theory. At least theoretically – problems will be discussed at a later stage – this is a positive development because it creates space for the unfolding of ideals and opportunities, and removes the focus on external dependency and limitation. Borrowing a term Wolfgang Welsch (1987) coined with regard to the theory of postmodernism, one could say the abolition of nature puts an end to the ecologist version of the *mourning process of modernity*. Much of the eco-movement, and the theoretical writing accompanying it, has so far been fuelled by the experience of alienation from nature and the resulting desire for reconciliation with it. As Giddens puts it, 'ecological politics is a politics of loss – the loss of nature and the loss of tradition' (1994: 227). Ecological politics can, however, also turn into a 'politics of recovery' (ibid.). With the abolition of nature, and ecologism's turn into social theory, this thinking in dualisms is abandoned. Neither alienation nor reconciliation will henceforth be possible. Whilst until the early 1990s the ecocentric search for nature as the *Other* of society was regarded as 'the most comprehensive, promising, and distinctive approach . . . in ecopolitical theory' (Eckersley 1992: 27), the abolition of nature necessitates the transition to a post-dualist, a post-ecologist approach.

Before I move on to exploring to what extent environmental sociologists have so far performed the necessary turn of ecological thought into social theory, it might be useful to offer some clarifications about the abolition of nature which may help to avoid fatal misunderstandings. Firstly, the thesis of the abolition of nature does not mean that human civilisation has become a closed system capable of reproducing itself without having to rely on external (natural) input. What has been abolished is merely the particular understanding of nature as a singular entity opposite society, that is in the present context nature is understood as a purely *cultural* concept. Secondly, the shift of emphasis from the material dimension of nature to the cultural dimension does not in any way reduce or deny the vital importance of the physical framework and conditions of human and other life. It merely aims to take account of the fact that we are unable to think and talk about these physical conditions without making a whole range of cultural assumptions. And what are at stake in the ecological discourse are, arguably, these cultural parameters in accordance to which physical and material issues are being framed and discussed rather than the material content itself. What I mean with the thesis of the abolition of nature is that these assumptions have radically changed. Contrary to what Carson, Goldsmith, McKibben and others might suggest, the abolition of nature is therefore not to be regarded as an event in the empirical environment, but as the collapse and replacement of certain patterns of perception. Thirdly, the abolition of nature does not mean that the concept of nature becomes irrelevant, or that political campaigning for it becomes obsolete. *Post-natural* and *post-traditional* societies (Giddens 1994) still require social values on the basis of which they can organise their material affairs and social relations, and establish systems of meaning. And even though we may know that the notion of nature as the *Other* that was given to humanity has never been more than a particular way of conceptualising the duality of *being* and *consciousness*, the ideas of nature and naturalness have by no means lost their intriguing attractiveness. Jagtenberg and McKie are therefore correct in joking that 'for a corpse, nature maintains a vigorous afterlife' (1997: 21). Beyond the abolition of the traditional single (modernist) nature which was assumed to be completely separate and independent from human civilisation, nature survives as a multiplicity of competing social constructions.

3.2 Ecological constructionism

Since the mid-1990s, the supposedly anti-ecological idea of the abolition of nature, or as Macnaghten and Urry put it, the idea 'that there is no singular nature as such, only natures' (1998: 15), has gained a lot in currency. Book titles such as *Contested Natures* (Macnaghten and Urry 1998), *Reconstructing Nature* (Dickens 1996), *The Social Construction of Nature* (Eder 1996a), *Faking Nature* (Elliot 1997), *Remaking Reality* (Braun and Castree 1998), to name but a few, indicate that for many environmental sociologists – as for me – 'queering what counts as nature' has become a 'categorical imperative' (Haraway 1994: 60). The portrayal of nature as a social construct (see also *FutureNatural* (Robertson et al. 1996)) has triggered controversial debates between *social constructionists* and *environmental realists*. Far too soon, this debate has, unfortunately, been denounced as 'rather dull' (Macnaghten and Urry 1998: 2) just because it has remained *largely academic* in the pejorative sense. Of course, social constructionist approaches do not directly contribute to practical policy making. They deconstruct rather than establish practical guidelines for ecological politics.

Social constructionist approaches tend to assume that ecological imperatives are already in place rather than to be installed, and that ecological action is already happening rather than to be incited. They are appropriate primarily as an interpretative instrument. They take a perspective that ecological activists or policy makers themselves can never take because every (ecological) decision and action – including the decision not to take action – has to prioritise certain values over others. In other words, decision makers and activists invariably have to be (ecologically) normative. And this is exactly what social constructionist approaches are trying to avoid. In social and political reality, however, *avoiding being normative* is not really an option, just as *not acting* is not an option either. From the policy oriented point of view, it is therefore understandable how and why constructionist approaches acquired their rather poor reputation. But to dismiss them altogether as a dead end in ecological thinking would mean to throw out the baby with the bath water, because *for the analysis* of the environmental discourse social constructionist approaches are extremely useful. I therefore want to explore in a bit more detail: (a) what ecological constructionists have achieved so far; (b) how environmental realists have criticised them; and (c) how constructionists may be defended against the realist attacks.

(a) The realisation that 'what counts as *nature* . . . is always historical' and 'related to a configuration of historically specific social and representational practices' (Braun and Castree 1998: 17) triggered a range of attempts to explore certain country- and culture-specific understandings of nature, and reconstruct the historical process of their emergence. The American *wilderness* (e.g. Cronon 1995), the British *countryside* (e.g. Macnaghten and Urry 1998) and the German *forests* (e.g. Bramwell 1989), to mention but a few well-researched examples, represent quite distinct and culturally (ideologically) charged conceptualisations of nature which lead to very different and non-transferable political demands and concepts of environmental protection. Beyond the level of such national accounts, the abolition of the traditional singular nature also motivated environmental sociologists to make a clearer distinction between empirically measurable environmental *change* and the social perception of environmental *problems* – a distinction that is thoroughly comparable, for example, to the feminist distinction between *sex* and *gender*. In the first half of the 1990s, theorists like Yearley, Eder or Hannigan could build on the work of constructivist pioneers, like Kitsuse and Spector, who had suggested much earlier that a clear distinction ought to be made between 'objective conditions and the subjective awareness of social problems' (1981: 199). In the contemporary debate it is now widely accepted that 'public concern about the environment is by no means automatic even when the conditions are visibly bad' (Hannigan 1995: 2). It has so far remained impossible to determine the exact relationship between physical environmental change and the social perception of problems, but there is agreement that there is no direct connection between the physical conditions and public environmental anxiety, just as there is no 'simple correspondence between the state of environmental consciousness in a country and the level of development of its environmental movement or the electoral fortunes of its Green party' (Rootes

1997: 320). Nevertheless, the idea that the social 'perception of environmental problems may . . . be independent of the magnitude of the problems themselves' (Hannigan 1995: 24), and that the relationship between the physical environment and public anxieties may actually be governed by a 'law of independence of protest and destruction' (Beck 1995a: 45), remains rather irritating.

The recognition that 'public concern is at least partially independent of actual environmental deterioration and is shaped by other considerations' (Hannigan 1995: 24) firstly raised the question to what extent and in what way science, environmental pressure groups, the media and other players contribute to the shaping of environmental discourses and eco-political agendas. Trying to reach beyond this primary level of social construction, Beck, for example, drew attention to 'the profound significance of the *cultural dispositions to perceive*' and the central importance of 'cultural norms' which 'decide *which despoliations are put up with and which are not*, and how acceptance of the unacceptable arises and persists'[2] (Beck 1995a: 45). This new emphasis on the fact that 'the particular *objective* environmental problems and issues which society recognises at any one moment are shaped and determined by processes of human judgement and social negotiation, *even in their very definitions*', that is that environmental problems are in a sense actually 'human inventions' (Grove-White 1997: 109), initiated a shift of sociological interest: away from the physical conditions towards the social mechanisms of problem construction and the 'cultural dispositions' on which they rely.

This shift had already been demanded by Kitsuse and Spector who regarded the task of accounting 'for the emergence and maintenance of claim-making and responding activities' as the 'central problem' for further sociological research (1981: 201). Making explicit reference to their work, Steven Yearley suggested that environmental sociologists 'should suspend any interest in whether the objective circumstances merit the existence of a social problem or not', but concentrate instead 'on the social processes involved in bringing an issue to public attention as a social problem' (Yearley 1991: 50). Widening the perspective slightly to include Beck's 'cultural dispositions to perceive', John Hannigan pointed out that 'from a sociological point of view, the chief task here is to understand why certain conditions come to be perceived as problematic and how those who register this *claim* command political attention in their quest to do something positive' (Hannigan 1995: 2f). The most important point about this change in the research agenda is that it 'encourages us to examine processes *internal* to the green movement' (Yearley 1991: 52; my emphasis). Against the background of my demand for a turn of ecological thought into social theory, this new *inward* orientation is certainly a step in the right direction. It leads to a reinterpretation of the eco-movement as a 'society-oriented, inward movement' rather than an 'outward-oriented movement for and about the environment'[3] (Beck 1995a). Such an

---

2 Original emphasis (dropped in the translation).
3 The official translation probably fails to get Beck's crucial point across: 'The ecological movement is not an environmental movement but a social, inward movement' [Beck 1995b: 55].

inverted approach to the ecological issue gives rise to the challenging thesis that 'it is not the despoliation of nature, but the jeopardization of a *specific cultural model of nature* . . . that provides the sounding-board for the ecological alarm of . . . society'[4] (Beck 1995a: 54).

So there is now a widespread consensus that both nature and ecological problems are, at least in part, social constructions which are subject to a continuous process of discursive deconstruction and reconstruction. A range of different social constructionisms – of which David Demeritt (1998), for example, provides a useful typology – has emerged in order to analyse and explain this process. John Hannigan correctly points to three major advantages of a social constructionist approach in environmental sociology. First, such an approach is more critical than much of the traditional environmental literature in that it does not simply 'accept the existence of an environmental crisis brought on by unchecked population growth, over-production, dangerous new technologies' (Hannigan 1995: 30). Instead of reproducing the stereotypes of the eco-debate, it focuses on 'the social, political and cultural processes by which environmental conditions are defined as being unacceptably risky and therefore actionable' (ibid.). Second, a social constructionist approach 'recognises the extent to which environmental problems and solutions are end-products of a dynamic social process of definition, negotiation and legitimation both in public and private settings' (ibid.: 31). And finally, by deflecting attention from the so-called objective external conditions which are traditionally the realm of the natural rather than the social sciences, 'a social constructionist approach grounds the study of environmental matters in a distinctly sociological discourse' (ibid.). Certainly a constructionist approach to ecological issues will never reveal the full and only truth, but it is evident that this specific perspective reveals insights which remain inaccessible to both natural scientists and eco-campaigners. After all, it questions what both of these uncritically presuppose: nature and the environmental problem.

(b)   However, ecological constructionists have to face powerful opposition from those refusing to accept the abolition of nature. Environmental realists like Benton, Dickens, Dunlap and Catton, Martell, and also to some extent Ulrich Beck, concede that constructionist approaches are – 'daft as they are' – 'currently very fashionable among intellectuals' (Benton 1993: 66), but believe that they are, 'in the end, not . . . worth the amount of intellectual effort' put into them (Dickens 1996: 72). Many of them agree that because 'all concepts have evolved from human societies', 'all knowledge must in some sense be a social construction' (ibid.: 71). But when it comes to environmental deterioration, they insist on the independent existence of nature and the objective reality of environmental problems, without which it would in their view 'be difficult' for the social constructionists 'to define such problems as existing or arouse popular concern over them' (Martell 1994: 132). Soulé heavily criticises 'the social siege of nature' (Soulé 1995). Martell warns

---

4   Original emphasis (dropped in the translation).

that 'the objective basis of environmentalism in problems in the environment can be sociologized away' (1994: 132). And Benton suggests that social constructionists favour 'a perspective in which the independent presence of the non-human world in our lives is marginal to the point of disappearance' (Benton 1994: 45). Making explicit reference to Yearley's social problems perspective and emphasis on analysing the societal processes of problem construction, he argues:

> It is, of course, both interesting and important to be aware of these social processes, but in the case of environmental issues this approach has the consequence of bracketing out of sociological analysis any consideration of the 'objective conditions' which give rise to environmental concern. It is all the same, as far as the sociologist is concerned, whether we do, in fact, face ecological catastrophe, or whether environmentalists have conjured this threat out of their fevered imaginations.
>
> (Benton 1994: 46)

Arguing along the same lines, Dunlap and Catton point out that 'treating global environmental change . . . as a social construction discourages investigation of the societal causes, consequences and amelioration of global environmental problems'. They insist that such an approach is 'particularly unwise in the case of global environmental change' (1994: 20).

Attacks on social constructionist approaches tend to become particularly merciless when constructionist thinking is seen to be inspired by elements of postmodernist thinking. When it comes to polemicising against the *postmodernist threat*, there is striking accord between ecological realists and positivist scientists. The latter are aggressively trying to defend the objective validity of their scientific truths, which has come under siege from counter-science, disbelief, and the realisation that in real life and real politics, images, moods, perceptions and *feel-good-factors* are at least as influential as the so-called scientific facts. But as for the ecological realists, their harmony with the positivist sciences is actually rather surprising. After all, the empirical sciences are fiercely defending a world-view which ecologists would normally strictly reject, namely the modernist dualism of nature and society, which is itself merely a construction of modern scientific rationality – and as ecologists have often pointed out, a rather anti-ecological one. Nevertheless, ecological constructionists find themselves confronted with a phalanx of ecological realists and positivist scientists. And the onus of proof seems to be on the constructionists because they are challenging what has become the established truth. Even though ecologists themselves have often pointed to this very *truth*, that is the dualism of nature and society, as the deepest root of the ecological crisis, they still seem to regard it as the lesser evil compared to the constructionist pluralisation of nature, for ecological constructionism undermines 'the objective basis for moral concern' about environmental issues (Martell 1994: 132). Postmodernist deconstructionists have therefore been identified as the new political enemy, and they are themselves regarded as part of the ecological problem.

As if the process I described as the abolition of nature could be stopped or reversed by militating against theoretical models for its conceptualisation, post-modernist deconstructionism has been denounced as a 'contemporary form of intellectual and social relativism' that 'can be just as destructive to nature as bulldozers and chain saws' (Soulé and Lease 1995: xvi). According to Soulé, post-modernist deconstructionism is a coalition of 'conservative free market capitalists, humanists concerned with the emancipation and empowerment of certain social and ethnic groups, and others, including animal rights organisations' (Soulé 1995: 146). Supposedly, these actors are all united in the attempt to 'justify further exploitative tinkering with what little remains of wildness' (ibid.: xv). Postmodernist deconstructionism is assumed to be driven by the 'belief that a world beyond our control is so terrifying that we can – indeed, must – believe only in the landscapes of our imagination' (Shepard 1995: 22f.). Whilst the environmental movement is seen as 'essentially a reawakening to the truth . . . that we must depend on other forms of life to survive' (Worster 1995: 79), 'deconstructionist postmodernism rationalizes the final step away from connection: beyond relativism to denial' (Shepard 1995: 25). Shepard expresses a widespread concern when he says that constructionism effectively means taking 'refuge from overwhelming problems by announcing all lands to be illusionary' (ibid.).

Of course, this summary is, once again, a simplification. In a brief overview I cannot take account of the different degrees of realism, just as the differences between mild and more radical forms of constructionism have to remain unexplored (see e.g. Dickens 1996: 73ff.). With a view to my theory of post-ecologist politics, I just want to draw attention to the core message of environmental realism, which is the ever repeated warning against the 'idealist tendency in modern social theory' (Benton 1994: 45), and the insistence 'that the world, including its living components, really does exist apart from humanity's perceptions and beliefs about it' (Soulé and Lease, 1995: xv). As Benton puts it, the 'reality external to discourse' must not be reduced to 'an unknowable ghostly presence' (Benton 1994: 45). The 'natural world' cannot simply be seen 'as an extension of human consciousness and activity', but it remains 'an ultimate constraint on the life of humans and other animal species' (Gray 1997: 158f.). And the basis for this realist imperative is that the postmodern pluralisation of nature undermines ecological imperatives and opens the gates to moral relativism: 'If all truth claims have validity, then there is no basis for endorsing some over others, and thus no basis for becoming proactive' (Dunlap and Catton 1994: 22). Accordingly, social constructionists are accused: (i) of undermining the possibility of taking a critical stance *vis-à-vis* ecologically damaging societal practices; (ii) of impairing the moral credibility of ecological campaigns; and (iii) of promoting political quietism by destroying the motivational basis for ecological action. Undoubtedly, all these accusations will be raised against my projected theory of post-ecologist politics. I will respond to them in some detail in Chapter 9, but in the context of these preliminary explorations, it seems useful to pre-empt at least some of the most dubious allegations.

(c) There is, firstly, the bizarre idea that social constructionists are aiming to 'justify further exploitative tinkering' with the natural environment, and that they

themselves are partly responsible for the ongoing destruction of nature. Of course, the constructionist project implies the deconstruction of certainties which have so far provided the basis for the ecological discourse. However, these certainties cannot be said to have been a particularly adequate foundation for environmental politics. As we have seen, ecologist thinking and the eco-movement have clearly failed to reach the objectives they had formulated for themselves, and have ended up in a situation of comprehensive crisis. In this situation, demonstrating that the ecologist certainties were no more than social constructions – which can be deconstructed and reconstructed in a different way – may bring considerable relief. It can, firstly, help to prevent further ecologist disappointment and frustration and, secondly, perhaps provide the foundation for a more contemporary and appropriate politics of nature. Apart from this, it seems hardly justified to say that environmental constructionists themselves are destroying these traditional certainties, when in fact they merely theorise and conceptualise societal processes which – in a quite realist sense – evolve and take effect irrespective of their being sociologically observed and theorised. Environmental realists, in particular, will surely have to concede that there is a clear difference between the intellectual exercise of deconstructing social constructions and the physical exercise of effecting empirical changes in the so-called natural environment. What I described above as the abolition of nature is not the work of environmental sociologists, but their constructivist approaches are the attempt to respond to it.

Secondly, it is a fundamental misunderstanding if social constructionists are seen to be terrified by the existence of a world which is beyond their control, and that they seek to perfect modernity's claim to absolute power by denying the existence of anything uncontrollable. If constructionists take a social problems perspective, and emphasise that processes of political agenda-setting and environmental policy making respond first and foremost to socially constructed concerns rather than to the so-called objective empirical realities, this certainly enhances rather than reduces the complexity of ecological issues. Particularly in their postmodernist variety, constructionists acknowledge that after the abolition of the great constant of modernity, that is the single nature as the Other of society, we are confronted with the emergence of multiple, and equally legitimate, conceptual representations of the world around us which can no longer be forced under one unifying umbrella. It is therefore difficult to see how constructionist approaches can be said to increase human power and control. As some realist critics have correctly pointed out, the opposite is much more likely to be the case.

Thirdly, there is the allegation that constructionists are denying the reality of overwhelming environmental problems and taking refuge in the virtual reality of their imagination. If constructionists really were to deny, firstly, that the physical environment is subject to processes of change which are accelerated by the impact of human civilisation and, secondly, that contemporary societies devise concrete policies in response to these changes, they would certainly not deserve to be taken seriously. But they would, of course, never contest, for example, that in 1998 hurricane Mitch killed thousands of people in central America, that hurricane George devastated the Caribbean, that unprecedented floods ravaged parts of China and huge fires destroyed the forests of Indonesia. It is undeniable that almost every month there are reports about the worst-ever drought, rainfalls, heat wave, famine, ice storm, mud slides, forest fires, and so on. However, to what extent these undeniable facts and physical changes can be described as environmental problems, and the societal responses as remedies, is a completely separate issue. Here we are confronted with the question of where and how contemporary societies find their measure or normative standard for both environmental *deterioration* and *remedial* action. Traditional environmentalism, although far from simply equating environmental change and environmental problems, has devoted amazingly little thought to the distinction between the two. Certainly, nobody would identify environmental problems where change has not been classified as deterioration, but any such classification invariably relies on a set of norms and parameters which are socially mediated. Hence environmental problems, unlike physical environmental change, are always and necessarily social constructions which may legitimately be deconstructed and tested for their validity. And those engaging in this complex activity can hardly be accused of wanting to escape from reality into a fantasyland. On the contrary, social constructionists seek to face the realities we have constructed.

In this context it also seems appropriate to say something about constructionism's alleged tendency towards idealism. This criticism is based on a superficial understanding of idealism and is strongly influenced by general prejudice against theoretical approaches. Constructionists are indeed idealists in so far as they distinguish between being and consciousness, and assume that problems and crises are primarily a matter of the latter. But as Marx correctly pointed out when he polemicised against the *German Ideology*, the crucial point of idealism is not this distinction, but that idealists prioritise consciousness over being and demand that the material world ought to be determined by a transcendental consciousness. And in this very crucial sense, ecological constructionists are not idealists because they do not accept any ecological certainties or imperatives, least of all any demands that claim *a priori* validity. It is, on the contrary, the dubious idealism of (allegedly realist) ecologists which provides the very driving force behind the deconstructionist efforts. Over the past three decades it has been the ecologists who have been idealistically convinced that their consciousness should determine the empirical world and who became increasingly surprised that social and political reality largely ignored their prescriptions. But the failure of their idealism does not restrict us to realism in the positivistic sense. The objective is rather to explore why reality does not correspond to theory and improve the latter in such a way that it eventually does correspond. This is exactly what ecological constructionists are trying to achieve, and to the extent that they restrict themselves to trying to *understand* rather than to *prescribe*, they are precisely not idealists.

This finally takes me to the question of whether the abolition of nature and the resulting constructivist approach may imply the discursive abolition of the so-called environmental crisis. If nature and the environmental problem have to be regarded as social constructions which have no ontological reality outside the societal discourse, the ecological crisis might turn out to be significantly less worrying than it had previously appeared. With regard to this question, social constructionists may be criticised for causing substantial confusion by failing to introduce clear terminological distinctions. This will be discussed in some detail in the next section, where I will also make suggestions as to how the constructivist approach could be improved. In direct response, however, to the realist allegation that constructionists reduce nature and the ecological problem to 'an unknowable ghostly presence', I want to make one point of clarification: The whole debate about the independent reality of the physical environment outside the realm of social discourse may be an interesting question for epistemologists, but in the context of environmental sociology it simply misses the point. Environmental constructionists may happily accept that the physical environment 'including its living components, really does exist apart from humanity's perceptions and beliefs about it'. Whether or not this is the case will neither be verifiable for them, nor is it particularly important as long as we realise that concrete environmental politics is not based upon such a hypothetical reality anyway, but responds first and foremost to *concerns* and *anxieties* which are quite evidently social constructs. So contrary to the realist criticism, the project of social constructionism is not at all concerned with denying or confirming *a priori* reality, but rather with exploring the origin of the feelings and the composition of the images on which modern societies base their politics, including their environmental politics. Whatever the *external* realities, for constructionist environmental sociologists the focus is on the question of how contemporary societies frame and process their *knowledge* about this *external* world. Certainly, their approach can only complement and never replace that of the sciences, but this exclusive focus on internal representations and their societal negotiation has, in itself, to be regarded as a valuable and unique contribution to the environmental debate.

3.3   A post-ecologist research agenda

So the social constructionist approach can easily be defended against much of the realist criticism levelled against it. In particular, no realist insistence on the objective existence of nature and the ecological problem will reverse the cultural process I described as the abolition of nature. It remains a fact that pristine nature has almost completely been converted into human environment, that there is no consensus about the nature we want to protect, preserve or restore, and that there is no quasi-metaphysical normative standard of naturalness which could guide our policy towards our environment(s). In other words, no realist criticism will remove the pressure on environmental sociology to devise theoretical models which take account of Hajer's 'new environmental conflict'. Of course, this does not mean that the existing constructionist approaches are already fully developed and satisfactory. Undeniably, they display significant weaknesses which the suggested theory of post-ecologist politics will have to try to iron out – yet not by returning to realist positions, but by radicalising the constructionist perspective. Anticipating the argument that will be fully developed in the following chapters, I would suggest that social constructionists themselves do not take the abolition of nature sufficiently seriously. There are at least four specific respects in which the suggested theory of post-ecologist politics will have to radicalise their approach.

To begin with, it is striking that most environmental sociologists who favour a social constructionist perspective are rather inconsistent in the way they handle or talk about the abolition of nature. When Beck, for example, argues that the environmental movement does not respond 'to the *despoliation* of nature, but the jeopardization of a specific cultural model of nature' (1995a: 54; my emphasis), and that 'cultural dispositions' decide 'how acceptance of the *unacceptable* arises and persists' (ibid.: 45; my emphasis), he clearly assumes the extra-discursive *objective* existence of 'despoliations' and 'unacceptabilities'. In other words, Beck presupposes a problem-standard which exists prior to and independent of social discourse. Beck evidently preserves a conception of the normal and natural that has survived the abolition of nature. The same applies if Hannigan, for example, distinguishes between the '*perception* of environmental problems' and 'the magnitude of the *problems themselves*' (1995: 24; my emphasis), if he notes that environmental concern 'is at least partially independent of *actual environmental deterioration*' (ibid.; my emphasis), and if he highlights that public problem perceptions do 'not necessarily reflect the *reality of actual problems*' (ibid.: 25). A further example of this half-hearted abolition of nature is Yearley's suggestion that environmental sociologists should focus on the mechanisms by which a social problem 'comes to public attention', or 'comes to the fore' (1991: 50). It seems to be implicit that there are also problems which come neither 'to public attention' nor 'to the fore'.

In other words, what most social constructionists seem to share with their realist counterparts is the belief that there exist two clearly distinguishable worlds: the extra-discursive, empirically verifiable objective world, and the world of subjective impressions and socially constructed realities. Both these worlds are assumed to be accessible to scientific exploration. However, whilst the realists insist on investigating the *objective* conditions with the *real* problems as well as the *discursive* reality with the social problem *perceptions*, we have seen that constructionists believe they should 'suspend any interest in . . . the objective circumstances' (Yearley 1991: 49), in order not to 'deflect attention from investigation of the definitional process' (Kitsuse and Spector 1981: 200). But the recommendation to leave the 'objective' conditions on one side is wrong. It firstly forgets that the natural sciences cannot come up with anything but social constructions of knowledge either. Secondly, it denies the subjective impressions and social constructions their full validity. But however *subjective* and *constructed* concerns and anxieties may be, they are still thoroughly real. And if they are shared by a sufficiently large number of people, or carried forward by sufficiently radical individuals, they will undoubtedly have very real effects on political agendas. Therefore the recommendation to social constructionists should not be to leave the 'objective conditions' unobserved, but to take the social constructions seriously. Social constructions are the most real and most objective reality we have got, and nothing more real or more objective is accessible to us. This Kantian focus on the subjective and social consciousness preserves the existence of an *a priori* world beyond the social constructions, yet it ensures that the latter can claim full and unlimited validity. Hence the first suggestion for a post-ecologist research agenda is to take account of the full epistemological implications of the constructionist approach. The two equations *social = subjective–invalid*, and *natural = objective–valid* are both wrong. The same may be said of the opposition *social ≠ natural*. If the abolition of nature is taken seriously, the essentially modernist dualisms of *nature–society* and *subjective–objective* need to be given up or merged into the formula *natural = social = objective*. This does, of course, not mean to deny the ontological distinction between material and non-material. Neither does it dissolve the difference between 'social capital' (resources which can be socially produced and reproduced) and 'natural capital' (external input into social processes) (e.g. Dobson 1998).

The reasons why even constructionists hesitate to give up the belief in extra-discursive *objective* problems are, firstly, that they are looking for an objective source of environmental concern – because people do, indeed, not get upset about nothing. Secondly, health hazards, resources shortages, the extinction of species, and other issues which trigger such concern do, indeed, seem to be 'objective realities' outside the realm of societal discourse. With regard to the first point, it may be said that it is certainly correct to assume that environmental concerns need – and have – an *objective* basis, yet there is no reason to believe that this basis necessarily needs to be located in the material world. It may just as well be a non-material necessity originating from a certain (modernist) way in which we conceive of ourselves. As I will argue in the following chapters, taking the abolition of nature seriously means locating the objective basis of environmental concern on the side of the human subjects and their self-conceptualisation as an identity. With regard to the second point, I will argue that it is never the material side of a phenomenon of environmental change which triggers environmental concern, but always and exclusively the violation of established cultural norms of naturalness and acceptability. Therefore my second suggestion for a post-ecologist research agenda is that we look here rather than in the material world for the objective basis of environmental concern.

As these considerations suggest, social constructionists have so far not really started to explore the objective basis of environmental concern, erroneously believing that it must be located in the extra-discursive material world. Most of them have so far focused on science, pressure groups, the media and other 'moral entrepreneurs', and explored by what means these social actors turn environmental facts into political issues. However, if the emergence of social problem perceptions is exclusively explained as the work of 'moral entrepreneurs', this seriously overestimates their power and influence. Apart from the fact that they frame and publicise phenomena of physical environmental change, these social actors are tapping a second resource which may provisionally be described as a *pre-existing vital interest in nature* – not as an accumulation of physical conditions, but as a metaphysical norm and context of values which is projected onto these conditions. For the social construction of environmental problems this second resource is not just indispensable, but it is arguably even more important than the physical input. Problem perceptions may well correspond to empirically verifiable physical changes, yet this is neither a necessary nor a sufficient condition of their emergence. Hence the third suggestion for a post-ecologist research agenda is that we do not only focus on 'moral entrepreneurs' and the political career of single issues. Above all, an adequate theory of contemporary (post-ecologist) politics of nature has to explore what is behind this pre-existing interest in nature and in the standard of naturalness. It has to clarify why humans tend to get concerned about nature, and what nature means to us beyond the accumulation of physical conditions.

In particular, when exploring how the ongoing evolution of modernity affects the need for and interest in this *meta*-physical nature, environmental sociology is well advised to work together with contemporary philosophy and social or cultural theory. Following the abolition of the singular nature and the emergence of its multiple successors, there is the danger that (constructionist) environmental sociology exhausts itself in the empirical description of an unlimited number of individual or societal 'patterns to perceive' of nature and construct the environmental problem without ever coming to the point where conclusions may be drawn which reach beyond the case studies themselves. But what is the benefit of just mapping the manifold 'socially patterned *ways of sensing*' (Macnaghten and Urry 1998: 106)? What is the point of exploring the 'particular combinations of the senses . . . that may produce what is interpreted as an environmental *bad*' (ibid.) if the only result is the diagnosis of radical plurality? Ultimately, the task must be to establish systematic order and unity in this plurality because there is no other way of moving beyond arbitrariness and towards generalisable conclusions – not in the sense of ecological prescriptions, but conclusions (interpretations) about the content of the ecological discourse and about ongoing changes in the human–nature relationship. This, however, is not a matter of empirical description, but of theory formation and philosophical thinking. And due to their anti-theoretical stance, environmental sociologists have, in this respect, so far largely failed. The fourth suggestion for a post-ecologist research agenda is therefore to enhance the co-operation between environmental sociology on the one hand, and contemporary philosophy and social theory on the other.

What is at stake is that environmental sociology finally takes on board 'the huge cultural changes which have been sweeping through modern societies', that it takes account of 'the new ways in which individuals perceive their own lives and their collective identities' (Jacobs 1997: 6). As regards the 'new set of cultural filters' (Grove-White 1997: 109) which undoubtedly change the perceptions and definitions of environmental problems and priorities, philosophy and contemporary social theory can be of considerable help to environmental sociology. And such co-operation can also help environmental sociologists to overcome their reservations about postmodernist approaches. As I explained above, there are evident reasons for these reservations, but they are a remnant of the subordination of environmental sociology to ecological campaigning. In the interest of a more comprehensive understanding of the internal structure of the social discourse about nature and ecology, a post-ecologist environmental sociology will therefore try to fully emancipate itself from any ecological imperatives (idealism) and embrace the postmodernist paradigm of thought. Taking the abolition of nature seriously means taking account of its postmodern pluralisation. But embracing the postmodernist paradigm of thought does not necessarily imply the uncritical acceptance of all postmodernist beliefs. In central respects, postmodernists remain – consciously and deliberately – deeply modernist. A post-ecologist environmental sociology will have to remain critical, for example, of the postmodernist focus on the individual, and the belief in its legitimate emancipation and normative autonomy. A post-ecologist approach will have to take account of the fact that such beliefs merely 'replicated an ancient western humanist tradition that is now long outworn' (Gray 1997: 159).

In conclusion to this section one may finally ask where such a post-ecologist research agenda is going to take us. In this context I want to emphasise once again what has been pointed out so many times before: for post-ecologist thinking, the prime interest is not to *solve* the ecological crisis or to *save* nature. A theory of post-ecologist politics is not meant to be ideological and politically prescriptive. Instead, it seeks to be analytical and understand exactly what this crisis consists in, how contemporary society communicates about it, what the concept of nature means to us, and why we want to save nature at all. So whilst the reader had better not expect post-ecologist thinking to devise more effective strategies for the protection of nature, it may well be expected to explain why environmental politics has so far had a rather modest record of success. If we want to understand how and why ecological claims are made, sustained and (not) translated into actual policies, a constructionist approach is certainly much more promising than its realist alternative. But only a radicalised constructionist perspective which takes full account of the abolition of nature will help to show that in advanced industrial societies, the 'cultural dispositions to perceive' physical environmental change have, since the late 1980s, undergone a significant metamorphosis.

The crucial hypothesis that underlies this study and leads to the suggested theory of post-ecologist politics is that late modern societies are running out of the central non-renewable resource for ecologist politics: the demand for the metaphysical norm and standard of naturalness is in decline. A network of multiple, socially negotiated, mutually exclusive, and as I will demonstrate, often not at all subject-centred value systems has taken over the function formerly fulfilled by the idea of an all-inclusive nature. A post-ecologist approach is likely to reveal that the ecologist interest in nature was itself a (specifically modernist) social construction which is gradually superseded by a different world-view and politics of nature.

This takes us to the end of Part I of this book. The purpose of this comprehensive introductory part has been to introduce and discuss the three fundamental assumptions of this study:

1   that the ecological discourse still has rather weak theoretical foundations;
2   that around the turn to the 1990s, both the eco-movement and ecological thought hit a stage of crisis or transformation; and
3   that this transformation indicates the exhaustion of the ecologist paradigm of thought.

The preliminary discussions in these first three chapters have underlined that the centre-piece of the ecological discourse – nature – is significantly more than just the physical environment. Yet our understanding of what else this concept may stand for, that is what exactly ecologists want to protect, is still superficial. Secondly, we have established that environmental concern is not simply the immediate reflection of certain conditions in the physical environment, but the result of complex processes of social construction and mediation. But as yet, we know very little about the exact causes and conditions for the emergence of environmental concern. Thirdly, I suggested that we are witnessing the emergence of a new social attitude towards nature, environmental change and environment-related problems. Yet, we only have vague suspicions so far about what triggered this change, what exactly it implies, and how fundamental and lasting it really is.

As I pointed out, one could attempt to follow these issues up by undertaking empirical surveys of established patterns of sensing nature, or by providing historical accounts of the evolution of particular concepts of nature and environmental problem perceptions. For the reasons outlined above, I will not take this approach, but turn instead to philosophy and its contemporary successor, social theory. Questions like what nature means to human beings, why they tend to get concerned about it, and what exactly they find problematic about environmental problems, ultimately have to be answered against the background of comprehensive theories about the human–nature relationship and extensive models for the evolution and functioning of contemporary societies. Arguably, the most powerful contemporary theories of this kind are *critical theory* and *systems theory*. They are, therefore, the focus of the following two parts.

Part II

Understanding ecologism – critical theory

4 Alienation and reconciliation – Horkheimer and Adorno

In accordance with Hegel's dictum that Minerva's owl does not spread her wings before dusk, the deepest concerns of the ecologist project and the reasons why it has always been doomed to failure might reveal themselves only as the ecologist paradigm is in decline. And if philosophy and social theory are really not able to make (ecological) prescriptions about how the world ought to be, then they may at least be expected to fulfil the function of midwife to the process of this revelation. In the previous chapters I argued that ecological thought is, contrary to its pluralistic and radically democratic ambitions, fundamentally 'uncommunicative', hostile to theoretical enquiry and incompatible with rational justification. This seems to suggest that ecological thought is essentially *premodern*. When I was outlining my 'refined constructionist research agenda', I then insisted that the contemporary ecological discourse can only be theorised in an adequate way on the basis of a *postmodernist* approach. And I am now setting out to interpret ecological concerns within the framework of critical theory, which is a clearly *modernist* model. This raises the old question of the relationship between ecology and modernity. There is no need here to engage in the huge debate on this question, but in order to justify why I regard critical theory as an appropriate framework for the interpretation of the ecological critique, some clarification seems to be necessary to do with whether ecological thinking has to be considered as modern, premodern, antimodern, postmodern, or perhaps, as Ulrich Beck argues (see Chapter 5), as reflexively modern.

All of these positions have been defended in the literature, and although I believe that an unambiguous answer can and has to be given, the different perspectives at least have to be taken into account. If modernity is the age and movement that pulls everything into doubt and demands a rational explanation and legitimation for every phenomenon, action and belief, then ecological thinking can indeed be described as premodern. As I outlined in Section 1.2, ecological thinking is concerned with the Other of rationality, the pre-rational. I highlighted that for ecologists, the issue and value of nature is not open to debate, and that even ecological pragmatists are, to some extent, necessarily fundamentalists. But surely any kind of fundamentalism is radically incompatible with modernist thinking, and to the extent that ecologists rely on ecological fundamentalisms, they are evidently premodern. From a slightly different perspective, however, they can also be described as anti-modern. Ever since the end of the nineteenth century, certain currents within the ecological movement have argued against technological and scientific progress. Industrial development, economic growth, the accumulation of material wealth, mass consumption, jet-set mobility, the high-tech culture, genetic enhancement – much of what is widely associated with modernity and modernisation meets the disapproval of ecological thinkers and is high on the list of *must-nots* in many green utopias. The anti-modernist reputation of ecological thought is further confirmed by the fact that ecologists have always been deeply sceptical *vis-à-vis* the European movement of the Enlightenment, which has undoubtedly provided the very foundations for all achievements of modern society. Ecologists have often criticised the Enlightenment's exclusive focus on human interests and humanity's emancipation from nature, and have pointed out that its anthropocentric and instrumental rationality has to be regarded as the prime evil leading to the current ecological crisis.

At the same time, however, ecological thought has always continued the Enlightenment tradition, and must therefore be described as clearly modernist. Admittedly, it rejected the belief that unrestricted techno-scientific progress implies the linear improvement of human welfare, that ever-increasing human control over the non-human world will promote the goal of human happiness and fulfilment, and that this goal has absolute priority over all other possible considerations. But it firmly believed in the power of human rationality, and in the possibility and necessity of human emancipation from the irrational. Ecological thinkers were critical of the pact between science, technology and political power, however, they strongly relied on rational argument and scientific evidence. In line with the critical strand of Enlightenment thinkers, ecologists insisted that the rationality determining social and political reality in modern societies must not be equated with reason. They aimed to give a voice to the powerless, the socially marginalised and those who cannot speak for themselves. They struggled for the old emancipatory goals of liberty, equality and solidarity (for all forms of life), and demanded that the dominant form of (exploitative) rationality be replaced by a new and more comprehensive form of (ecological) rationality. In other words, despite their criticism of instrumental and anthropocentric rationality, ecologists clearly continue the tradition of European Enlightenment and modernity. Time and again, ecologists have argued for a 'reconstructed enlightenment', for 'ecological enlightenment' (Hayward 1995; Beck 1995b), although they have also, time and again, failed to achieve it.

So there are obviously premodern, anti-modern and modern elements in ecological thought. But I still want to contend that, ultimately, ecological thinking is always and necessarily modernist. For the purposes of my argument, I want to understand modernism as the movement that subjects everything to the rule of reason, but does not question the character of rationality itself. In other words, modernism is the paradigm of thought that does not tolerate any fundamentalisms, but relies on the fundamentalism of reason, that is the belief in a single, uniform and all-embracing rationality. I would argue that ecological thought cannot be premodern because it is concerned with problems emerging from the dualism of nature and society, which is (as I shall argue below) a typically modernist construction. Ecological thought discusses the juxtaposition of the rational and the non-rational, which is a fundamentally modernist constellation. But, of course, the above definition of modernity implies that with its unquestioned belief in reason, modernity itself contains an essentially premodern element. And to the same extent that modernity itself is premodern, this also applies to ecological thought. Ecological thinking cannot be anti-modern exactly because it is so firmly based on the typically modernist fundamentalism of reason, and on belief in the all-embracing system of rationality, against the background of which the currently dominant civilisatory rationality can and must be exposed and criticised as irrational. Surely a complex of ideas that relies on rationality as its critical tool is clearly modern rather than anti-modern. And ecological thinking also cannot be postmodern because, as I argued above, in its fundamental convictions it is hostile to discourse and plurality. It believes in the necessity, possibility and normative validity of ecological imperatives and a green morality. If ecological thinking wanted to embrace the principles of postmodernist thought, it would have to give up its critical stance. Whilst the sociological analysis of the ecological discourse may of course be continued from a postmodernist point of view, ecological thinking itself can never become postmodern. As a matter of fact, from a postmodernist perspective, its specific problems and concerns, which emerge from – and depend on – the cognitive constellation of modernity, would probably dissolve (see Chapter 8).

On the basis of this clarification, it is evident why I believe it to be most appropriate to interpret ecological concerns within the paradigm of modernist critical theory. Critical theory will help me to demonstrate that ecological concerns and problem perceptions emerge from the modernist world-view, and depend on the cognitive constellations of modernity. Admittedly, the two theoretical models which provide the focus of this and the next chapter clearly point to the limitations of a modernist approach. This implies that for the analysis of the ecological discourse in contemporary society, the modernist framework of critical theory can only be a transitionary stage. But rather than jumping immediately to the weaknesses of critical theory, I first want to explore its considerable benefits.

The works of the Frankfurt School of Critical Theory belong undeniably to the most influential philosophical and sociological writings of the twentieth century. A number of analysts have pointed out that long passages of Horkheimer and Adorno's *Dialectic of Enlightenment* (1944/1972; henceforth DE), Horkheimer's *Eclipse of Reason* (1947; henceforth ER), and Adorno's *Negative Dialectics* (1966/1973; henceforth ND) read as if they had been written by contemporary ecological thinkers (e.g. Link 1986; Eckersley 1992; Dobson 1993; Hayward 1995). This would seem to suggest that ecological theorists ought to take these writings very seriously and investigate to what extent ecological thought can benefit from critical theory. However, references in the ecological literature to early critical theory are conspicuously rare. Even in core texts on ecology and social theory (e.g. Redclift and Benton 1994; Hannigan 1995; Goldblatt 1996; Lash, Wynne and Szerszynski 1996; Conley 1997; Darier 1999), the Frankfurt School of Critical Theory is hardly mentioned at all. In order to explain the fact that contemporary ecological theorists have taken virtually no account of this particular current of western post-Marxism, Hülsberg points to the 'coded language' of the Frankfurt School (1988: 9). Eckersley highlights 'the early Frankfurt School's pessimistic outlook' and its 'increasing preoccupation with theory rather than praxis' (1992: 99). She also notes that 'their overriding objective was the liberation of "inner" rather than "outer" nature' (ibid.: 11). And Dobson comes to the conclusion that critical theory is fundamentally incompatible with ecological thought because instead of providing 'Greens with a sophisticated theory of social change', it presents us with 'a sophisticated theory suggesting its impossibility' (1993: 207). It may well be true that the message of early critical theory appears strategically and politically unacceptable to committed ecologists. Nevertheless, there are good reasons why ecological theorists should not simply regard critical theory as a 'failed promise' (Eckersley 1992: ch. 4), but listen very carefully to what it has got to say. At least for the sociological analysis of the contemporary ecological discourse, there are very important lessons to learn from it.

As I mentioned before, early critical theorists have never been concerned with nature and ecology in the sense of contemporary ecologists. Also, the evolution of political and social theory has left Horkheimer and Adorno behind because their concept of modernity was not sufficiently complex to capture the structure and development of contemporary societies. However, it is just this wider (*pre-ecological*) understanding of 'nature', and just their position at the threshold between plain modernism and concepts of post- or reflexive modernity that ought to make early critical theory interesting for contemporary ecological thought. A closer analysis of Horkheimer and Adorno's thinking will certainly not tell us how we may preserve the integrity of the natural environment and achieve the ideal of sustainable development. But in at least four respects, such an analysis can be tremendously useful: Firstly, critical theory offers a culture-theoretical model for the human–nature relationship and its historical development that is significantly more sophisticated and convincing than anything ecologists have suggested so far. Secondly, the theory of the emancipation of the human subject and the dialectic between its *alienation from nature* and its *dependence on nature* provides a most powerful conceptual framework for the interpretation of contemporary ecologist concerns. Thirdly, Adorno and Horkheimer convincingly demonstrated why the project of the desired reconciliation with nature can and will never be successful. And finally, the reasons why Adorno's model was criticised and replaced by more contemporary theoretical models are, arguably, exactly the reasons why ecologist thought has to be replaced by post-ecologist thought. Were it not in the context of ecological thought, there would, of course, be no need for a further review of Horkheimer and Adorno's thinking. But with a view to the above mentioned issues, it does indeed make sense to tell their story once again.

4.1   The Self and the Other

Horkheimer and Adorno conceptualise the cultural history of modern man (and not just *men*) as the history of the constitution of the human Self and its struggle for self-determination. This history is the history of enlightenment, yet Horkheimer and Adorno's notion of enlightenment is considerably more comprehensive than the cultural epoch represented by Kant's rationalist philosophy: it goes right back to ancient mythology. At the beginning of this history was the split of Being (*Sein*) into the Self and the Other. The birth of the Self, that is the first awareness of potential subjective autonomy, immediately implied the need for Self-preservation and Self-development. Opposite the Self was nature, the Other. And according to Horkheimer and Adorno, the Other, nature, did not exist prior to the Self. Contrary to those who uncritically equate nature to the physical environment (which obviously existed long before human kind and the modern subject), Horkheimer and Adorno suggest that the 'unity of nature' was only established as the correlate to 'the identity of the spirit' (DE: 10). In other words, in line with the view that the singular nature and the human–nature dualism are specifically modernist constructions, they suggest that neither the *subject* nor *nature* have ontological reality: the unity of nature was presupposed 'as little as the unity of the subject' (DE: 9).

Ever since the emergence of the *subject*, however, nature has represented a threat to the Self. In the very act of subjective Self-constitution, nature emerged as the paragon of heterodetermination (*Fremdbestimmung*), and in the interest of human self-determination it had to be brought under rational control. Horkheimer and Adorno therefore argue that 'the awakening of the self is paid for by the acknowledgment of power as the principle of all relations' (DE: 9). According to their model, the relationship between the Self and the Other, that is the human subject and nature, has always been a relationship of one dominating the other. And the restless attempt to expand human control over nature has always been spurred by the constant fear of 'a reversion of the self to that mere state of nature from which it had estranged itself with so huge an effort, and which therefore struck such terror into the self' (DE: 31). In other words, the preservation of the human Self and the subjugation of nature are inseparably intertwined.

When reflecting on human domination and control of nature, Horkheimer and Adorno are not so much interested in the visible transformation of physical nature through human civilisation and the process of labour. They focus on the underlying level, that is the intellectual means of dominating nature. They argue that in the name of human emancipation from nature, and for the maintenance and defence of the human Self *vis-à-vis* the threatening powers of nature, reason has adopted a specific form, which they call *formalised* or *instrumental* reason. Instrumental reason transforms 'everything in heaven and on earth into means' for the sole end of Self-preservation (ER: 97). This exclusive focus on subjective Self-preservation turns objective reason into subjective reason. Instrumental reason is not interested in recognising things as they might be independently of human ends, but with this particular kind of rationality, humans 'distance themselves from nature, in order to present it to themselves in such a way that it can be controlled'[1]

---

1   Official translation: 'In thought, men distance themselves from nature in order thus imaginatively to present it to themselves – but only in order to determine how it is to be dominated.'

(DE: 39). As Horkheimer and Adorno point out, instrumental reason is the prime tool of modern science, and anticipating the concerns of ecologists in the 1970s and 1980s, they suggest that science 'behaves toward things as a dictator toward men': it 'knows them' only 'in so far as' it 'can manipulate them' (DE: 9).

Making explicit reference to the Kantian system of rationality and knowledge, Horkheimer and Adorno suggest that 'in the Enlightenment's interpretation, thinking is the creation of unified, scientific order and the derivation of factual knowledge from principles' (DE: 81f.). Formal logic, 'the grand school of uniformity'[2] (DE: 7), provides the set of rules on the basis of which instrumental reason constantly works towards its ideal of 'the system from which all and everything follows' (DE: 7). The more successful instrumental reason is regarding the emancipation of the human Self, that is the more of the non-rational world that can be integrated into the system of rationality, the more complex this system becomes. Assuming that 'enlightenment is totalitarian' (DE: 6), Horkheimer and Adorno anticipate that 'pure immanence' will be the 'ultimate product' (DE: 16). 'Nothing at all may remain outside, because the mere idea of outsideness is the very source of fear' (ibid.). Whatever resists integration into the system, is denied its existence; it is refused its status 'as being or occurrence' (DE: 7). Yet, in this process of the rational penetration and systemisation of the Other, everything in the non-rational world is 'brought to a common denominator, and reduced to the human subject' (DE: 7). Horkheimer and Adorno point out that 'the identity of everything with everything else', that is the integration of everything into the system of subjective reason, 'is paid for in that nothing may at the same time be identical with itself' (DE: 12). In other words, in the interest of subjective identity formation and self-preservation, all objects of human cognition are forced to adopt a subject-oriented identity and are alienated from their independent identity.

In order to capture the difference between the things and occurrences as they are for themselves and their appearance within the system of instrumental reason, that is in order to conceptualise how the process of rational identification alienates things from themselves and completely replaces their independent identity with a subject-dominated identity, Horkheimer and Adorno distinguish between *nature* and *second nature*. In *Dialectic of Enlightenment* this distinction is only hinted at, but in *Negative Dialectics* Adorno is more explicit. *Second nature* – to some extent it can be described as the epistemological equivalent to Goldsmith's 'surrogate nature' (see Section 3.1) – is the systematic representation of nature which is produced by instrumental reason in the interest of bringing nature under rational control and preserving the human Self. The more embracing and complex second nature becomes, the more difficult it will be to remember, or to become aware of, first nature. Whilst first nature gradually disappears, second nature – although only a construct of human rationality – successfully claims the status of genuine naturalness:

---

2   Official translation: 'the major school of unified science'.

What is truly ϑεσει – produced by a functional context of individuals, if not by themselves – usurps the insignia of that which a bourgeois consciousness regards as nature and as natural. To that consciousness nothing appears as being outside any more; in a certain sense there actually is nothing outside any more, nothing unaffected by mediation, which is total. What is trapped within, therefore, comes to appear to itself as its own otherness . . . . The more relentlessly socialisation commands all moments of human and interhuman immediacy, the smaller the capacity of men to recall that this web has evolved, and the more irresistible its natural appearance. The appearance is reinforced as the distance between human history and nature keeps growing . . . .

(ND: 357f.)

For Horkheimer and Adorno the central aim of all philosophy is to expose this false appearance of naturalness, and preserve the memory of nature as it might be independent of all human aims. To second nature, that is to the mutilated image instrumental reason creates of nature, they also refer as a 'delusive context' (*Verblendungszusammenhang*). This delusive context becomes ever more universal the less there remains unpenetrated by rationality. The dangerous implication of this *Verblendungszusammenhang* is not only that it shuts human thinking off against what nature could be independent of human perception, but more importantly, it installs as natural what in reality is no more than the product of the mind. What Adorno calls the 'bourgeois' concept of nature is not only oppressive towards first nature, but it transfigures as natural what in reality is man-made. Specifically human (ideological) interests are presented as nature and natural. The bourgeois concept of nature pretends to be speaking about the radically different, from which it wants to derive ethical and political imperatives, while in reality it only captures a tamed and fully calculable nature. 'The bourgeois ideal of naturalness intends not amorphous nature, but the virtuous mean' (DE: 31), that is whatever it conceptualises is under full rational control.

The crucial point Adorno wants to make is that wherever human reason reflects on nature and the natural, that is on the Other, it tends to be speaking – without admitting it – only about itself, about the 'spirit as a second nature' (ND: 356). On the one hand, Adorno rejects this identification as ideological, yet at the same time, he suggests that there is no alternative, that the human mind *can* only capture second nature, and that wanting to conceptualise original nature is a contradiction in terms. Following 'a fatal dialectics', all efforts through which 'consciousness hopes to escape from that entanglement', merely 'reinforce the spell of the second nature' (ND: 68). According to Adorno, already 'the question about nature as the absolute first, as the downright immediate compared with its mediations' is ideological, for 'what the question pursues is presented in the hierarchic form of analytical judgment, whose premises command whatever follows, and it thus repeats the delusion it would escape from' (ND: 359). Against this background, it hardly comes as a surprise that, as a safeguard against all ideological transfiguration, Adorno demands 'to see all nature, and whatever would install itself as such, as history' (ibid.). In other words, anticipating crucial elements of the constructionist argument presented above (see Section 3.2), he favours a completely social concept of nature. Nevertheless, this does not stop Adorno from insisting that the effort to get beyond the constructions of instrumental reason must never be given up. For him, 'to breach the walls which thought has built around itself, to pierce the interjected layer of subjective positions that have become a second nature' (ND: 78f.), always remains the prime aim of all philosophy, for the awareness of the Other is the only remedy against the 'incapacitation of the subject' (ND: 66) which results from the so-called dialectic of enlightenment.

4.2   The dialectic of enlightenment

According to the famous beginning of *Dialectic of Enlightenment*, the progress of human rationality 'has always aimed at liberating men from fear and establishing their sovereignty' *vis-à-vis* nature, but 'the fully enlightened earth radiates disaster triumphant' (DE: 3). Contrary to its own intentions, the process of the constitution and emancipation of the human subject eventually culminates in 'the revolt of nature' (ER: ch. 3), or in Adorno's words, in a 'logic of disintegration' (ND: 144). On the one hand civilisatory progress has achieved that 'nature has lost its awesomeness, its *qualitates occultae*' (ER: 103), but on the other, 'nature seems to be taking its revenge' (ER: 104). In *Negative Dialectics* Adorno points to 'a universal feeling, a universal fear, that our progress in controlling nature may increasingly help to weave the very calamity it is supposed to protect us from' (ND: 67). Horkheimer and Adorno argue that the system instrumental reason erects for the preservation of the Self and the domination of nature quickly becomes so complex that it becomes a source of *Fremdbestimmung* itself. Once again anticipating the concerns of contemporary ecologists, they fear that 'the more devices we invent for dominating nature, the more must we serve them if we are to survive' (ER: 97), and the more must individuals 'model their body and soul according to the technical apparatus' (DE: 29f.).

What Horkheimer and Adorno here suggest is that nature and second nature are identical in that they are both sources of *Fremdbestimmung* undermining the claim to self-determination. It is the dialectic of enlightenment that second nature, as a secondary source of *Fremdbestimmung*, builds up at the same pace as first nature is brought under rational control. According to this model, the cumulative potential of *Fremdbestimmung* therefore remains by and large the same, whatever the progress of human rationality. All that changes is its source. To the extent, however, that in the enlightened world *Fremdbestimmung* means the domination of rational beings by other rational beings, or by rational structures whose complexity has grown beyond the capacities of the individual, and the control over which is unequally distributed within society, this condition is even worse than the pre-enlightened one. Horkheimer and Adorno therefore note that 'irresistible regression' is 'the curse of irresistible progress' (DE: 36). The explanation they offer for this dialectic of progress and regression is that 'the human being, in the process of his emancipation, shares the fate of the rest of his world' (ER: 93). In *Eclipse of Reason* Horkheimer points out that 'the history of man's effort to subjugate nature is also the history of man's subjugation by man' (ER: 105). And in *Dialectic of Enlightenment* the authors note that 'men had to do fearful things to themselves before the self, the identical, purposive, and virile nature of man, was formed' (DE: 33).

Taking account of the fact that humans themselves are a part of nature, Horkheimer and Adorno distinguish between *outer nature* and *inner nature*, and suggest that the domination of the former necessarily implies that of the latter:

> Domination of nature involves domination of man. Each subject not only has to take part in the subjugation of external nature, human and nonhuman, but in order to do so must subjugate nature in himself. Domination becomes 'internalized' for domination's sake.
>
> (ER: 93)

In other words, the project of the constitution and emancipation of the modern Self and subject by means of subjugating nature implies, at the same time, 'the destruction of the subject' (DE: 54) because nature is an inseparable unity of outer and inner nature. Horkheimer and Adorno emphasise that as long as the emancipation of the Self is 'paid for by a denial of nature in man for the sake of domination over non-human nature' (ibid.), the project of human self-determination and subjective autonomy cannot be successful. The inevitable domination of inner nature is an obstacle to subjective self-realisation. It alienates the human subject from itself. Alienation from nature and alienation from the Self are the dialectical counterpart of emancipation and self-determination. So there is something fundamentally flawed and contradictory in the way in which the enlightenment process tries to establish and preserve the human Self. It is not just, as was indicated above, that 'mankind pays[3] for the increase of their power' over external nature 'with alienation from that over which they exercise their power' (DE: 9), but beyond this:

> Man's domination over himself, which grounds his selfhood, is in essence[4] the destruction of the subject in whose service it is undertaken; for the substance which is dominated, suppressed, and dissolved by virtue of self-preservation is none other than that very life as functions of which the achievements of self-preservation find their sole definition and determination: it is, in fact, what is to be preserved.
>
> (DE: 54f.)

The process of enlightenment was meant to emancipate humanity from nature, increase human self-determination and replace myth by rationality. But the idea of the emancipated subject and its control over nature itself turns into a myth: 'enlightenment returns to mythology' (DE: 27). As Horkheimer points out, the 'end result' of the enlightenment process is, on the one hand, 'the abstract ego emptied of all substance', and on the other hand, 'an empty nature degraded to mere

---

3   Official translation: 'men pay'.
4   Official translation: 'is almost always'.

material, mere stuff to be dominated' (ER: 97). And since the domination of nature (outer and inner) obviously does not lead to the emancipation of the subject, but instead to the destruction of both the subject's own substance as well as the substance of what the subject wanted to dominate, it ceases to make sense. It serves no purpose apart from the perpetuation of the principle of domination. According to early critical theory, the continued belief in the progress of human rationality thus becomes 'the germ cell of a proliferating mythic irrationality' (DE: 54). Horkheimer and Adorno actually raise a suspicion that is very interesting with regard to an argument I will develop at a much later stage in this book: they suggest that under the conditions of advanced capitalist societies, this continued – if irrational – belief in the progress of rationality and human control over nature turns 'into an instrument of rational administration by the wholly enlightened as they steer society toward barbarism' (DE: 20). What Horkheimer and Adorno mean is that social elites ('the wholly enlightened') strategically abuse the cherished, but illusionary, belief in rational progress towards a better society as a social tranquilliser while they concentrate material wealth and social opportunities in their own hands and keep the masses at bay. This is a gloomy idea that smacks of conspiracy theories. Nevertheless, it is a very interesting idea that deserves closer consideration (see Chapter 11). Horkheimer and Adorno, however, had no intention of resigning to the powers that be. They sought to break free from the vicious circle of the enlightenment project. For humanity to escape the downward spiral towards *barbarism*, they demand that the 'non-identical' integrity of the Other *vis-à-vis* the Self be acknowledged. The 'remembrance of nature in the subject' (DE: 40), so they argue, may be the first step towards a reconciliation with nature which is the only way to achieving real happiness, fulfilment and a meaningful modern Self.

4.3   The project of reconciliation

Horkheimer and Adorno want to get beyond the ill-conceived pattern of subjective Self-constitution that was outlined above. In their view, this pattern demands and relentlessly implements the reification and domination of nature, whilst the ideal of the fully emancipated Self always remains an unfulfilled promise. Their philosophical project is the critique of 'identifying thought', that is of the tradition of European thought that forces whatever exists into an all-embracing system of subject-oriented instrumental rationality. As Adorno phrases it in *Negative Dialectics*, the aim is to expose the 'barricading' and 'mutilating'[5] (ND: 9) character of human rationality which is the basis for the domination of nature, and the explanation for the illnesses of modern capitalist society. Horkheimer and Adorno aim to detect, assist and reinstate the Other, the natural, the non-identical, which has not yet been reified and subjected to the interest of the modern Self. Their utopia is the reconciliation with nature which 'would release the nonidentical, would rid it of

---

5   Official translation: 'the preparatory and concluding'.

coercion' and 'open the road to the multiplicity of different things' (ND: 6). To them reconciling human rationality with nature would mean to abandon the project of forcing everything into the system of rationality, and to allow 'the thought of the many as no longer inimical' (ibid.). In line with what I said about ecologist thought, Adorno points out that this idea of plurality is 'a thought that is anathema to subjective reason' (ibid.). The attempt to overcome the split between the Self and the Other (human thinking and its object; nature and second nature) at the same time implies the attempt to defend reason against the inbuilt movement of the enlightenment towards irrationality. What is required is enlightenment about the enlightenment, that is that human rationality becomes self-critical and self-correcting. Yet, Horkheimer and Adorno had significant doubts regarding the capability of human rationality to rid itself of its suppressive character and bring about its genuine reconciliation with nature.

Horkheimer and Adorno first point to the constant temptation to look for reconciliation in an allegedly better past. Mythologies of a bygone golden age when humans and nature were living in perfect harmony have been around ever since the ancient Greeks, and the ecologist literature of the past three decades provides plenty of evidence that they still have not lost their attractiveness. But Horkheimer and Adorno are adamant that the only path to reconciliation with nature is through the progressive self-critique of the dominant civilisatory rationality and, most certainly, not through a reversal of the historical process and progress of human civilisation. They argue that trying to reinstall a historically earlier – allegedly more reconciled or less alienated – human–nature relationship would neither benefit the project of eliminating the irrationality of civilisatory reason, nor the project of liberating nature. Instead, any backward-oriented approach would necessarily amount to promoting anti-modernism and irrationality. In *Eclipse of Reason* Horkheimer insists that 'we are the heirs, for better or worse, of the Enlightenment and technological progress'. This implies that 'the permanent crisis' scientific and technological progress have brought about cannot be alleviated 'by regressing to more primitive stages'. In Horkheimer's view, any such attempt would only lead 'from historically reasonable to utterly barbaric forms of social domination' (ER: 127).

So any romantic orientation to the past and the attempt to go *back to nature* would further aggravate the crisis and contribute nothing to the liberation of nature. Horkheimer actually suggests that, as a matter of principle, human ideas or ideals of nature and the natural are *generally* inappropriate as a standard and justification for the critique and self-correction of rational progress and societal development, because any rational conceptualisation of nature 'has largely accepted the very principle that it is ostensibly combating' (ER: 123). Anticipating what Beck describes as 'the naturalistic misunderstanding of the green movement' (1995a: 36) (see Chapter 5), Horkheimer points out that 'whenever man deliberately makes nature his principle, he regresses to primitive urges' (ER: 127). He suggests that 'the equation of reason and nature, by which reason is debased and raw nature exalted, is a typical fallacy of the era of rationalization' (ER: 125). However, if nature cannot be used as 'a supreme principle', as 'a weapon of thought against thinking' (ER: 123), it becomes all the more questionable what else may serve as the normative standard for the self-critique of human rationality. If every rational critique of 'the growth of rationality has actually furthered the formalization of reason, and has served to fetter rather than to free nature' (ER: 122), this creates an extremely unfavourable framework for the project of reconciliation.

In order to avoid any ideological misconceptions, Horkheimer and Adorno do not sketch out any concrete scenarios of a reconciled condition or a liberated nature. This is in line with the fact that they conceptualise the subjugation of nature in intellectual rather than in empirical terms. They focus on the critique of the '*ideal*' rather than the '*material* tools' (DE: 39; my emphasis) by which nature (inner and outer) is suppressed and exploited. By the same token, they avoid concrete political recommendations, but restrict themselves to trying to 'unshackle . . . independent *thought*' which they consider as '*the sole way* of assisting nature' (ER: 127; my emphasis). But there is, of course, a contradiction implicit in the hope that 'the concept can transcend the concept . . . and can thus reach the nonconceptual' (ND: 9). Horkheimer and Adorno were well aware of this, but they were still not prepared to abandon the hope that there is a certain reflexive potential in philosophical thinking which can, and has, to be mobilised. Even though modern rationality has so far reified and enslaved rather than acknowledged and liberated nature, they still believe that, in philosophy, thinking can reflect 'its very own self as nature which has lost awareness of itself' (DE: 39). If nothing else, philosophical thinking can perhaps achieve that modern instrumental rationality 'no longer mistakes the ramparts that it erects against necessity . . . for guarantees of the freedom to come' (DE: 40). In Horkheimer and Adorno's view, this is the humble contribution philosophical thinking can make to the project of reconciliation. But there remains the fundamental problem that even philosophical thinking has to rely on rational conceptualisations and thus reproduces the domination of nature which it seeks to avoid.

Horkheimer and Adorno suggest that the 'cognitive utopia' to 'unseal the nonconceptual with concepts, without making it their equal' (ND: 10) may best be achieved if instrumental reason is counterbalanced and restricted by *mimesis*. Mimesis is a kind of behaviour towards the Other of formal rationality that does not conceptualise, capture and reify nature. It does not mutilate nature by forcing it into a system which serves only the interests of the Self. It rather adapts itself to nature, it seeks to imitate nature. Mimesis acknowledges the equality and integrity of the Other, and does not look to dominate or instrumentalise it. In many respects mimesis can be described as the conceptual precursor of Habermas's *communicative rationality*, but also of the ecologists' *ecological rationality*. According to *Dialectic of Enlightenment*, mimesis was the kind of behaviour towards nature that was characteristic of pre-enlightened mythology. The ancient myths animated nature and may therefore be described as 'mimesis unto life'. In contrast to this, 'the *ratio* which supplants mimesis' is 'mimesis unto death' (DE: 57). But Horkheimer and Adorno are implicitly aware that their dualistic model of the Self and the Other, subject and object, self-determination and *Fremdbestimmung*, leaves no space for the excluded third. As they conceptualise human rationality and social progress as the explication of formal logic, it remains unclear where exactly mimesis is supposed to fit into the system. It remains an ideal, and Horkheimer and Adorno do not spell out exactly how it might be applied in philosophical, let alone political, practice.

In the model of early critical theory, the fundamental obstacle to mimesis and reconciliation is what Horkheimer and Adorno call the *Naturverfallenheit* of human beings and social history. '*Naturverfallenheit* consists in the subjugation of nature, without which spirit does not exist'[6] (DE: 39), and which 'cannot be separated from social progress' (DE: xiv). What Horkheimer and Adorno describe as the *Naturverfallenheit* of human thinking is the impossibility of escaping the *natural* 'mechanism of compulsion' (DE: 39) which perpetuates the logic of domination and destruction. Although in the process of enlightenment nature becomes ever more mutilated and suppressed, it still persists as the ultimate driving force of history and its own destruction. Within the framework of the 'universal delusive context', *Naturverfallenheit* is the only way in which nature still expresses itself and remains invincible. As Adorno notes in *Negative Dialectics*, 'human history, the history of the progressing mastery of nature, continues the *unconscious history of nature*, of devouring and being devoured' (ND: 355; my emphasis). This belief in the *Naturverfallenheit* of human rationality and social history seals the futility of the project of reconciliation and gives Horkheimer and Adorno's theory its pessimistic outlook. As *Naturverfallenheit* is common to all rational beings, reconciliation will never find a historical subject.

As if he was looking back to *Dialectic of Enlightenment* and desired to revise the hope he and Adorno had placed in philosophy, Horkheimer notes in *Eclipse of Reason* that it had once been the project of philosophy 'to express the meaning of things and of life, to be the voice of all that is dumb, to endow nature with an organ for making known her sufferings, or, we might say, to call reality by its rightful name'. But 'today', Horkheimer writes, 'nature's tongue' has been 'taken away', that is even philosophy – not to mention politics – has failed. And anticipating both the fate of radical ecological protest since the 1970s as well as a common criticism of the contemporary practice of *ecological modernisation* (see Chapter 10), Horkheimer states:

> Typical of our present era is the manipulation of this revolt [the revolt of nature and ecologist protests] by the prevailing forces of civilization itself, the use of the revolt as a means of perpetuating the very conditions by which it is stirred up and against which it is directed. Civilization as rationalized irrationality integrates the revolt of nature as another means or instrument.
>
> (ER: 94)

---

6 Official translation: '*The decline, the forfeiture, of nature* consists in the subjugation' [DE: 39; my emphasis]. Contrary to what this translation suggests, the term *Naturverfallenheit* does not actually say anything about nature or the state it is in. Rather it signifies that mankind is and remains a slave to nature and is, however much nature is subjugated, ultimately unable to free itself entirely from nature's power. In order to avoid misinterpretations I will stick to the German term.

4.4   The pre-ecological imperative

Early critical theory was thoroughly concerned about the suppression and exploitation of nature. Its strongest desire was the liberation of, and the reconciliation with, nature. Yet its most daunting fear was neither the collapse of the ecological equilibrium and the loss of biodiversity, nor the possible destruction of the natural foundations of human and other life. If, nevertheless, Horkheimer and Adorno describe the domination of nature as a 'permanent crisis' and a 'disaster'; if they talk of the 'revolt' and the 'revenge of nature' in a way that closely resembles the warnings of contemporary ecologists, this begs the question what, in their view, this crisis actually consists in. Why did they think nature has to be saved? What kind of revenge did they foresee in case the domination of nature continued? I described early critical theory's concept of nature as a *pre-ecological* concept and their concern for nature as a *pre-ecological* concern. By the same token, their imperative to save nature, the Other, the non-identical, may be described as a *pre-ecological* imperative. What would be interesting to know is how Horkheimer and Adorno justify this imperative. In the context of the above discussion of the dialectic of the enlightenment, I already indicated where Horkheimer and Adorno see the catastrophe and the revenge of nature, but with a view to an analysis of the contemporary ecological discourse, it appears useful to look at this question in a little more detail.

As the above explorations demonstrate, the project of early critical theory was not just to preserve nature, but there are at least four other concerns which are inseparably connected to the concern for nature as well as to each other. As a matter of fact, they all seem to be more or less congruent and only conceptually distinguished from each other: to save reason, to save the subject, to save the critical standpoint, and to save meaning. Amongst these four concerns, the one for the loss of meaning adopts a prominent position. Reiterating the traditional sociological critique of modernity (Weber), Horkheimer and Adorno point out that 'on the road to modern science, men renounce any claim to meaning' (DE: 5). The process of enlightenment and the progress of rationality, they suggest, imply the 'disenchantment of the world', 'the extirpation of animism' (DE: 5), which is – for the lack of a functional equivalent of animated nature – tantamount to the extirpation of meaning. According to their model, the main deficiency of civilisatory rationality is that it 'substitute(s) formula for concept' (DE: 5), that is it implements the rules of formal logic but is indifferent regarding the aims of such formalisation. Making specific reference to the (in exactly this respect insufficient) Kantian ideal of the form of *purposeless purposiveness*, Horkheimer and Adorno highlight that formal reason itself 'posits no substantial goals' (DE: 89). Unless these goals are defined elsewhere, its uninhibited progress invariably culminates in a kind of 'organization of life in all its dimensions[7] which is deprived of any substantial goal' (DE: 88).

Ideally, these goals should be defined by a form of reason that is not reduced to

---

7   Official translation: 'life as a whole'.

instrumental rationality. However, as I outlined above, this form of reason has not yet been established; and as a result, the ongoing process of rationalisation remains purposeless beyond the merely formal goal of self-determination. At the very beginning of his chapter on 'The Revolt of Nature', Horkheimer notes that 'if reason is declared incapable of determining the ultimate aims of life and must content itself with reducing everything it encounters to a mere tool, its sole remaining goal is simply the perpetuation of its co-ordinating activity' (ER: 92). In Horkheimer and Adorno's model, reason – in its appearance as instrumental reason – is indeed declared incapable of determining any substantive goals, and whilst it gradually 'cancels the animation of nature' (DE: 57), the system it establishes represents 'a purposeless purposiveness which might thus be attached to all ends' (DE: 89). This dialectic of form and content will become very important at a later stage in my argument (see Chapter 7). At the risk of overstating the point I will therefore try to rephrase why exactly Horkheimer and Adorno believe that the enlightenment process destroys meaning without itself having an intrinsic value or goal.

Horkheimer and Adorno see instrumental reason as a purely formal mechanism. It may be compared to a machine that needs to be fed with some kind of raw material (external input) in order to be able to produce something. But being no more than 'the organ of calculation' which is 'neutral in regard to ends' (DE: 88), human rationality is itself unable to generate any substantive purpose for its formalising activity. It is 'planning considered solely as planning' (DE: 89); 'its element is coordination' (DE: 88). The only source of substantive purposes which make the process of formalisation meaningful is the Other of instrumental reason. Theoretically, this Other could be absolute reason, but given that absolute reason is not accessible, this Other can only be *nature*. Only the existence of *nature* can infuse formalised reason with meaning. The enlightenment process, however, 'puts back coherence, meaning and life into subjectivity, which is properly constituted only in this process' (DE: 89). In other words, the enlightenment process seeks to define meaning exclusively on the basis of subjectivity, ignoring the fact that the latter only emerges against the background of nature, and cannot be defined without reference to nature. On the one hand, meaning only emerges from the duality of and the tension between the Self and nature, but on the other hand, instrumental reason negates nature (outer and inner), and tries to find its justification and purpose solely in the subject. By denying nature and considering 'substantial goals as the power of nature over mind, as the erosion of its self-legislation' (DE: 87), formalised reason not only becomes abstract and counterproductive regarding the aim of subjective self-constitution, it also becomes self-referential and tautological. The congruence of means and ends leads to absurdity:

> with the denial of nature in man not merely the *telos* of the outward control of nature but the *telos* of man's own life is distorted and befogged. As soon as man discards his awareness that he himself is nature, all the aims for which he keeps himself alive – social progress, the intensification of all his material and

spiritual powers, even consciousness itself – are nullified, and the enthrone-
ment of the means as an end, which under late capitalism takes the form of[8]
open insanity, is already perceptible in the prehistory of subjectivity.

(DE: 54)

Coming back to the questions why nature has to be saved, what the threatening
catastrophe consists in and how the concern for nature is connected to the various
other concerns mentioned above, we can hence establish that in Horkheimer and
Adorno's model, nature has to be saved as a safeguard of meaning. Without nature
instrumental reason becomes irrational, subjectivity becomes empty and human
rationality can do nothing but reproduce the already existing. With the abolition or
denial of nature, 'factuality wins the day; cognition is restricted to its repetition; and
thought becomes mere tautology' (DE: 27). The catastrophe early critical theory
anticipated is that human rationality becomes pure form, bereft of any substance.
Horkheimer and Adorno feared that the enlightenment process would force individuals to adapt to societal structures and comply with formal regulations without
having any benefit from doing so. They were anxious that the subjugation of outer
and inner nature would render life completely meaningless, and that nothing
would remain against which the *status quo* could be measured and criticised. What
Horkheimer and Adorno spell out is the elaborated version of McKibben's horror
that 'without nature there is nothing but us'. In the context of their theory, nature
becomes the symbol of meaningfulness and liberty (autonomy); it becomes the substitute (functional equivalent) for absolute reason. Without nature there is nothing
but domination for domination's sake, which is equally pointless and barbaric.
Against this background the fundamental function of the critique of instrumental
reason is to expose the danger of formalised reason becoming self-referential.
Enlightenment about the Enlightenment seeks to demonstrate that human rationality at the same time destroys the integrity of nature and depends on it as its only
source of substantive goals. It attempts to achieve 'the self-cognition of the spirit as
nature in disunion with itself' (DE: 39).

So in the model of early critical theory, reconciliation with nature, the 'remembrance of nature in the subject', is necessary in order to avoid the self-referentiality
of formalised rationality. The *pre-ecological* imperative emanates from the necessity
to secure meaning. With regard to my further enquiries, this pre-occupation with
meaning, this fear of self-referentiality, and this quality of nature as a symbol are
important points. We will come back to these issues at a later stage, when I will
argue that the contemporary ecological imperative is not so radically different
from critical theory's pre-ecological imperative as it might seem. At this present
point, the question that immediately springs to mind is why Horkheimer and
Adorno believe that there is no alternative to their ultimately metaphysical concept
of meaning. Why did they insist on a concept of meaning that makes them so
dependent on the metaphysics of nature? If, as I quoted above, it was their aim to

---

8   Official translation: 'is tantamount to'.

'release the non-identical' and to 'open the road to the multiplicity of different things', why did they presuppose the unity of reason? What made them believe that human rationality integrates everything into one all-embracing systematic whole? Suppose they had abandoned this idea of uniform rationality, they could have adopted a concept of meaning that does not rely on transcendental sources, that is that does not emanate from nature as the Other of rationality. In such a scenario meaning would still – as it always and necessarily does – come from the Other, yet if rationality and the systems it erects are multiple, meaning can be generated immanently, that is by means of distinguishing different forms of rationality, and without reference to the completely pre- or extra-rational.

The evident explanation for this peculiarity of Horkheimer and Adorno's model is, firstly, their belief in the modernist idea of the identical subject and, secondly, the attempt to preserve critical theory's critical stance. Their ultimate concern is neither outer nature, nor, as some critics have suggested, inner nature, but the idea of the unified and autonomous subject which depends on the idea of uniform rationality, and which measures (criticises) the world around itself by this rationality. There is, however, no reason to assume that this particular mode of subjective self-construction and self-understanding is in any way more valid than, or normatively superior to, other forms of self-construction. As a matter of fact, contemporary sociology has abandoned this notion of the subject in order to take account of the principles of plurality and discontinuity (see Chapters 6 and 7). Equally, contemporary sociology has given up the idea of uniform reason. It is empirically evident that Horkheimer and Adorno wrongly assumed that human rationality integrates everything into one all-embracing logical system, and that it exhausts itself in reproducing the already existing structures of domination. Social history clearly demonstrates that even within the framework of capitalist systems, multiple mutually exclusive rationalities serving multiple mutually exclusive purposes have emerged and are competing with each other. As will be discussed at a later stage, the pluralisation of reason has significant effects for Horkheimer and Adorno's critical project. Unsurprisingly, contemporary social theory has become extremely sceptical regarding the critical paradigm as a whole. Of course, suspending the quasi-metaphysical ideas of the modernist subject and uniform reason not only destroys the normative foundation for critical theory's *pre-ecological* imperative. As we will see in the following chapters, abandoning these fundamentally modernist assumptions also has repercussions for the societal critique of contemporary ecologists.

4.5   Lessons to learn

Horkheimer and Adorno's work has to be read as the attempt to theorise and explain the discrepancy between the optimistic and ambitious goals of the enlightenment project and the historical reality the founding fathers of the Frankfurt School experienced at their time. Their immediate point of reference was the barbaric reality of Soviet Stalinism and German fascism. In their philosophy the concept of nature adopts a central position, yet as we have seen, Horkheimer and

Adorno do not define or describe nature in the empirical terms favoured by contemporary ecologists: nature – be it in its alienated and suppressed or in its envisaged reconciled state – remains an abstract concept. The fact that Horkheimer and Adorno are primarily concerned with meaning, identity and the autonomous subject rather than with biodiversity, human health, social justice, or animal rights, seems to make early critical theory and its discussion of nature incomparable and incompatible with the contemporary ecological discourse. Nevertheless, there are a variety of respects in which Horkheimer and Adorno anticipated concerns, observations and strategies that are characteristic of ecologist thought of the 1970s and 1980s. What makes their work exceptionally interesting from my particular perspective is that Horkheimer and Adorno respond to a historical constellation, which is thoroughly comparable to the one I seek to explain in this book: just as Horkheimer and Adorno were wondering why the project of enlightenment had failed so miserably, it is my objective to clarify why three decades of ecological campaigning (*ecological* enlightenment) have still not led to the ecological U-turn of late modern society. And just like early critical theory aimed to 'explain mistaken Marxist prognoses, but without breaking with Marxist intentions' (Habermas 1987b: 116), I would ideally wish to explain mistaken ecologist prognoses without having to abandon the ecologist intentions. It hence becomes all the more understandable why early critical theory appeared an attractive framework for the interpretation of ecologist concerns. As a matter of fact, it can offer explanations for a whole range of problems which were identified – but not solved – in the preliminary chapters in Part I:

(a)   When I discussed whether ecological thought qualifies as an ideology in its own right, I noted that ecologists have so far neither produced an attractive utopia nor a convincing strategy, and that they have also failed to nominate a promising agent for social change towards the ecologist ideal (see Section 2.1). I came to the conclusion that ecologism therefore has to be regarded as a *failed* ideology, but I could neither offer an explanation *why* it failed in all three respects, nor predict whether ecological thought might be able to resolve these issues in the future. On the basis of critical theory, we can now suggest that it is so difficult to sketch out a concrete ecologist utopia because human rationality is, as a matter of principle, incapable of conceptualising the reconciliation with nature. There are, as Wellmer puts it, 'no concepts available which could capture the state of reconciliation, whose idea appears [if at all], *ex negativo*, on the horizon of . . . philosophy' (1985: 19). And even if ecologists were successful in conceptualising this utopia beyond alienation, humanity's *Naturverfallenheit* would still make it impossible to devise effective strategies for the practical transition to this radically different world. If human thinking and action cannot break away from the 'compulsive mechanism' of domination, programmes and strategies of social change may achieve superficial reforms, but will never affect the basic structures of the *status quo*. And if human rationality cannot escape from the 'universal delusive context', it is no surprise that, as I noted above, agents of radical change cannot be found, and that all activists, whatever their intentions, ultimately just reproduce the alienating structures they are trying to oppose.

So Horkheimer and Adorno's theory helps us to explain why the ecologist ideology necessarily had to remain a failed ideology. If their theory is correct and really applicable to the contemporary ecological discourse, ecologists could have learnt from them that ecologism will never be able to resolve its deficiencies and that humankind's reconciliation with nature will never become a social reality. Ecologists will of course find this message politically unacceptable. They will criticise these considerations as excessively abstract and refer to partial successes. They will insist on the practical necessity of having regulative ideals even if it is known that they will never become fully true. Rather than discussing at this theoretical level, they will point towards much more concrete obstacles to radical ecological change. All these objections have to be taken seriously, but they do not affect the validity of Horkheimer and Adorno's theoretical evidence that ideologies of the reconciliation between the Self and the Other, between modern society and nature, are generally and necessarily doomed to failure. Although it admittedly is at the most abstract level, Horkheimer and Adorno's theoretical model does seem to provide some help with explaining the failure of ecologist ideology.

(b)   When I argued that around the turn to the 1990s there was a fundamental shift in the environmental movement, I suggested that this is due to 'the abolition of nature' (see Section 3.1), following which both the experience of alienation from nature as well as the resulting desire for reconciliation – both major motivating factors of the eco-movement – are in radical decline. After the discussion of critical theory, we can now see that Horkheimer and Adorno clearly anticipated and theorised this end of nature. According to their model, the enlightenment process establishes a 'universal delusive context', which aims at 'pure immanence' and tolerates nothing outside. This complete transformation of first nature into second nature is tantamount to the abolition of nature. It implies the end of duality. The experience of the nature–society split (the awareness of which Horkheimer and Adorno are trying to preserve) becomes increasingly impossible. This experience, however, is a prerequisite for the experience of alienation and the desire for reconciliation. And we may therefore expect that civilisatory progress increasingly undermines the motivational basis of the ecology movement. In other words, early critical theory provides a plausible – though of course once again very abstract and purely theoretical – explanation for the observation that the traditional eco-movement is in decline (see Section 2.2). If Horkheimer and Adorno's model is correct, ecological thought could have learnt from them that what ecologists seek to preserve has long been abolished. And as the memory of the Other (nature) fades, it will become ever more difficult to mobilise support for the ecologist cause.

(c)   Implicit in this is Horkheimer and Adorno's warning to contemporary ecologists that we have to be extremely cautious with the concepts of nature and the natural. They remind us that (especially since the abolition of nature) whatever we may perceive as nature and natural is most likely to be a social construct corresponding to particular social interests and needs. What assumes the status of naturalness is in effect purely ideological. The idea of the abolition of nature

implies that the concepts of nature and naturalness have lost their innocence. Admittedly, ecologists make an effort not to use these concepts at all. They have found substitutes like sustainability, biodiversity, and the like. However, these concepts can hardly be substantiated – and the related practical guidelines justified – without making reference to nature and the natural (see Chapter 7). And these underlying concepts of nature and the natural therefore need to be revealed and discursively defended. So assuming Horkheimer and Adorno's theory is correct, ecologists could have learnt from them that after the abolition of singular nature, the idea of an eco-centric critique of contemporary society is a contradiction in terms. After the end of modernist dualism there is nothing but society and its social constructions – including the multiple constructions of nature and the natural. Any social critique, including the ecological critique, becomes a societal self-critique. Ecological thought – as I noted above – has to turn into social theory.

(d)   When I discussed the constructionist responses to the abolition of nature (see Chapter 3) and tried to set out a refined constructionist research agenda, I pointed towards a pre-existing vital interest in nature which has not yet been sufficiently theorised. We noted that concern for nature goes far beyond the narrow concern for certain material conditions and physical phenomena. We pointed towards 'cultural filters' mediating the physical conditions (Grove-Whiet 1997) and highlighted that 'all statements on risk contain built-in standards of tolerance and acceptance relying on morality, cultural standards and perceptions' (Beck 1997c: 24). But we could not say very much about these *cultural filters* and, in particular, we were unable to clarify where the *moral interest* in nature originates from. On the basis of Horkheimer and Adorno's *pre-ecological* theory, we can now suggest that this pre-existing fundamental interest in nature emerges from nature's crucial function as the Other of the modernist Self. As we have seen above, the modernist idea of the autonomous subject depends on the idea of nature as a larger context or horizon, against which it constitutes and stabilises its identity. In other words, assuming that Horkheimer and Adorno's model is correct, ecological thought could have learnt that the whole of the ecological discourse is ultimately not about physical nature but about identity. Of course, this idea needs to be explored in much more detail, but Horkheimer and Adorno seem to suggest that concern for nature is ultimately concern for the modernist subject. On the basis of early critical theory, we begin to understand that the ecological *Angst* to which I pointed in Chapter 1 (and to which I will return in Chapter 7) is the fear of meaninglessness and the disintegration of the subjective identity. It is the fundamental *Angst* of *Fremdbestimmung* and the 'reversion of the self to that mere state of nature from which it had estranged itself with so huge an effort'.

(e)   At the same time, Horkheimer and Adorno's model of the Self and the Other does offer a very plausible explanation why nature has been constructed and installed as a singular nature in the first place. Environmental sociologists have often pointed to the fact *that* 'nature has historically been made singular, abstract and then personified', and *that* this singular nature is now once again breaking

down into a 'multiplicity of lived experiences' (Macnaghten and Urry 1998: 8). But there are surprisingly few attempts to explain *why* nature has been socially constructed in this and not in any other way. As Horkheimer and Adorno's model suggests, nature had to be conceptualised (and preserved) as a singular entity because this is the precondition for the emergence and stability of the identical subject. So Horkheimer and Adorno's model does not just confirm the suggestion that the ecological discourse ultimately centres around two social constructions (nature and the identical subject) rather than two ontological entities (human beings and the physical environment), but it also reconfirms that this discourse is a specifically modernist discourse and that its concerns are specifically modernist concerns, for both singular nature and the identical subject are specifically modernist constructs. As a matter of fact, early critical theory thus also confirms that the ecologist discourse is indeed a conservative rather than a progressive discourse (see Section 2.3) because it seeks to preserve modernist constructions which have arguably lost their cultural basis.

(f)   Beyond the points addressed so far, Horkheimer and Adorno also point to fundamental methodological problems inherent in the project of rationality's self-critique. Their attempt to 'transcend the concept by means of the concept', that is to criticise human rationality by means of this same rationality, leads into problems of self-referentiality. If ecological thought had taken critical theory more seriously, it would have realised that the fundamental contradiction of the project of enlightenment about the Enlightenment also affects the project of *ecological enlightenment*. How would ecologists justify their *ecological* critique and make it empirically meaningful? As I demonstrated above, for Horkheimer and Adorno the struggle to find a normative basis for their critique of modern society is the very nucleus of their whole philosophy. In the end, they evaded the problem by leaving the ideas of *mimesis* and reconciliation virtually undefined. We saw that this did not protect them from falling back into metaphysics, but it is still early critical theory's major achievement to have highlighted the problem of post-metaphysical normative standards, and to have tried to confront it. Ecologists, in contrast, seem to have forgotten about this fundamental problem. They have never given much thought to the normative foundation of their ecological imperatives; and they are either unaware of the self-referentiality of ecological discourse or not concerned about it (see Chapter 7). This takes me to the final point I want to address in this context.

(g)   Horkheimer and Adorno were clearly aware that human rationality is unsuitable as a basis for objectively valid, empirically meaningful moral imperatives. In this respect they were radically critical of Kant, who had been convinced that the morally good can be deduced from pure reason. Making specific reference to Nietzsche, whose philosophy marks 'the entry into postmodernity' (Habermas 1987b), Horkheimer and Adorno point to the fundamental error of believing 'that formalistic reason is more closely allied to morality than to immorality' (DE: 118). Yet although early critical theory had

clearly demonstrated that human rationality is purely formal, that is empirically empty, and that beliefs about the morally good cannot be given an objectively valid basis, ecologists continued to believe in a rationally justified eco-ethics, which was meant to provide the central motivation and guideline for the ecologisation of society. Horkheimer and Adorno even went a step further than diagnosing the end of rationalist ethics. They were on the very threshold of postmodernist thinking. And long before the actual emergence of the postmodernist discourse, they issued a warning to anyone trying to confront enlightenment thought with postmodernist reasoning. Anticipating exactly the kind of aggressive reaction I documented in Section 3.2 they noted:

> Not to have glossed over or suppressed but to have trumpeted far and wide the impossibility of deriving from reason any fundamental argument against murder fired the hatred which the progressives (and they in particular) still direct against Sade and Nietzsche.
>
> (DE: 118)

Horkheimer and Adorno were surely right with their observation that the message of the end of uniform rationality and rationalist ethics provokes 'hatred'. And as we have seen, the believers in ecological enlightenment are thoroughly comparable to the 'progressives' Horkheimer and Adorno were talking about: rather than using the thesis of the end of modernist reason as an incentive for further theoretical and sociological enquiry, they respond with 'hatred' whenever it is suggested that absolute reason does not provide any argument against the 'murder' of nature. Horkheimer and Adorno themselves sought to avoid the *pre-ecological* precursor of the *hatred* that contemporary eco-postmodernists have to confront by holding fast to their bourgeois beliefs, even when they were themselves arguing that their project was irrational and necessarily futile. It is, however, blatantly evident that this solution is not consistent with their own theory. What contemporary ecological theorists could therefore have learnt from early critical theory is, firstly, that they will never succeed in constructing a binding rational foundation for any ecological ethics and, secondly, that it will be necessary to embrace the postmodernist paradigm rather than trying to evade it. The inconsistencies of early critical theory could have functioned as an incentive for trying to find other ways out of the dilemma in which Horkheimer and Adorno got caught up. Ecological theorists could, for example, have thought through the idea that with the full abolition of nature and the arrival of postmodernist plurality, the very need for an ethics of reconciliation might disappear. This idea has already surfaced at various points above; I will keep coming back to it until it is fully developed in Part IV. But at this stage I will first of all focus on those weaknesses in Horkheimer and Adorno's theory which make it unconvincing as a theoretical model for the analysis and interpretation of contemporary ecological discourse. This exercise will sharpen the focus for what may be expected from contemporary attempts to revise and modify early critical theory.

4.6   Theoretical limitations

Apart from the fundamental question to what extent, or whether at all, it is really possible to compare Horkheimer and Adorno's pre-ecological *concern for nature* to contemporary *ecological concern*, the most striking inconsistency *within* early critical theory was that it stuck to the modernist model of linear modernisation although it was evident that this model had reached its limits. Horkheimer and Adorno's 'principle of dissolvent rationality' (DE: 6) is always directed towards the Other of the human mind, which is gradually penetrated until everything has been integrated into the system. Despite pointing out that the replacement of nature by second nature is so complete that the delusive context is practically universal, Horkheimer and Adorno hold fast to the distinction between nature and second nature, between the Self and the Other. On the one hand, their philosophy wants to tell us that nature has disappeared, that it cannot be conceptualised, and that reconciliation is therefore impossible, but on the other hand, the whole aim of their philosophy is to remind us of the existence of nature and to give it a voice.

Horkheimer and Adorno realise that *Fremdbestimmung* increasingly originates from the system itself rather than from its Other, yet in their model, the efforts of rationality remain oriented exclusively towards primary nature: *Naturbeherrschung* (subjugation of nature) for Self-preservation. By assuming that systemic *Fremdbestimmung* is merely the extension and continuation of the Other, of nature, they manage to preserve the dualism which they cannot give up because in their model, the unity and identity of the Self depends on the existence of the Other. In other words, in order to secure their (bourgeois) concept of the subject, they shy away from implementing the abolition of nature and thus contradict their own thesis about the universality of the delusive context. Because they could not imagine that there might be historical successors for the modernist subject, they replace analysis by prescription. Yet irrespective of the consequences this may have for the subject, they have to accept that eventually 'the principle of dissolvent rationality' will turn against rationality itself, against the 'spirit as the second nature' (ND: 356). And if the *Verblendungszusammenhang* really becomes universal, this implies, as I noted above, that the experience of alienation as well as the desire for reconciliation will become impossible. It then becomes very difficult to justify the almost ontological quality Horkheimer and Adorno accredit to both these feelings, for this absolute status is neither consistent theoretically, nor verifiable empirically. Furthermore, with the delusive context becoming universal, 'dissolvent rationality' begins to undermine its own foundations, that is to question its hitherto uncontested assumptions like the unity of reason, the unity of the subject, and the unity of nature. Early critical theory's idea of the *reflective* confrontation of instrumental rationality with reason then gives way to the *reflexive* process of rational self-dissolution.

With the abolition of nature, the single dualism of *nature* and *second nature* becomes irrelevant, and the project of emancipation continues as an inner-societal project. Uniform reason and the modernist concept of the subject become subject to processes of pluralisation and differentiation. This post-metaphysical differentiation of rationality and the societal subsystems it generates had already been observed and conceptualised by Max Weber. Yet rather than developing this idea, Horkheimer and Adorno once again tried to unify rationality under the heading of self-preservation. It is exactly this historically outdated attempt to resuscitate the old dualist thinking of modernity that makes early critical theory so gloomy and pessimistic. The reason why Horkheimer and Adorno could never get beyond bemoaning the 'irresistible regression' which they saw as 'the curse of irresistible progress' is that they did not allow reason to become truly reflexive. Horkheimer and Adorno were longing for a reconciliation which they knew would never be possible. What they did not realise is that as soon as the concepts of reason and nature are pluralised, there is new scope for optimism because there is new scope for reconciliation: reconciliation that is between particular forms of rationality and particular ideas of nature. In this respect, however, contemporary society has clearly developed beyond early critical theory's conceptualisations. Habermas was therefore right in suggesting that Horkheimer and Adorno's cultural pessimism has become obsolete: 'we no longer share this mood, this attitude' (1987b: 106). Early critical theory's one-dimensional conceptualisation of human rationality as nothing but a tool for the domination of nature and the preservation of the Self is no longer suitable as a basis for the analysis of highly complex contemporary societies. As Adorno famously states in the last sentence of *Negative Dialectics*, his thinking sympathises with 'metaphysics at the time of its fall' (ND: 408). At the beginning of the twenty-first century we have surely moved beyond this point, and for interpreting contemporary ecological discourse we therefore require more contemporary theoretical models.

So early critical theory can clearly offer significant assistance regarding my three main objectives in this study. Although it is *pre-ecological* and although it cannot help to solve, politically, the so-called ecological crisis, it still contributes to the project of ecological enlightenment by helping us to understand what ecological concern is all about, and where and why ecological thought still requires consolidation. On the basis of Horkheimer and Adorno's model, we managed to fill in a range of theoretical gaps. Early critical theory also helped to conceptualise and explain the crisis of ecologism and the eco-movement. And beyond that it provided important hints for the exploration of the future of the ecological issue and eco-politics. The ideas of the social constructedness of nature and the modernist subject, of the abolition of nature and of the possible decline of the modernist constellations of thought are important signposts for the projected theory of post-ecologist politics. But Horkheimer and Adorno's thinking also displays weaknesses which go far beyond the (dubious) allegations that their concept of nature is incompatible with that of ecologists, and that their model remains subject-centred instead of becoming eco-centred. It raises questions which we might be able to answer on the basis of Ulrich Beck's modernised version of critical theory.

5 Pluralisation and reflexivity – Ulrich Beck

Undeniably, there is a big leap between the founding fathers of the Frankfurt School and Ulrich Beck, who might be considered as a *third generation* (Munich-based) critical theorist. Already, *second generation* critical theorists like Marcuse and Habermas had criticised the pessimism and inner contradictions of Horkheimer and Adorno's thinking. Habermas, in particular, introduced radical and important changes into critical theory. Yet from the specific perspective of this study, his writings are less interesting than those of Ulrich Beck. Whilst in Habermas's work the themes of nature and ecology find only marginal representation (Eckersley 1990, 1992), Beck shares Horkheimer and Adorno's immediate concern for nature and reconciliation. As I indicated above, he focuses their critical project on ecological issues in the contemporary sense. He performs the transition from early critical theory's *concern for nature* to today's *ecological concern*, and thus provides an opportunity to explore how far early critical theory's insights and theses about nature are applicable to the contemporary ecological discourse. And what makes Beck's work even more interesting from my particular perspective: he considers the abolition of nature as the starting point for his theoretical inquiry.

Up to the present, Beck's most important book is his well-known *Risk Society* (1986/92; henceforth RS). Here he develops all the fundamental ideas he cites, varies and elaborates in his innumerable later writings. The book is a provocative and polemic crusade against the rationality that dominates modern civilisation. It thus clearly continues the tradition of the Frankfurt School. Undoubtedly, *Risk Society* has to be considered as a sociological core text no less important and influential than Horkheimer and Adorno's *Dialectic of Enlightenment*. Compared to the latter, however, and compared to the writings of first- and second-generation critical theory in general (Adorno, Habermas), Beck's essayistic – at times almost journalistic – style makes fairly easy reading. Like Anthony Giddens – and together with him – he programmatically seeks to cross the dividing line between academic and popular discourses about the development of contemporary society. It has often been observed that Beck's analysis of contemporary society lacks theoretical consistency and is not sufficiently supported by empirical evidence (e.g. Baumann 1993; Goldblatt 1996; Hamm 1996). As a matter of fact, in both his own country and in the English-speaking world, Beck is widely denied the status of a social or political theorist in the proper sense. Nevertheless, Beck – alongside his intellectual partner Giddens – very quickly became one of the most widely read and debated sociological writers of the 1990s (apart from the above, see e.g. Lash 1993; Prittwitz 1993a; Hajer 1995; Hannigan 1995; Lash, Szerzynski and Wynne 1996; Dryzek 1997; Darier 1999). In the eco-sociological literature his concepts enjoy enormous popularity. Far beyond the *ecological* discourse, one might actually say that at the beginning of the twenty-first century, the Beck–Giddensian rhetoric of the risk society, reflexive modernisation, ecological democratisation and the *third way* towards a global civil society exerts something like a hegemonic influence, pushing all other discourses into the margins. A comprehensive critical analysis of Beck's thinking is therefore a very important task. However, as Goldblatt correctly points out, 'there has as yet been no proper survey of his recent work', nor 'have the precise implications of that work for the understanding of environmental degradation and environmental politics been properly explored' (Goldblatt 1996: 156).

In the context of this study, a systematic 'survey of Beck's recent work' would be out of place, not least because – quite in line with the central thesis of this book – his interest has, since the mid-1990s, moved away from ecological issues in the narrow sense towards the wider issues of globalisation, the future of work, and the prospects for democracy and a global civil society (Beck 1997b, 1998a, 1998b, 1999, 2000a, 2000b). But a systematic exploration of the implications of Beck's work 'for the understanding of environmental degradation and environmental politics' would be very helpful, indeed. The eco-oriented review of early critical theory has left plenty of unresolved issues for which Beck's updated version may give us some hints. Also, most of the existing eco-sociological literature arguably approaches and criticises Beck's work from a misguided perspective and therefore fails to uncover both its crucial achievements as well as its fundamental weaknesses. In my own analysis I will focus on Beck's declared goal to replace the older critical theory of society with an ecologically oriented 'theory of societal self-critique' (1993: 54). More precisely, I am interested to see: (i) how Beck integrates specifically ecological issues into critical theory's sociological model; (ii) whether Beck is more consistent than Horkheimer and Adorno regarding the abolition of nature; (iii) to what extent he dares to cross the threshold to postmodernist thinking; (iv) how Beck manages to overcome the pessimism of earlier critical theory; and (v) how he handles the problem of self-referentiality. With regard to a better understanding of ecologist thinking and with a view to my three objectives in this book, an answer to these questions would mean significant progress. Apart from *Risk Society*, I will base my analysis mainly – but by no means exclusively – on *Ecological Politics in an Age of Risk* (1995a) and *The Reinvention of Politics* (1993 and 1997a; henceforth EP and RP[1]).

---

1 *The Reinvention of Politics* is more than a translation of Beck's German book *Die Erfindung des Politischen*. For the English version, the first three chapters of the German text have been replaced by a new Chapter 1. For this reason I use two abbreviations: EP refers to the German text (my own translations); RP signifies the revised English version.

5.1   The risk society

Towards the end of the twentieth century Beck saw himself confronted with societal structures which he believed to be categorically different from the ones
characteristic of earlier parts of the century. Whilst Horkheimer and Adorno had
been theorising advanced industrial societies, Beck suggested we are now living in
a *risk society*. For Beck this implies 'not just a change *in* the frame of reference of
classical sociology, but a categorical change, a change *of* the frame of reference, that
is a change of society and politics that distinguishes contemporary societies in a significant way from earlier phases of social evolution' (Beck et al. 1999: 8). For the
definition of the *risk society* and its distinction from industrial society, 'irreversible
threats to the life of plants, animals and human beings' (RS: 13) play a central role.
In other words, ecological issues, which were only marginally or indirectly touched
upon in early critical theory, become the focal point of attention. For Beck, the crucial difference between the risk society and its classical industrial precursor is that
the latter centres around issues of the generation and distribution of wealth, whilst
the former is predominantly concerned with the generation and distribution of
hazards and risks. This does not mean to say that earlier stages of human civilisation had not been confronted with risks. Also, wealth remains for Beck a central
issue in contemporary societies. However, Beck suggests that 'while in classical
industrial society the *logic* of wealth production dominates the *logic* of risk production, in the risk society this relationship is reversed' (RS: 12). And this shift of
emphasis is not the result of 'malevolence' or a conspiracy, but, according to Beck,
it follows the 'internal dynamic' of contemporary society (RS: 51). Advanced
industrial society automatically transforms into a risk society which 'is *not an option*
that in the process of political discourse could be chosen or rejected', but that
'emerges automatically [*im Selbstlauf*] through self-perpetuating processes of modernisation which are blind to any consequences and deaf to potential dangers' (EP:
36; also Beck 1997c: 28).

The historical event that symbolises for Beck the arrival of the risk society was
the nuclear catastrophe in Chernobyl. Just as Auschwitz provided for Horkheimer
and Adorno the historical evidence that the rationality of industrial society has
become perverted, so the disaster in Ukraine demonstrated for Beck that societal
development has entered a phase 'where the hazards generated on the path of
industrialised society become dominant' (EP: 37f.). In 'the age of side-effects' (RP:
ch. 1) the latent threats of technological progress 'add up to self-endangerments
which question, dissolve and transform the foundations of industrial society' (EP:
36). In the risk society 'the motor of social transformation' is no longer 'instrumental rationality, but rather the side-effect' (RP: 23). We are, evidently, confronted
here with a further variation of the old Marxian thesis of the self-undermining of
modern society and its dialectic progress towards a new evolutionary phase. What
Beck perceives as the radically new quality of the risks governing contemporary
societies may be summarised in four main points:

In the risk society we firstly have to deal with threats which cannot be attributed
to nature, the immortals or any other external powers. We are 'essentially'

concerned 'with problems resulting from techno-economic development itself' (RS: 19), that is problems which raise fundamental questions of responsibility. Whilst Horkheimer and Adorno's thinking centred around forces which are beyond human control – *Fremdbestimmung* originating from nature – and tried to conceptualise even systemic *Fremdbestimmung* as an extension of nature (*Naturverfallenheit*), Beck shifts the focus of attention to the fact that contemporary risks are self-inflicted and man-made. Secondly, the threats emanating from modern technology have a completely new spatial and temporal dimension. As the example of nuclear technology demonstrates, the side-effects of certain human activities may affect even parts of the globe which are far removed from the place where they were originally caused. Also, it might take several generations until these side-effects become visible at all. Political, administrative and judicial decision makers are thus in a difficult position: whilst it was formerly comparatively simple to identify the source and originator of man-made hazards or devastation, the threats which are typical of the risk society cannot easily be attributed to definite causes. And even where direct causes *can* be identified and individual perpetrators *can* be held accountable, this still does not mean that compensation for those affected is possible at all.

Closely connected to this point is the fact that the risks which in Beck's perception are the distinctive feature of the contemporary type of society are to a significant extent the outcome of processes of social construction. The identification and definition of risks depends on the instruments and knowledge of scientific experts, because 'more and more, the center comes to be occupied by threats that are . . . neither visible nor tangible to the lay public' (RS: 162). In as much as they '*require the sensory organs of science . . . in order to become visible and interpretable as threats at all*', contemporary high-tech risks are 'not only transmitted by science, but in the strict sense . . . *scientifically constituted*' (RS: 162). But apart from science, there are also other players involved in the process of social risk construction, for 'behind all the objectifications, sooner or later the question of *acceptance* arises' (RS: 28). As I indicated in Chapter 3, Beck emphasises that statements on risks always contain 'implicit cultural value notions of a life worth living' (RS: 58). All statements of risks 'ultimately come down to the question: how do we want to live?' (Beck 1997c: 24). Obviously, 'this is a question that can never be answered by experts alone' (ibid.). The sciences have no monopoly on the implicit value notions. Quite irrespective of what scientific experts may or may not define as risky, political decision makers have to take into account that 'if people experience risks as real, they are real as a consequence' (RS: 77) (see Chapter 3). As the example of Chernobyl clearly demonstrated, public risk perceptions may unfold a political dynamic which does not follow the logic of scientific rationality, and which cannot be rationally controlled.

The fourth characteristic of the risks which according to Beck define the categorically new status of contemporary society is that they 'display an equalizing effect within their scope and among those affected by them' (RS: 36). Beck concedes that 'poverty attracts an unfortunate abundance of risks' (RS: 35) and that 'the possibilities and abilities to deal with risks, avoid them or compensate for them are probably unequally divided among the various occupational and educational strata' (RS: 35). Nevertheless, he is convinced that sooner or later, the side-effects of modern technology affect also the rich, and that 'in this sense risk societies are exactly *not*[2] class societies' (RS: 36). From an ecologist point of view, it is interesting to note that Beck's 'community of the endangered' (RS: 47) is not just meant to transcend the boundaries of social class and nation states, but his 'utopia of a world society' (RS: 46) also includes plants and animals. This seems to indicate that Beck's concerns are not only much more concrete and material than those of Horkheimer and Adorno, but that Beck is also significantly less anthropocentric. Whilst in early critical theory it was merely the integrity of an abstract concept, the modernist human subject, which was at risk, Beck conceptualises the self-inflicted risks of late modern society as implying the possible 'self-destruction of *all* life on Earth' (RS: 21). In a quite ecologist sense, the risk society therefore generates a community of fate that goes far beyond the human species.

Although the centrality of ecological issues in today's sense seems to distinguish Beck's model of contemporary society sharply from that of earlier critical theory, even this brief outline already points towards significant lines of continuity. It is, firstly, striking that for early critical theory, too, the central problem was the *side-effects* of the progress of modernity, which in a dialectical process undermined the very goal of the enlightenment project (the constitution of the subject). In both models civilisatory rationality turns into *irrationality*, and in both of them this dialectical process is *beyond human control*. Its automatism or internal dynamic which Horkheimer and Adorno sought to capture with their concept of *Naturverfallenheit*, recurs in Beck's model as the idea of the *Selbstlauf* (self-propellation) of the transition from industrial society to the risk society. Furthermore, it seems obvious that Beck's experience of *risks* and the related imperative of *risk-avoidance* are variations and the functional equivalent of early critical theory's experience of *alienation* and the related imperative of *reconciliation*. Both risk and alienation cause existential *Angst*. Horkheimer and Adorno's fear (*Angst*) for the loss of the (abstract) Self recurs as the fear for (concrete) health and survival. What these structural parallels between early critical theory and Beck's updated version seem to suggest is that the risk society is perhaps not quite as different from the society Horkheimer and Adorno were theorising as Beck would want to believe.

As a matter of fact, critics have often pointed out that Beck's categorical distinction between the risk society and its classical industrial precursor does not really hold. Time and again they have questioned all of Beck's characteristics of the risk society. One of the most commonly voiced objections is that 'the thesis of the *risk society* in which we all – beyond the boundaries of class and cultures – are equally affected by a crisis is wrong and ideological' because 'it obscures the perspective onto continuing and even increasing *inequalities*' (Hamm 1996: 20; also see e.g. Baumann 1993; Goldblatt 1996; Benton 1997). Many analysts have come to the conclusion that the changes Beck describes 'do not add up to the

---

2 Official translation: '*not* exactly'.

kind of epochal transformation that Beck seems to be pointing to', and that 'it is difficult to argue that the evidence unambiguously supports the emergence of a radically different type of politics and polity in Western societies that would truly herald the emergence of a risk society' (Goldblatt 1996: 179). Most certainly, this criticism is justified. But the question arises whether this focus on the alleged categorical novelty of the risk society is very productive. At least in the context of my argument, it does not really matter whether or not contemporary society is categorically different from classical industrial society. The much more interesting questions are, firstly, whether and how exactly the ecological questions Beck seeks to tackle distinguish themselves from the *pre-ecological* questions addressed in early critical theory; and, secondly, how Beck believes modern society may escape the *dialectic of enlightenment* or the Weberian *cage of modernity*. In order to establish whether Beck really addresses concerns which are fundamentally different from those of early critical theory, we have to take a closer look at his concept of risk.

Unfortunately Beck never spells out what exactly these risks actually comprise. In very general terms he talks about the natural foundations of human and other life; in a seemingly more concrete fashion he also refers, for example, to nuclear threats, BSE, fertility, life-planning, or the fate of the modern family. But he never clarifies *why exactly*, in *what respect*, to *what extent* and *for whom* these issues represent a risk. He does not seem to see any need for further explanations, simply assuming that the reality and experience of fundamental threats is uncontroversial. Correctly, Goldblatt notes that it is 'almost as if Beck assumes that we accept and agree with his estimations of the dangers we face' (1996: 158). However, it is obvious that the concept of risk describes a relationship between human subjects and certain physical conditions. And it is therefore crucially important to find out which of the two sides accredits risk their status as risks. As we have seen, Beck himself points to the significance of *subjective values* and *cultural parameters* (see above and Chapter 3). Such considerations push his thinking into the direction of early critical theory. If Beck wants to prove that he is talking about more than just the subject and its identity, that is if he wants to demonstrate that his theory really goes beyond early critical theory's interest in nature, he has to demonstrate that the ecological risks of his risk society exist as risks irrespective of their being perceived.

Beck himself, however, seems to be undecided whether ecological risks have to be conceptualised as objective empirical realities or as subjective perceptions and social constructions. This undecidedness surfaces at several points in his analysis: on the one hand, he suggests that risks are real when people experience them as real, which seems to imply that they have no reality beyond their social perception. But on the other hand, he also states that whilst the '*perception* of risks' may be suppressed, this is not the case with 'their reality or their effects' (RS: 45). As I indicated above, Beck believes that one of the characteristic features of the risk society are its 'definitional struggles' and 'antagonistic definitions' of risks (RS: 29). But at the same time, he seems to suggest that ecological risks are unambiguous and 'occupy a special place' because they 'express the *common good* and the vote of those who themselves have neither vote nor voice' (RS: 31). On the one hand, the idea that politics in the risk society centres around the *distribution* of risks seems to suggest that risks are objectively there and need to be distributed. But on the other hand, we have also seen that in Beck's view, ultimately 'norms of acceptance' and 'implicit notions of cultural value' decide what is perceived as a risk and what is not. And finally, Beck's talk of the 'equalising effect' of risks once again seems to suggest their independence from individual circumstances. Yet at the same time, Beck himself concedes that risk perceptions and the exposure to risks are to a significant extent determined by the factors of knowledge and financial solvency.

These contradictions seem to indicate that Beck's conception of risk is not fully thought through. And to the same extent that the concept of risk remains fuzzy, the distinction between the risk society and its classical industrial precursor becomes questionable. Beck's claim that the risk society is categorically different from industrial society – that is that his *ecological* theory really goes beyond the *pre-ecological* theory of the early Frankfurt School – rests on the idea that ecological risks are not social constructions, but physical realities whose status as risks is uncontested and incontestable. Only under this condition is the whole of society challenged and required to react in all its parts. If, on the other hand, risks are social perceptions, that is if their status as risks is defined primarily by subjective norms and expectations, this shifts the focus of attention back to the questions of identity which we know from Horkheimer and Adorno's theory. For early critical theory, the question of nature and the question of identity were one and the same. Beck's claim to be radically different rests on the promise to keep these two questions separate. It is still too early to come to any definite conclusions here, but it seems doubtful whether Beck really manages to talk about more than questions of subjective identity. The concept of risk, rather than being the central difference between Beck and early critical theory, may point to a further parallel between the two models: Horkheimer and Adorno's *metaphysics of nature* reappears in Beck's model as the *metaphysics of risk*. And just as early critical theory did not manage to resolve the contradiction between its metaphysics of nature and its thesis that nature survives its own abolition only in the form of (multiple) social constructions, Beck seems to be unable to resolve the contradiction between his metaphysics of risk and his insight into the social constructedness of risks, that is the multiplicity of risk perceptions. But the emergence of ecological risks is not Beck's only defining criterion for the risk society. Before drawing further conclusions, we will therefore have to clarify in what other ways Beck may go beyond early critical theory, and whether and how Beck's metaphysics of risk fits together with other aspects of his theory of contemporary society.

5.2 Reflexive modernisation and second modernity

According to Beck, the risk society is defined in two different ways, one being the ecological risks addressed in the previous section, the other the experience of cultural uprootedness resulting from processes of pluralisation, individualisation and the dissolution of established certainties, which destroy the basis of traditional patterns of social organisation and identity formation. Beck points out that 'both sides together, the sum of *risks* and *disrupting experiences*, . . . constitute the social and political dynamic of the risk society'[3] (RS 87; my emphasis). In Beck's model, their systematic connection is the above-mentioned idea of the *abolition of nature*: whilst ecological risks are the consequence of modernity's impact on the *natural physical environment*, the experience of disruption is the consequence of modernity's impact on the set of *cultural beliefs and assumptions* which we have come to perceive as *natural*. In both cases, the *natural* provided safety and security, whilst the *abolition of nature* exposes us to risk and uncertainty. However, despite this connection, the two dimensions of Beck's model seem to be poorly integrated. As a matter of fact, I would suggest that they are mutually exclusive, and that contrary to the common criticism of Beck's thinking, *this* is where its crucial fault is located. Arguably, Beck's attempt to ecologise early critical theory and at the same time radicalise its thesis of the abolition of nature represents an inherent contradiction. In order to substantiate this assertion I will explore in some more detail how Beck develops the idea of the abolition of nature. In terms of theorising contemporary society, this means making a completely new start. Beck retains the label *risk society*, but what is at the centre of interest in this second approach is no longer the ecological risks discussed above, but the *political economy of uncertainty* (Beck 2000b; also Baumann 1999).

According to Beck, the arrival of the risk society was secondly signalled by '*the end of the antithesis between nature and society*' (RS: 80). As I indicated in Section 3.1, he argues that the opposition between the two sides was a typical construct of the nineteenth century, which has now lost its validity. Towards the end of the twentieth century, modernisation had finally '*consumed and lost its other*' (RS: 10). It is now confronted with nothing but itself. Whilst 'the concept of the classical industrial society is based on the antithesis between nature and society', the idea of the 'risk society proceeds from *nature* as integrated by culture' (RS: 81). In other words, the radically new feature of the risk society is the amalgamation of nature and society: 'nature *is* society and society is also *nature*' (ibid.). Once again the parallel to early critical theory is evident. What Horkheimer and Adorno conceptualised as 'total immanence' or the 'universal delusive context', appears in Beck's model as the idea of a 'nature–society'[4]. Echoing Marx's amalgamation of the nature–society dualism into 'an historical nature and a natural history' (1977: 174), Beck suggests that the nature-society emerges 'either by nature becoming societalized or by society becoming naturalized' (RP: 115). Picking up the terminology we know from Horkheimer and Adorno, Beck speaks of a 'domestic nature' and a 'second nature' that is 'internal' to society (RS: 81). Nature has become 'a highly synthetic product', an 'artificial nature', and 'not a hair or crumb of it is still *natural*' (RS: 81). Yet with the end of the Other, with the abolition of nature, the

3 The official translation suggests 'insecurities' instead of 'disrupting experiences'. In the German text, however, the word is *Verunsicherungen* rather than *Unsicherheiten*. Furthermore, the official translation speaks of the 'political dynamic of *industrial* society'. This is an obvious error.

4 Official translation: 'natural society'.

process of modernisation does not come to a halt. Where Horkheimer and Adorno had diagnosed the end of modernity and been unable to see the beginning of anything new, Beck identifies the beginning of a 'second modernity', a 'reflexive modernity'. At the threshold to the twenty-first century 'modernization within the horizon of experience of *pre*-modernity' was 'displaced by *reflexive* modernization' (RS: 10). Following the abolition of primary (pre-modern) nature during the phase of first modernity, we now experience the abolition of second (modern) nature through the process of second modernity. Whilst during the phase of first (linear) modernity the sciences were 'applied to a *given* world', the phase of second (reflex-ive) modernity means that 'the sciences are confronted with their own products', that is that they 'encounter a *second creation in civilization*' (RS: 155).

Horkheimer and Adorno had pointed out that second nature, civilisation's 'second creation', gradually assumes the status of naturalness. They believed that second nature, once it has installed itself, cannot be removed, that the 'universal delusive context' is permanent and inescapable. In Beck's process of reflexive modernisation, however, this second nature, the '*seemingly natural*[5] ways of life and certainties of industrial society' (RS: 153) are once again dissolved. In the same way that 'the forms of living and working in feudal agrarian society were dissolved at the turn of the nineteenth century', we are now witnessing the decline of 'those of developed industrial society' (RS: 153). Whilst Horkheimer and Adorno were the-orising the dissolution of *nature* (inner and outer), Beck is concerned with the dissolution of the socially constructed *natural*, that is the *internal* Other industrial society had created for itself. From this perspective, early critical theory actually appears to be closer to the concerns of contemporary ecologists than Beck. Whilst Horkheimer and Adorno were talking about the external Other of rationality and society, Beck clearly speaks about society's traditions, values and expectations, that is the subject and its understanding of what is *natural* in the sense of *normal* and, although man-made, *non-negotiable*.

Only with the abolition of second nature are the project of modernity and the abolition of nature really complete. What early critical theory had conceptu-alised, namely the transformation of primary nature into second nature (of *nature* into the *natural*) during the phase of first modernity, was no more than the *semi*-abolition of nature. And the phase of first (linear) modernity was only a *semi*-modernity. Beck himself points out that the belief 'that industrial society is a modern society' is just a 'nineteenth century myth', whilst in reality the 'project of modernity' has so far always been '*truncated*' (RS: 153). Only by theorising the second half of modernity, does Beck fully implement Horkheimer and Adorno's thesis of the abolition of nature. The project of modernity was the project of abolishing the Other, nature, and this includes the abolition of both first as well as second nature. With the complete abolition of nature, the project of modernity comes to an end, and the modernist principle of unity (the singular dualism) is replaced by the principle of plurality.

---

5 Official translation: '*apparently naturally ordained*'.

The reason why the first (linear) modernity remained a semi-modernity or a 'restricted modernity' (RP: 68ff.) is, according to Beck, that it relied on a 'bisection of scientific rationality' (RS: 164). As Horkheimer and Adorno had shown, scientific rationality was the main tool of the modern enlightenment process, yet as I argued above, the 'principle of dissolvent rationality', or as Beck calls it, the 'methodical scepticism of the sciences' (RS: 163), was never applied to scientific rationality itself. It remained 'limited to the *objects* of science' (RS: 163). Only with the entry into second (reflexive) modernity, 'science begins to extend the methodological power of its scepticism to its own foundations and practical results' (RS: 156). The invariable result of this reflexive application of scientific scepticism is the 'demystification of scientific rationality' (RS: 71) and 'a momentous *demonopolization of scientific knowledge claims*' (RS: 156). In the phase of second modernity, the unity of reason which Horkheimer and Adorno were not prepared to give up makes room for multiple and competing forms of rationality, each of which 'relate the entire *hocus-pocus of science* to different principles and different interests – and therefore reach exactly the opposite conclusions' (RS: 161). What Beck describes somewhat airily as the 'hocus-pocus of science', is of course the old problem that scientific rationality is no more than a set of formal principles. Already, Horkheimer and Adorno had argued that scientific rationality is empirically empty, and that science therefore always makes certain assumptions which are not themselves questioned. In the process of reflexive modernisation these assumptions are exposed. They thus become accessible to debate and come under pressure of legitimation. This leads directly to Beck's thesis of the 'reinvention of politics'. Yet before I move on to exploring this idea, I want to discuss how the pluralisation of rationality affects Beck's concept of ecological risks.

5.3   Environmental problems and systemic problems

If, as Beck argues, the success of the industrial system 'causes the boundaries between nature and society to become blurred' (RS: 154), environmental problems lose their status as problems in the environment and turn into 'social, political, economic and cultural contradictions inherent in the system' (ibid.). Beck convincingly argues that the side-effects of the civilisatory process can no longer be off-loaded to the Other of society, that is they can no longer be externalised. He suggests that 'the reverse of societalised nature is the *societalisation* of the destructions of nature' (1986: 10), that is their transformation into systemic self-endangerments. In other words, the abolition of nature results in the abolition of *environmental* problems which become *systemic* problems. But if the abolition of nature does not just signify the end of the nature–society dualism, but beyond this the differentiation of scientific rationality, this has much more significant implications. With the end of uniform reason, environmental problems do not just lose their status as *environmental* problems, but arguably they also lose their status as *problems* in the traditional ecologist sense.

For Beck, the transformation of environmental problems into systemic problems implies, firstly, that these dangers are man-made and, secondly, that they threaten society itself rather than just the external environment. But what it does not imply is that these dangers and threats now have to be conceptualised as flexible social perceptions rather than objective physical realities. In other words, phenomena which from one perspective may appear as serious problems, may from a different point of view be perceived as rather irrelevant. Beck is of course aware of this novelty and tries to take account of it by referring to *definitional struggles* and numerous competing risk definitions. Yet, as I noted above, Beck continues to believe in the objectivity of ecological problems. Contrary to Beck's view, however, the complete abolition of nature in the process of reflexive modernity should theoretically decide, once and for all, that ecological risks are social constructions with very limited validity. Certainly, there can be no doubt about the objective reality of significant change – be it in the external environment or in the system itself – but after the pluralisation of rationality, there is no longer any guarantee that this change is generally regarded as a problem. We can therefore say that to the same extent that Beck continues to talk of 'objective threats common to everybody',[6] he does not implement the abolition of nature and remains in the phase of semimodernity where everything is subjected to the methodological scepticism of rationality except the alleged objectivity of ecological risks. This reconfirms the above thesis that Beck, rather than really implementing the end of the Other, merely replaces Adorno's metaphysics of nature by a metaphysics of risk.

In Beck's model we are confronted with the simultaneity of linear (first) and reflexive (second) modernity. The *indisputable* ecological risks which, according to Beck, are one central characteristic of the risk society, can only be conceptualised as the result of linear (*semi*-)modernisation. The experience of disruptions, however, which is meant to be the other central characteristic, is clearly the result of reflexive modernisation. But reflexive modernisation also undermines the objectivity of ecological risks and dissolves them into a plurality of subjective risk perceptions. Of course, this neither eliminates the civilisatory impact on the physical environment, nor the reality of risk perceptions, but it dissolves the risk society's integrating interest and concern, its 'environmental security consensus' (RP: 91). With the abolition of nature and the pluralisation of rationality, that is with the dissolution of objectivity, the ecological discourse loses its common point of reference. It thus becomes evident that the ecologisation of critical theory and the consequent implementation of its idea of the abolition of nature cannot coexist. At the current stage of the analysis I still want to avoid final judgements, but eventually we will have to determine which of the two dimensions in Beck's model ought to be regarded as dominant and as his central achievement.

5.4 The reinvention of politics

In a sense, the idea of the 'reinvention of politics' is meant to integrate the two dimensions of Beck's model. Already in *Risk Society*, Beck indicates that with the

---

6 In the English translation 'objective' is dropped. The neologism *Gefährdungsgemeinsamkeit* is erroneously translated as 'community of danger' [RS: 47].

reflexive abolition of the 'seemingly natural' forms of life and certainties of industrial society everything becomes political, that is open to debate. Institutional arrangements and the goals of modernisation can suddenly be socially (re-) negotiated, and thus there emerges the opportunity for removing the structural obstacles to the ecological reorganisation of modern society. In other words, reflexive modernisation (the abolition of second nature) has a constructive as well as a destructive dimension. In Beck's view it can even be considered as the precondition for the solution of ecological problems, which have been caused by the abolition of first nature. For Beck, considerable promise lies in the idea that through reflexive modernisation, 'all the conditions become, first, *structurable* and, second, *dependent on legitimation*' (RS: 175). Optimistically, he notes that 'the idea *it could be different* increasingly comes to dominate, overtly or covertly, all fields of action' (ibid.). The differentiation of scientific rationality 'opens up *new possibilities of influence and development*' (RS: 157). Echoing the tradition of early critical theory, Beck points towards 'the opportunity to emancipate social practice *from* science *through* science' (RS: 157). He realises that the deconstruction of established certainties always implies the threat of new ideologies and dogmas: 'constructed certitude' is 'the other side of modernity' (RP: 61ff.). Yet he believes that in the process of reflexive modernisation, 'a bit of enlightenment can also be brought into reality' (RS: 168). In particular, he sees the chance of 'ecological enlightenment' (1995b). Leaving Horkheimer and Adorno's pessimism behind, he once again dares to go the Marxian step beyond interpreting the world, towards actively changing and improving it.

In *Risk Society*, the idea that the softening of societal structures through reflexive modernisation could be a unique chance for resolving the ecological problems of contemporary society is only hinted at. Beck states that ecological risks do not just represent 'new sources of conflict', but also of 'consensus' (RS: 47). He hopes that they might give rise to a '*new ecological morality*' (RS: 77). Updating the old Kantian dream of a rational cosmopolitanism, Beck believes that ecological risks might finally implement what Kant's rationalism always failed to achieve: ecological risks are supposed to provide a common interest and to function as a powerful force of social integration towards the 'world society' (RS: 46ff.). In *The Reinvention of Politics*, these ideas are then fully elaborated. Here Beck almost welcomes the ecological crisis as an outstanding chance for contemporary societies. Almost euphorically he notes that rather than 'intensifying and confirming the general pointlessness of modernity, environmental dangers create a *substantive horizon of meaning centring around avoidance, prevention and helping*'[7] (RP: 159). For disoriented and increasingly individualised post-industrial consumer societies, Beck argues, the challenges of self-inflicted ecological hazards present a new source of moral inspiration and social integration. He believes that 'the ecological issue forms an ideal milieu for morality' (EP: 28). In his view, ecology may function 'as a fountain of moral rejuvenation' (EP: 24), and this 'moral climate and milieu' even 'intensifies with the size

---

7   Official translation: 'substantive semantic horizon of avoidance, prevention and helping'.

of the threat' (RP: 159). In his characteristic, powerful style Beck suggests that with the environmental issue, 'a postmodern, jaded, saturated, meaningless and fatalistic *paté de foie gras* culture creates a Herculean task for itself, which acts as a stimulus everywhere' (RP: 159f.). In view of the overwhelming task and opportunities, he demands enthusiastically that society finally 'awakes from the pessimism of the confrontational constellation and conceives of the environmental issue as a *providential gift for the universal self-reformation of a previously fatalistic industrial modernity*' (RP: 160).

As Beck assumes that the 'increasingly critical constellations of civilisatory risks' translate into an ever-'growing pressure to act' (EP: 282),[8] there seems to be little doubt for him that advanced industrial societies not only *can* master the ecological problem, but will hardly be able to avoid 'gaining impetus' from the ecological threats. And Beck is confident that they will not just 'conduct cosmetic ecology on a grand scale, but . . . actually assure sustainability'[9] (RP: 160). Here the idea of *Selbstlauf* (automatism) recurs. Just like the transition from industrial society to the risk society is brought about by the self-perpetuating processes of modernisation, the transition from the *world risk society* to the socially and ecologically sustainable *global civil society* seems to be induced 'not by political elections, the downfall of governments or by revolutions', but emerge 'as the latent side-effect of the usual' (EP: 57). Admittedly, this rather Marxian historical determinism ought to make us sceptical. But in *Ecological Enlightenment* Beck explicitly states that in the risk society, the automatism of reflexivity takes over the role formerly played by 'revolutionary subjects', and that it fulfils this function 'even more convincingly and effectively than opposing political movements could ever have managed' (1995b: 32). Beck's explanation for this is that 'the individualized society prepares the ground for new . . . alliances, which go beyond the scope of all hitherto existing schematizations' (RS: 101). In view of increasingly threatening ecological risks, '*temporary* coalitions between *different groups* and *different camps* are formed and dissolved, depending on the *particular issue* at stake and on the *particular situation*' (RS: 100).

In this restructuring process of the public sphere even the profit-oriented economy is assumed to become an important coalition partner for the eco-movement because risks and hazards supposedly lead to its internal differentiation along ecological lines. Taking up the central argument of the *theory of ecological modernisation* (see Chapter 10), Beck suggests that as soon as economic sectors emerge 'which build up their existence and their markets on the recognition and elimination of hazards', the anti-ecological phalanx of the economy breaks up 'into reformists and orthodox believers' (RP: 158f.). And Beck is convinced that not even economic recessions will stop the ecological and cultural '*Red Cross consciousness*' (RP: 159) of the public. Increasingly critical risk constellations prompt categorical ecological imperatives: 'Action must be taken, immediately, everywhere, by everybody, under all circumstances' (EP: 47). In this scenario the environmentally aware

---

8 The English translation skips pages 277–82 of the German text.
9 Official translation: 'viability in the future'.

sections of the public, as purchasers and consumers, act as society's environmental consciousness, and force ecological correctness on to all parts and institutions of society. Despite its obvious heterogeneity, Beck believes the ecological lobby is becoming so powerful that he even speaks of an emerging 'environmental Machiavellianism' (1998a: 154ff.).

This is an extremely positive view. Correctly, critics have commented that 'Beck's optimistic expectation of a recognised universal interest in addressing these (ecological) hazards is hard to sustain' (Benton 1997: 44). In line with the theoretical explorations of the previous chapters, Bauman points out that there is 'no direct line leading from availability and even the acquisition of knowledge' about the environment 'to knowledge-specific political action' (Bauman 1993: 208). Given the plurality of interests and risk perceptions, 'the range of possible reactions is wide' (ibid.), and there is no compelling reason why we should ever see 'the unification of sufferers into an harmoniously acting force of opposition' (ibid.: 206). As a matter of fact, empirical experience provides only very scattered support for the thesis that newly emerging political alliances and institutions bring about substantial improvements in the ecologist sense. In the context of economic globalisation, there is significantly more evidence for the further concentration of power (witness the recent wave of mergers between powerful international corporations) than for its redistribution between multiple smaller units. In a way that appears to be blind to the political realities, Beck seems to believe in the existence of a Habermasian *ideal speech situation* which provides a space for the rational, democratic and egalitarian negotiation of societal goals. Also, Beck seems to have overlooked the fact that the *political economy of uncertainty* has triggered a *silent counter-revolution* which leads to the rematerialisation of formerly post-materialist value orientations (Blühdorn 2000).

Undoubtedly, there is a strong trend towards the *depoliticisation* of the public sphere which counterbalances the potentially positive effects of the so-called reinvention of politics. *Depoliticisation* firstly means the ongoing shift of political control and decision-making capacities from democratically controlled institutions into research laboratories and executive boardrooms. Beck himself is referring to this development (RS: 183ff.; also see Beck 1999, 1998b, 2000b) which surely implies ongoing public disempowerment rather than the kind of re-empowerment Beck – and also Giddens (1998, 1999) – so strongly believe in. Secondly, *depoliticisation* means that public interest in politics, and confidence in the established political institutions and democratic procedures, are in radical decline. Beck's optimism presupposes a high level of public political awareness, interest and activity. Yet despite Beck's firm belief in the emerging (transnational) civil society (e.g. Beck 1997b, 2000a, 2000b), one may seriously doubt that there really are any new structures or agents emerging which are suitable for the bottom-up democratically negotiated reorganisation of political affairs. Given that at the macro level, conditions and developments increasingly seem to be beyond genuine influence and controllability, public political interest and activity clearly focuses on the micro level of personal interests and local life-worlds.

Furthermore, the fact that deregulation and competitiveness have established themselves as the new super-ideology just at the point of time when information technology and genetic engineering are beginning to revolutionise the most fundamental structures and principles of modern society seems to provide strong evidence against Beck's optimism. If Beck were right, we could expect the unprecedented range of new opportunities to be regulated through an equally unprecedented extent of societal debate about the application or non-application of these technologies. In actual fact, however, this debate is hardly taking place – be it because it is consciously being suppressed, or because the majority – willingly or out of political frustration – is prepared *to leave things as they are*. In any case, in the absence of political visions and control, the course of development is largely determined by economic considerations. Contrary to Beck's claims, the idea that *things could also be different* is rapidly becoming a farce. Whilst national governments – in a desperate attempt to present themselves as *proactive* and a still relevant political player – are forcefully pushing ahead the supposedly inevitable, private individuals – be it as taxpayers or as shareholders – are equally committed to economic rationality, and have an equally strong interest in cost-cutting and profit-maximising strategies for the reorganisation of political affairs and the public and private economy. Against this background the idea of an 'environmental Machiavellism' appears at best naive, but could also be described as politically highly dangerous. The suggestion that in contemporary society 'nature becomes politics' and a 'societal project' (RP: 114) – in which, using Böhme's words, we ourselves 'negotiate politically which nature we want at all' (1992: 24) – appears as rather cynical, unless, of course, we assume that the development towards GM-foods, designer babies, ever-increasing social inequalities, and so on *are* the kind of *nature* we want (see Part IV).

Interestingly, Beck himself sharply contrasts his optimism with the warning that 'the emerging age of action' must not be confused with an 'age of hope' (EP: 89). As I indicated above, he points out that 'risk politics relies on *faceless power*', which Beck describes as 'the most tyrannical form of the exercise of power, because under these conditions, no one can be held responsible for anything' (1997c: 25). In this context, Beck speaks of 'organised irresponsibility' (1995a; 1997c), which does not easily fit together with his thesis that we are moving towards 'a responsible modernity' (1997c: 32). Beck also emphasises the ambivalence of reflexive modernity, and that the dissolution of established certainties also opens the door for anti-modern tendencies. As he points out, the experience of cultural disruption may generate 'completely new hysterias and reflexes of escape' (EP: 89). Unmanageable uncertainty may trigger 'withdrawals into old certainties' (ibid.). Echoing the concerns of early critical theory, Beck therefore points towards the possibility of 'a new form of *constructed barbarism*' that might re-emerge 'at the culmination of civilization' (1997a: 53). So there are also reasons for pessimism. But Beck's optimism clearly prevails. Beck is convinced that 'the contours of a *utopia of ecological democracy*' are becoming visible (1997c: 32). And what is required to promote this process of late modern society's self-ecologisation is, first and foremost, 'that industrial society becomes an industrial society with a bad conscience, that it understands and indicts itself as a risk society' (1998a: 160). Beck obviously believes that this self-accusation is almost inevitable because as soon as the 'modernization risks have been *recognized*', the ecological issue begins to unfold its 'incredible political dynamic' (RS: 77). But one may wonder what happens if the risks are not 'recognized', and which preconditions must be fulfilled for them to be 'recognized'?

On the one hand, Beck seems to suggest that the risks are self-evident and simply impose themselves on public awareness. If this were the case, his ecological optimism would probably be justified. But Beck himself stresses that the 'recognition' of risks by no means comes automatically and that 'there is a lot involved in that' (RS: 77). What is required is 'not just knowledge, but *collective* knowledge' of the risks, 'belief in them, and the political illumination of the associated chains of cause and effect' (ibid.). In other words, the recognition of risks strongly depends on the success of their social construction. But once again one may ask: What are the conditions for this process of construction to be successful? What happens if the societal discourse about risks does not get beyond the level of multiple risk constructions leading to multiple, competing and mutually neutralising accusations and policies? Empirical practice seems to suggest that irreconcilable interest conflicts are a lot more likely than Beck's ecological consensus. Beck's optimism strongly depends on the old simplistic belief that modern society *as a whole* is fundamentally alienated and that eventually this *commonly shared* feeling of alienation will necessarily trigger revolutionary change.

The prerequisite for society to be able to accuse itself as a risk society and direct its 'incredible political dynamic' towards the goal of its own ecologisation, is that there is a consensus about risks and about their opposite, that is safety, certainty and security. The success of society's self-ecologisation depends, firstly, on the achievability of large-scale agreement regarding the ecologically necessary and desirable, and secondly on large-scale agreement regarding the social and political priorities. After the complete abolition of nature, however, this consensus is no longer possible. With the abolition of the Other and the differentiation of rationality – even within a single human individual – Beck's ecological optimism loses its basis. Certainly, the societal discourse will continue to generate and negotiate problem perceptions, including ecological problem perceptions, but as there is no longer any metaphysical point of reference (uniform nature, uniform rationality, or the uniform subject) which could function as the bottom line of discursive agreement, (ecological) problem constructions will probably always remain multiple and contradictory, and the same will apply to the resulting (ecological) policies. Beck's 'reinvention of politics' might therefore lead to a lot of ecological activism, but it seems unlikely that it will ever lead to the ecologisation of contemporary society. Political reality appears to confirm both parts of this contention. Beck's model is inconsistent because it relies in its ecological dimension on the continued existence of what it abolishes in its reflexive dimension. To assume that the process of reflexive modernisation could be a linear process towards any developmental (ecological) goal is a contradiction in terms. Beck's idea of the ecological reorientation of society depends on his metaphysics of risk, which is not consistent with his own theory and certainly not reconcilable with empirical experience. Yet if we abandon this element of his thinking, the funda-mental idea of the abolition of nature and the theory of reflexivity remain unaffected. Only the idea that they might lead to society's ecologisation becomes unconvincing. Coming back to the question I posed at the end of the previous sec-tion, we may therefore come to the conclusion that in Beck's model, the element of reflexivity is clearly the dominant and convincing dimension, whilst his eco-logical interests are a source of inconsistencies.

5.5   A theory of societal self-critique?

The last aspect of Beck's ecological thinking that needs to be addressed before we can come to a final assessment of his contribution to the eco-theoretical debate is how Beck intends to escape Horkheimer and Adorno's problem of self-referentiality and establish a normative basis for the ecological critique of society. In *The Reinvention of Politics*, Beck notes optimistically that 'the constellations for social criticism, even for radical criticism, have never been as favourable as they are now' (EP: 53). He argues that with the abolition of nature and of the modernist nature–society dualism, a phase is coming to an end where 'theorists apply more or less solidly justified normative standards to society, and judge and criticise it (often against the self-understanding of those affected) in accordance to these' (EP: 54). Compared with this older model of social critique where the normative standards were conceived by intellectuals and legitimated through their superior knowledge of the common good, the risk society has, according to Beck, the enor-mous advantage that it can generate its own standards of critique and thus become a truly '*self*-critical society' (RS: 176). In the risk society, the 'reference points and presuppositions of critique are always being produced as by-products[10] in the form of risks and threats' (ibid.).

A further advantage of the risk society's self-critique is, according to Beck, that it is not guided by substantive values. 'Imperatives of avoidance' (EP: 48) are replacing the 'substantial and *positive* goals' (ibid.) generated by traditional social criticism. As Beck points out, 'risks tell us what we must *not* do, but not, *what* we have to do' (EP: 48). The ecological critique is thus assumed to become much less vulnerable because, supposedly, it is 'not a normative critique of values' (RS: 176). With its ideal of 'safety', the risk society's self-critique 'remains peculiarly *negative* and *defensive*' (RS: 49). Beck is confident that all this strengthens rather than threat-ens the viability of the critical project. He firmly believes that in the risk society, ecological risks can function 'like a probe which permits us over and over again to investigate the entire construction plan' and 'structure of civilization for potentials of self-endangerment' (RS: 176).

With the transition from the older critical theory of society to his 'theory of soci-etal self-critique' (EP: 54), Beck hopes to solve the problems of utopia, motivation and agency which I described as part of my preliminary investigations (see Section

10   Official translation: 'are always being produced there'.

2.1). For the self-reformation of the risk society an ecological utopia does not seem to be required at all because immediately tangible risks always prompt concrete imperatives for immediate action. The problem of motivation does not occur because the avoidance of hazards and risks is a natural reflex. And the question of agency does not occur either, because 'smog is democratic', that is everybody is equally affected. In the framework of reflexive modernisation ecological risks are thus supposed to become the miracle tool for the self-critique of society as well as its automotive self-transformation. In a way, the question for the normative basis of the risk society's self-critique does not arise in the first place, for as Beck believes, 'despoliations of nature[11] are the morality beyond morality'. In his view, 'they permit a critique of society beyond social critique – with all of its double dutch and murky Marxism' (1995a: 55).

But in the previous sections it has become sufficiently clear that ecological risks can never provide a reliable normative basis for the critique and transformation of contemporary society. Beck relies on his metaphysics of risks, which contradicts both his own theory and everyday empirical experience. And Beck himself obviously knows that his theory of society's ecological self-critique is flawed. At least implicitly, he is aware that his theory of reflexive modernisation does not just put an end to (post-) Marxist critical theory, but also to the ecologist critique of society. In various places he criticises the eco-movement for its helpless attempts 'to use nature as a measuring standard against its own destruction' (1998a: 155). He points out that 'the nature to which they refer in order to stop its destruction' (1988: 62) has long ceased to exist, and that the nature that is now being 'rediscovered and coddled' (1998a: 155) by the ecology movement is 'a global fusion, rife with contradictions, of nature and society' (1995a: 38). Beck notes that if the ecology movement fails to realise that its normative standards are actually no more than fairly flexible social constructions, it 'has fallen prey to a naturalistic misapprehension of itself' (Ibid: 38; also 1998a: 155).

Beck criticises the eco-movement, firstly, for applying normative standards to contemporary society which are metaphysically conceived and not sufficiently legitimated; secondly, for failing to realise that the nature to which they refer has long been abolished; and thirdly, for the self-referentiality of their project. Beck is, of course, right in his criticism of the ecological critique, but it is not clear how his own model of society's self-critique and ecological self-transformation is meant to distinguish itself from the protest movements he criticises. How is the societal self-critique supposed to materialise if not in the form of social movements? How is it supposed to avoid the mistakes Beck exposes? Most certainly, a societal critique that is guided by social constructions of risk is not only structurally identical to a societal critique that is guided by social constructions of nature, but it actually depends on the latter.

We may thus come to the conclusion that the attempt to replace the critical theory of society by a theory of societal self-critique fails. With regard to the

---

11 Official translation: 'natural despoliations'.

project of establishing a normative foundation for the critique of modern society, Beck is just as unsuccessful as the founding fathers of critical theory. Not even nature and ecology, arguably the last resort of modernist thinking, will provide a common point of reference and a source of an overarching societal consensus. In a sense, Beck even falls behind the achievements of Horkheimer and Adorno. Whilst they were only trying to *theorise* society, Beck aims to produce a model of concrete societal (self-) *transformation.* To the extent that Horkheimer and Adorno refrained from making concrete political prescriptions, the question of their normative standards remained in the background. Of course, even sociological analysis and description are always based on normative assumptions. But a critique of society in the Kantian (philosophical) sense is more successful in trying to hide its normative problems, whereas Beck's social criticism in the Marxian (political) sense can hardly conceal that it makes reference to effectively contingent norms and values which are declared metaphysically valid.

5.6   Final assessment

Having discussed the key elements of Beck's (ecological) thinking, we may now try to assess what his model contributes to the solution of the problems we were unable to resolve on the basis of early critical theory. At the same time, this provides an opportunity to reformulate the research objectives for the following chapters. The analysis of Beck's theory of the risk society was meant to establish:

(i)   what contemporary ecological concerns are ultimately concerned about, and how different they really are from the ones discussed in Horkheimer and Adorno's *pre-ecological* theory;

(ii)   how the abolition of nature may be conceptualised in a more consistent way than in Horkheimer and Adorno's model;

(iii)   how ecological thinking may be reconciled with postmodernist thinking;

(iv)   how we may get beyond Horkheimer and Adorno's pessimism and take account of the much more optimistic outlook of contemporary society; and finally

(v)   whether the failure of Horkheimer and Adorno's critical theory anticipated the failure of the critical project as a whole.

With regard to the first point, we saw that Beck tries to ecologise early critical theory by shifting the concept of ecological risks into the centre of attention. He thus seems to be responding to the reproach that Horkheimer and Adorno's abstract notions of nature and the subject, as well as their preoccupation with reconciliation, do simply not reflect the ideas and concerns of the contemporary ecological debate. Beck's theory, in turn, could, of course, immediately be criticised for failing to reflect that under the conditions of globalisation, his 'logic of risk distribution' has once again given way to the older 'logic of wealth distribution'. But even if we accept that contemporary society is primarily determined by discourses of ecological risks, Beck has to be criticised for failing to explore exactly what these risks actually consist in. Rather than researching their constitutive parameters, Beck simply offers a *metaphysics of risk* which is not particularly convincing. Although he successfully draws attention to the importance of cultural norms and values which decide about the risk-status of particular experiences or conditions in the physical environment, he does not undertake any attempt to analyse these norms and values in any further detail. In the end, Beck remains ambivalent whether ecological risks are defined as such by objective physical criteria or by socially constructed norms of perception. For his thinking, this question is of no particular relevance.

Closer analysis actually reveals that Beck's work, which is supposedly centred around the core idea of ecological problems, is not primarily a contribution to ecological theory. It might be correct to say that 'in the beginning' there 'was the environmental issue' (1997a: 12). But historically as well as systematically, this issue was superseded by the *political economy of uncertainty* which gradually emerged as the real centre and focus of Beck's work. And while the emphasis incrementally shifted, the ecological issue experienced a most interesting fate: it dissolved into other questions. As Beck tells us, it 'must be broken down into other questions: technology and production design, product policy, form of nutrition, lifestyles, medical diagnosis and precaution, legal norms, organizational and administrative forms, foreign policy and development policy' (1998a: 160). Beck's comment confirms what was said towards the end of Section 2.1. Obviously, the ecological issue, the 'logic of risk distribution', the ecological rationality, has no substance of its own. Beck's failure to identify objective physical criteria for the definition of ecological risks, his emphasis on cultural parameters, as well as this *disintegration of the ecological issue* (see Chapter 8), all seem to confirm the thesis that ecological discourse and ecological politics only superficially centre around the Other of society in the ecologist sense, and that underneath the surface, the contemporary ecological debate ultimately negotiates questions of self-perception and identity. Also, these observations once again reconfirm the thesis that the academic and popular discourse about ecological threats and concerns is still fundamentally under-theorised (see Chapter 1). Given that Beck's own analysis of ecological concerns is so unsatisfactory, Horkheimer and Adorno's *pre-ecological* theory about human concern for nature and the sources of *Angst* surely remains an important interpretative tool.

As regards the idea of the abolition of nature, Beck is significantly more explicit and consistent than early critical theory. It is in this area that we have to look for his main achievements and his central contribution to the theoretical debate. However, in this area, too, there are fundamental problems. In Beck's model, the abolition of nature gives rise to the theory of reflexive modernisation, which dissolves the modernist dogma of uniform rationality, and draws the consequences of early critical theory's insight that rationality is purely formalistic. Beck clearly transcends the modernist dualism between singular nature and society. Using Adorno's words, one might say he 'releases the non-identical' and 'opens the road to the multiplicity of different things' (see Section 4.3). Couched in more contemporary terms, he opens the door for postmodernist plurality. However, Beck undermines his theory of reflexivity with his theory of the risk society. To the extent that he holds fast to his metaphysics of risk, he still fails to fully implement the abolition of nature. Beck therefore has to be considered – and considers himself – as a modernist rather than a postmodernist thinker. He speaks of the 'radicalization of modernity' and the endeavour 'to regain a voice and thus the ability to act' (1997a: 15). His project may be described as a last large-scale attempt to rescue the grand narrative of modernity and escape the collapse of Enlightenment humanism.

With his model of a 'second' modernity, Beck assumes a position between modernism and postmodernism which displays striking similarities to the one adopted by Horkheimer and Adorno. Just as they held fast to the idea of uniform reason and the liberation of nature at a stage where their own theory had abolished both, Beck holds fast to the objectivity of ecological risks and the possibility of an ecological consensus at a stage where his own theory has abolished objectivity and described risks as heterogeneous and contestable social constructs. So, although Beck is significantly more radical regarding the abolition of nature than early critical theory, he is in the end still inconsistent. His idea of a reflexive modernity which rejects both traditional modernity as well as postmodernity is not viable. It is a typical example of the kind of thinking that emerges in what Gray describes as the 'uneasy interregnum between modern hopes that are no longer credible and postmodern realities that many find intolerable' (1997: x). It is meant to reconcile ecologist and postmodernist thinking. But in line with my suggestion at the beginning of this chapter, it would seem that the two are not easily reconcilable. Beck's theoretical inconsistencies are forced upon him by his too traditionalist approach to the established certainties of ecological thinking.

With regard to the pessimism early critical theory had effectively taken over from Weber's analysis of the unstoppable spread of rationalisation and bureaucratic domination in modern society, it has become evident that Beck's theory provides considerably more room for a positive perspective on societal progress and development. In Beck's thinking the Weberian *cage of modernity* opens up. Contrary to the ecologist tradition, Beck considers the abolition of nature and the ecological crisis, at least potentially, as a source of optimism and of new chances for the self-reformation of late modern society. However, his idea of the reinvention of politics is highly ambiguous. Society can only unfold an ecologising political dynamic if a social consensus about the ecologically necessary and desirable is possible, that is if we presuppose the metaphysics of nature and risk which is abolished by Beck's own theory. Empirically, there is plenty of evidence that the risk perceptions of different individuals or social groups do not coincide, and in the *political economy of uncertainty* it is not difficult to provide examples of protest movements *for* rather than *against* nuclear powerstations, potentially contaminated beef or the production of GM-foods. Therefore, the new optimism that Beck's thinking shares with that of Giddens is not particularly convincing. It might have earned them their unrivalled position as intellectual leaders of late modern European politics and society, but it is not sociologically and theoretically grounded. Perhaps it has to be interpreted as a kind of *strategic* or *purposive* optimism.

However, the question arises whether to reject this (ecological) optimism necessarily implies a relapse into early critical theory's pessimism. Perhaps Beck's own theory provides access to other sources of hope. In Beck's view, contemporary societies have to choose between confronting and denying ecological risks. His main concern is that modern society, instead of discovering and exploiting the opportunities that come with the reinvention of politics, may prefer to eliminate risks by 'interpreting them away', by 'denying and trivializing' (RS: 75) them. But one may wonder whether it is enough to theorise this alternative of confronting or denying risks. If we fuse Horkheimer and Adorno's analysis of human interest in nature with Beck's analysis of the abolition of nature, this opens the perspective onto a third alternative. Horkheimer and Adorno suggested that human concern for nature is ultimately the concern for meaning, identity and the modernist subject. If the thesis of the abolition of nature is correct, if the dualistic paradigm of modernity has really been transcended, if reason has become pluralised and nature a multiplicity of social constructs, then this seems to suggest that the modernist construct of the subject is exhausted as well. This would imply that the subjective requirements for meaning and identity would change, too. And this, in turn, seems to suggest that beyond the modernist paradigm, the parameters and conditions for the emergence of concern (including ecological concern) are quite different from what they used to be. Suddenly conditions and experiences which used to be highly disturbing in the modernist framework (for the modernist subject) might become unproblematic. The question of the reconceptualisation of the modernist subject and its implications for the ecological question has to be postponed to the next chapter. But already at this stage, it seems evident that the dismissal of Beck's ecological optimism does not necessarily mean a reversion to Horkheimer and Adorno's pessimism. Beck's own theory points the way towards a post-ecologist stage beyond both ecological optimism and pessimism.

This finally takes me to the question whether the critical paradigm is still suitable as a theoretical framework for the conceptualisation of contemporary society and the interpretation of the ecological discourse. Beck's failure to construct a normative foundation on the basis of which the critical project might be continued reconfirms Horkheimer and Adorno's normative dilemma, and suggests that the critical paradigm has really reached its limits. At the end of the analysis of both early and contemporary critical theory, it seems evident that the critical paradigm has to be abandoned. After the abolition of nature and the transition into the age of reflexivity, we have to depart not only from the idea of uniform reason, but also from the modernist idea of the unity of society *vis-à-vis* the unity of nature. On the basis of their specific rationalities, the various subsections of society can of course continue to generate normative standards and apply them critically to themselves and to society as a whole, but their claim to validity is no more justified than the validity claims of any other subsection. Even the ecological issue no longer provides a consensual and uncontested normative standard. In order to reconceptualise contemporary society in this sense and to explore what this implies for the ecological issue, the next chapter will turn to the sociological model suggested by *systems theory*. In terms of sociological analysis – though not in political terms – this move endorses Gray's view that 'what we most need . . . is to put the Enlightenment behind us' and 'accept that all Enlightenment projects have by now become dead ends' (1997: 61).

The discussion of Beck's model has provided important cues for the *systems theoretical* continuation of my analysis of the contemporary ecological discourse Beck's ecological theory is evidently wrong in a number of respects , and perhaps this is the reason why in his more recent work, Beck has moved away from ecological issues. But the analysis of his eco-theoretical model has certainly helped to sketch the research agenda for the following chapters: We have to investigate further into the origins and internal structure of environmental concerns and clarify whether they can really be conceptualised as concerns for meaning, identity and the modernist subject. We have to take the idea of the abolition of nature even further than Beck's model does and thus try to avoid the inconsistencies Beck got caught up in. We have to gain a fuller understanding of the relationship between ecologist and postmodernist thought, and find a way of resolving their evident contradiction. Furthermore, we have to provide an explanation for the prevalent developmental optimism that is more convincing than Beck's ecological hopefulness. We have to follow up the idea of the abdication of the modernist subject and explore its implications for the ecological issue. And, finally, we have to investigate how the ecological discourse and the politics of nature may develop beyond the critical paradigm. All of these questions initially emerged from the discussion of Horkheimer and Adorno's model. They were further developed through the discussion of Beck's model. And they will, hopefully, be fully resolved on the basis of Niklas Luhmann's model. After we have already departed from the idea of *linear* reasoning and progress, we will now also abandon the concept of *reflexivity*, and replace it by the notion of *self-referentiality*. This will lead to the complete deconstruction of traditional ecological thought and, in a second step, to the construction of a postecologist theory.

Part III

Deconstructing ecologism – systems theory

6 Autopoietic systems and functional differentiation – Niklas Luhmann I

The transition from critical theory to systems theory as the theoretical framework for the further analysis of the ecological discourse and contemporary eco-politics marks a turning point in this study. In terms of social theory formation it marks a change of paradigm. Such changes of paradigm imply the complete replacement of the concepts and parameters which previously determined human enquiry about truth. The Copernican Revolution, for example, removed the earth from the centre of the universe thus giving rise to a radically new understanding of the world. By removing metaphysical truth from the centre of epistemology, Immanuel Kant initiated a similar revolution in the field of philosophy. He established that the scientific knowledge we have is valid *for all rational beings* but not *in itself*, that is *a priori*. Contemporary philosophy goes yet a step further in announcing that the Kantian belief in uniform reason and the transcendental subject is not defensible either. In his *Theory of Communicative Action*, Jürgen Habermas demands that 'we give up the paradigm of the philosophy of consciousness' and replace it with that of 'intersubjective understanding or communication' (Habermas 1984: 390). Within the framework of communication theory, truth is no longer anchored in the rational consciousness of the transcendental subject, but it has to be established in the intersubjective sphere of communication. In actual fact, the concept of *truth* is fully replaced by that of *agreement*.

Changes of paradigm do not just lead to the generation of completely new knowledge, but they also necessitate the revalidation of all established knowledge. In the discussion of Beck's model we have already seen that the shift from transcendental reason to discursively negotiated social norms has very significant effects for ecological thought, too. Yet Beck did not fully implement the idea of the discursive construction of nature, ecological risks and ecological rationalities. In particular, he paid very little attention to the concept of the subject and the possible effects of its abdication. Like Beck, ecological thought as a whole has so far been very reluctant to embrace the idea of the linguistic turn in social theory. As I pointed out in Chapter 2, there *is* actually talk about a paradigm shift in the eco-movement and ecological thought (Hajer 1995; Eder 1996a; Jagtenberg and McKie 1997). Discourse *has* become a central category (e.g. Dryzek 1997; Darier 1999). The lively debate around the concept of deliberative democracy (e.g. Dryzek 1990, 1995; Giddens 1994; Mathews 1996; Lafferty and Meadowcroft 1996; Beck 1997a;

Jacobs 1997), as well as the above-mentioned controversy between ecological constructionists and realists (see Chapter 3), all indicate that a reorientation in
ecological thought *is* taking place. Nevertheless, the ecological implications of the
communicative turn in social theory have not yet been fully thought through.

The theoretical model upon which I will base my further analysis in this chapter and the next is that of Niklas Luhmann. Admittedly, the European thinker who
is generally most closely associated with communicative theory is Jürgen
Habermas. Luhmann's thinking, on the other hand, has so far been radically
unpopular and, particularly in the English-speaking world, largely neglected (rare
exceptions e.g. Miller 1994; Neckel and Wolf 1994; Beck 1997a; Rutherford 1999).
The major reason why I prefer Luhmann's systems-theoretical interpretation of the
linguistic turn to that of Habermas is that Habermas retains a lot of the modernist,
humanist, idealist Enlightenment heritage. He seeks to establish a post-
metaphysical concept of communicative rationality on the basis of which he
intends to continue the project of critical theory (see e.g. Goldblatt 1996; Kneer
1996). His ideal of completely uncoerced communication, which unfolds 'a rationality that is inherent in communicative action' (Habermas 1984: 397) and
supposedly allows us to achieve an intersubjective understanding and consensus
that rests exclusively 'on the authority of the better argument' (Habermas 1987a:
145), is still reminiscent of the Kantian metaphysics of reason. Niklas Luhmann,
on the other hand, seeks to make a much more radical break with the philosophical tradition. In many respects he goes along with the Habermasian understanding
of the change of paradigm from transcendental to communicative reason. But
whilst Habermas continues to believe in the possibility of a normatively valid
rational criticism of society, Luhmann restricts himself to analysing the mechanisms that make a rational critique *appear* authoritative, meaningful and credible
even in a post-metaphysical context of self-referentiality, that is universal contingency. Furthermore, Luhmann's more radical systems-theoretical abolition of the
subject seems to correspond more closely to the radical abolition of nature. Also,
Luhmann's fundamental distinction between *system* and *environment* appears closer
to ecological concerns than Habermas's emphasis on the sphere of intersubjectiv-
ity and its fundamental dualism of *system* and *life world*. Finally, whilst 'Habermas
and green political thought' have indeed remained 'two diverging roads' (Eckersley
1990), Luhmann himself at least tentatively applies his theoretical findings to the
ecological debate.

In contemporary European social theory Niklas Luhmann is certainly the one
who departs most radically from the philosophy of the subject and the paradigm
of critical theory. Whilst Beck, Giddens or Habermas take a clearly continuist
approach, Luhmann realises, to use John Gray's words, that the 'unflagging labours
to save the modern self-image from dissolution, is in truth the principal blockage in
our thinking about the present' (1997: xi). His reasoning is a venture into a categorically different paradigm of thought: 'Everything needs to be thought anew –
and not starting from the concept of unity, but starting from the concept of difference' (Luhmann 1996a: 56). During the last three decades of the twentieth
century, Luhmann produced a philosophical-cum-sociological work which is, in

terms of its thematic inclusiveness and systematic coherence, unique in contemporary European thinking. It represents the seemingly paradoxical attempt to take full account of postmodern discontinuity and plurality, whilst still integrating this heterogeneity into a single all-embracing theoretical model without forcing uniformity into the diversity. Only a short time before his death in 1998, Luhmann completed his breath-taking project by presenting what he had intended to be the final volume: *Die Gesellschaft der Gesellschaft* (1998a; The Society of Society (double volume comprising well over 1,000 pages)). Luhmann makes the greatest effort to combine a lucid and comprehensible style with terminological accuracy and theoretical consistency. Yet the paradoxity of his project forces him to argue at a level of theoretical abstraction and complexity which cannot be said to be easily accessible.

Luhmann not only departs from the philosophy of the subject, but in a much more fundamental sense, he seeks to depart from philosophy in general. In accordance with Marcuse's predictions in *Reason and Revolution* (1941: 251ff.), Luhmann ascribes the function and place traditionally held by philosophy to social theory. Echoing Marcuse's argument, Luhmann points out that the ultimate goal of philosophical reasoning is the principle of unity. The aim of all philosophical reflection is to show how the disparate parts, the phenomena of the world, are interconnected to form one whole. The philosophical approach, Luhmann argues, starts out from the concept of unity, and to this concept it returns, if need be overcoming 'the insufficiency', 'the corruptibility of all things beneath the moon' by means of 'idealisation' (Luhmann 1995: 6; also see Habermas 1984: 1ff.). The philosophical approach remains *prescriptive* to the extent that, in order to ensure that unity can be, it will 'abstract to the greatest extent from social phenomena' (Luhmann 1995: 6). Social theory, on the other hand, is merely *descriptive*, that is it analyses the evolution and structural principles of contemporary societies without being bound to any imperative of unity. 'There is no unity in the end. Any cognitive observation is and remains the generation of differences starting out from the difference' (Luhmann 1990: 547). Critical theory, and in particular Adorno, tried to be both philosophy and social theory. Ultimately, this is where the inconsistencies of critical theory originate from. The concept of *communicative reason* provides evidence that even Habermas does not fully abandon the philosophical imperative of unity. In order to avoid the normative dilemmas critical theory gets caught up in, Luhmann tries to go yet a step further. Of course, even Luhmann cannot do more than undertake *an attempt* to be non-philosophical, and we always have to be aware that the success of any such attempt can only be relative. To the extent that Luhmann's whole work aims for systematic closure, that is unity, even Luhmann remains a philosopher. And even the fact that he uses several thousand pages in order to ensure that there is sufficient space for plurality and difference to unfold, cannot conceal that, ultimately, a single idea integrates – unifies – Luhmann's reasoning.

Apart from *Die Gesellschaft der Gesellschaft*, Luhmann's most comprehensive work, laying the theoretical foundations for the almost innumerable studies which were to follow, is *Social Systems* (henceforth SS). The book was published in 1984, and amongst German-speaking sociologists, it quickly became one of the most widely

read and influential theoretical works of the post-war era. An English translation
was not available until 1995. One major reason why since then the book has still
not really found its way into the Anglo-American academic debate might be that
the translation is rather unsatisfactory. Particularly in the ecological discourse,
which could potentially benefit a great deal from Luhmann's approach, there are
only very scattered references to Luhmannite ideas (e.g. Papadakis 1996; Beck
1997a; Rutherford 1999). A detailed analysis and authoritative assessment of his
thinking and writings is not yet available. Chapters I, II and V of *Social Systems* are
the main basis for my own attempt to sketch out a theoretical framework for a
Luhmannite interpretation of the ecological discourse. I will begin by providing
some introductory clarification of Luhmann's terminology, which in many ways
deviates from the philosophical and sociological tradition and thus represents an
obstacle to an adequate appreciation and eco-theoretical exploitation of
Luhmann's work. Readers who do not require that sort of introduction may wish
to jump from here directly to Section 6.6, or even Chapter 7 which focuses specifically on Luhmann's eco-sociological writings and a systems-theoretical
interpretation of ecological discourse.

6.1   Systems and environments

The most fundamental conceptual distinction in Luhmann's and any other systems-
theoretical approach is the one between the *system* and its *environment*. It is important
to point out right at the start that the systems-theoretical concept of the environment has got nothing (or very little) in common with the so-called natural
environment in the ecological sense. As regards the concept of the system, this idea
was traditionally constituted by the dualism of the whole and its parts. The central
question it raised was the one of the relationship between the two sides, that is the
question in what way the former would be represented by or reflected in the latter.
This 'intra-unit orientation' (SS: 8) not only relied on the unsubstantiated assumption that something like the whole as 'composed of its parts, plus something else'
(SS: 5) does at all exist; it also reduced the perspective to the internal structure and
organisation of the system, believing its outside to be irrelevant or even non-
existent. Luhmann, by contrast, bases his reasoning upon a 'concept of a system
related to an environment' (SS: 8). Systems are integrated by mechanisms of inclusion which are, necessarily, at the same time also exclusive. Being part of *something*
automatically means not being part of *something else*. Hence systems do not exist
without environments, that is they always have to be looked at in conjunction to
each other. Luhmann tries to take account of this, and therefore he shifts the focus
of attention from the 'intra-unit' perspective to the question of how systems constitute and stabilise themselves in relation to their environment, that is how they
produce and maintain their difference from their environment.

Like the 'intra-unit oriented' tradition, Luhmann places the analytical emphasis
on the system rather than its environment. However, this does not imply that the
former should in any way be regarded as more important or valuable than the
latter. Luhmann insists that the environment is not merely 'a kind of residual

category', but that 'relationship to the environment is *constitutive* in system formation' (SS: 176). The identity of the system depends on the difference from its
environment because – just as in the case of Horkheimer and Adorno's *Self* –
'identity is possible only by difference' (SS: 177). The internal structure of the
system establishes itself in response to the environment; 'both are what they are
only in reference to each other' (ibid.). The relationship between systems and their
environments varies according to the category of system under consideration.
Following the tradition of systems theory, Luhmann distinguishes between open
and closed systems. The latter can maintain themselves without any external input,
but the former are connected to their environment through processes of exchange.
For both types of systems, the environment emerges – by way of exclusion – in parallel to the process of system formation. In as much as the system itself draws the
demarcation line towards its environment, 'the unity of the environment is constituted by the system' (SS: 181). It is, however, important to note that – once again
as with early critical theory's Self and Other – the environment is a unity only from
the system's point of view. It comprises whatever the system excludes, but as
regards their internal structure, environments themselves do not have system status.
This represents a major difference between the systems-theoretical and the ecological concept of the environment. Systems-theoretical environments are
'delimited by open horizons, not by boundaries that can be crossed' (SS: 17).

Luhmann's key concept for the analysis of the difference between systems and
their environments is that of complexity, and the main reason he gives for the formation of systems is the necessity of reducing complexity. When speaking about
system formation, Luhmann does not intend to undertake a historical reconstruction of evolutionary processes. Also, his considerations 'do not begin with
epistemological doubt' (SS: 12), that is the question of whether reality really is systematic. Luhmann proceeds from the assumption 'that there *are* systems' (ibid.; my
emphasis), and he suggests that their difference from their environments can be
conceptualised by comparing their internal structural complexity with the external
complexity of relations.

In a hypothetical pre-systemic condition, the relations between whatever the
world consists of are hyper-complex; in some way, everything is likely to be related
to everything else. By means of distinctions, particular elements can be isolated
from this amorphous chaos and identified as *something*. Any such identification
implies that this something is not its opposite, that is every distinction has a positive
as well as a negative side. In the systems-theoretical model, the positive side qualifies the item as belonging to a system and relates it to other parts of the same
system. The negative side marks the item as excluded from the system's environment. In as much as any distinction establishes specific relations between particular
items at the cost of excluding other relations which, initially, would have been
equally possible, every distinction reduces complexity. But particular items are not
defined through just one distinction. Other distinctions qualify and extend the initial distinction and thus further reduce complexity. The respective item thereby
enters into ever-more specialised, that is less likely relations towards other items
both inside particular systems as well as in their environments. The process of

system formation is, in other words, a process of complexity reduction which establishes a permanent 'difference in relative degrees of complexity' (SS: 176) between the system and its environment. Accordingly, Luhmann's 'analyses of the difference between system and environment' begin with 'the assumption *that the environment is always more complex than the system itself*', and that 'this holds true for all systems that we can imagine' (SS: 182).

Once the distinction between the system and its environment, that is different levels of complexity, have been established, this relative difference between internal and external complexity begins to translate into priorities of attention: 'whereas internal events/processes are supposedly relevant to the system and can trigger connective action, events/processes in the environment are supposedly irrelevant to the system and can remain unheeded' (SS: 183). But in Luhmann's model, systems never remain static. As will be discussed below, they have inbuilt mechanisms of further reducing what they treat as relevant and what triggers connective action. Through processes of internal differentiation, they can achieve ever higher levels of specialisation in specific fields and narrow their perspective to ever less likely constellations of events. Any such reduction of complexity within the system is, of course, reflected in an increase of complexity outside, that is in the environment.

6.2   Communication and meaning

Having outlined the distinction between systems and environments, we can now turn to the question of what systems consist of. All systems are composed of elements. The nature or quality of these elements varies in accordance with the sort of system under consideration, but, in line with his epistemological disinterest, Luhmann never conceives of the elements as empirical or physical objects. Against the background of the epistemological tradition, he describes his own project as the 'radical de-ontologizing of objects as such' (SS: 177). He focuses the perspective not on empirical phenomena as separate cognitive units, but on the constitutive relationship between different items. Hence the constituents of a system are described as 'operationally employable system/environment differences' (SS: 7), that is they are defined in terms of their contribution towards the formation or reproduction of the system rather than in terms of ontological qualities.

The system/environment paradigm does not stipulate ontological differences. The aim is not to 'cut all of reality into two parts: here system, there environment' (SS: 178). In Luhmann's model it is not even possible to locate any item unambiguously in either the system or the environment. As the number of existing or potential systems is unlimited, the 'either/or is not an absolute', but 'pertains only in relation to the system' (ibid.). Any phenomenon in the world 'belongs to a *system* (or to many systems) and *always at the same time to the environment of other systems*' (SS: 177). There is nothing which would appear or could be looked at in isolation, but everything exists and has to be viewed in the context of particular systems and from the perspective of a particular system. So the traditional objects of cognition are decomposed, or broken down into a number of limited perspectives none of which could, on its own, reveal a full and exhaustive view. Depending on the system in the context of which they are considered, they display a different character and develop different relations to other items. It goes without saying that structural relationships and functional differences, that is the constitutive elements of Luhmann's systems, do not exist without physical or empirical objects, but whilst the tradition placed the emphasis on these objects, Luhmann focuses on the sphere of their *between*.

As a sociologist Luhmann focuses almost exclusively on *social* systems, which he distinguishes from other types of systems like, for example, machines, organisms and psychic systems (SS: 2). According to the sociological tradition, social systems are composed of human beings as their smallest and irreducible elements. Contrary to this tradition, and in line with his emphasis on the sphere of the *between*, Luhmann suggests that the elements which alone can constitute social systems are *communications*. With a view to the further analysis, it is very important to note that with this idea, Luhmann radically departs from the humanist tradition and regards the human individual as largely irrelevant for the structure and development of social systems. Luhmann neither accredits system-status to individual human beings, nor does he see them as the constitutive elements of social systems. In human beings, so Luhmann points out, we find a number of different systems like, for example, neural systems, systems of consciousness and various biological systems. But although 'a human being may appear to himself or an observer as a unity', Luhmann insists that 'he is not a system', and that it is 'even less possible to form a system out of a collection of human beings' (SS: 40).

Social systems in Luhmann's sense are sequences or networks of individual communications held together by a communicative context which they jointly produce and reproduce. They cannot be composed of human beings because, as Luhmann insists in a seemingly paradoxical way, human beings 'cannot communicate, not even their brains can communicate, nor can the conscience communicate. Only communication can communicate' (Luhmann 1988b: 884). Of course, Luhmann's point is not to deny that human beings physically generate, receive, interpret and respond to sound signals. Undeniably, human beings are necessary for social systems in as much as there is no other source of (verbal) communications. But they are comparable to other items, which may also be indispensable for social systems and can still not be regarded as their constitutive elements:

> Magnetism and acidity, air that carries sound waves and doors that one can close, clocks and telephones[1]: all seem more or less necessary. But the paradigm of the system/environment difference teaches us that not everything that is necessary can be combined into the unity of the system.
>
> (SS: 174)

By insisting that human beings cannot communicate and must therefore be conceived of 'as parts of the societal environment' (SS: 212) rather than as elements of

---

1 Official translation: 'ears and telephones'.

the social system, Luhmann wants to emphasise the considerable autonomy of his social systems *vis-à-vis* both the material world and the views or intentions of those who generate communications. In order to become part of the social system, any item, event or process in the material world first of all has to be linguistically coded, that is translated into communication. If it enters the system, it does so as its own communicative duplicate but never in its original form. To say that human beings cannot communicate thus means that they themselves, as material entities, cannot link into a purely communicative system. Certainly, they can produce communications which may qualify as elements of communicative systems, yet communications are distinct from their generators. Whether or not a communicative event can link to other such events, that is become part of a certain communicative system, furthermore depends on criteria of selection which are entirely determined by the communicative context rather than by those who produce communications.

Communicative contexts evolve along internal structures which emerge exclusively from the system itself and cannot be controlled from outside. Human beings may try to produce new communications in order to fit into existing contexts, but the rules of this production are dictated by the existing context, not by the producer himself. These distinctive criteria which qualify communications as elements of social systems need to be discussed in more detail, but it already becomes evident that Luhmann's model allows us to see human beings as involved in several social systems at the same time. Depending on the communication under consideration, they can – and are, indeed, most likely to – contribute to several social systems, each of which is constituted by certain communicative operations which are exclusive to this particular system and which establish its outside boundaries. Whilst the sociological tradition assumed social systems to be integrated by sets of norms and values held, shared and institutionalised by communities of human beings, Luhmann's approach leads to a *non-normative* theory of society's structure and functioning.

So, social systems consist of communications, and nothing but communications, that is they are communicative systems. It was suggested above that all systems can be distinguished from their environment in terms of the relative degree of complexity. At two different levels Luhmann demonstrates how social systems, too, can be seen to function as mechanisms of complexity reduction. If, firstly, society is understood as an all-embracing system composed from the totality of all communications, its internal organisation is inevitably significantly less complex than the world of possible objects of communications, which is its environment. As Luhmann points out, society necessarily has to be highly selective regarding the communicative options it actualises. In the same way in which a map reduces the complexity of the physical landscape along the lines of specific selection criteria, societal communication focuses on and evolves along certain aspects while excluding others:

> However complex its linguistic possibilities and however subtle the structure of its themes, society can never make possible communication about everything

that occurs in its environment . . . . Therefore, like every system, it must compensate for its own inferior complexity by superior order.

(SS: 182)

What Luhmann refers to as the 'superior order' of social systems points to the second dimension of their complexity reduction. This superior order is established by the category of *meaning*, which may further reduce complexity by distinguishing between meaningful, that is important, and meaningless, that is negligible, communications. Communicative systems in Luhmann's sense are integrated by structures of meaning. Their 'particularity' is 'that they orient themselves to complexity in the form of meaning' (SS: 194). In other words, the 'difference between system and environment is mediated exclusively by *meaning-constituted boundaries*' (ibid.). To the extent that social systems consist of communications which, by definition, are carriers of meaning, everything occurs to them in the form of meaning. This does, of course, not mean that, ontologically, everything *is* meaningful, that is to say meaning-free objects do not exist. However, '*for* meaning-constituting systems, everything has meaning; *for them*, there are no meaning-free objects' (SS: 73). In other words, whatever social systems can process has to be coded in such a way that it appears meaningful. As this idea of coding will become very important in the following chapter (see Section 7.6), it is worth explaining in some detail.

The coding of events may be seen as their entry ticket into the system. As indicated above, coding can be understood simply as the translation of events into language which is required because communicative systems can only process communicative events. Within social systems only linguistically 'coded events operate as information in the communication process', whilst uncoded events are perceived as a 'disturbance', as 'noise' (SS: 142). At a more abstract level, however, the process of coding can also be conceptualised as the conversion of meaning-free objects or events into their meaningful duplicates. Strictly speaking, the coding procedure leaves the external event itself unchanged, that is it 'leave(s) it outside' (SS: 142), yet it produces a meaningful duplicate that can be internally connected. Such duplication is inevitable because 'everything that can be perceived and processed in the world of meaning systems must assume the form of meaning' (SS: 63). If it does not, 'it remains a momentary impulse, an obscure mood, or even a crude shock without connectivity, communicability, or effect within the system' (ibid.). So, answering the question for the constitutive elements of social systems, we can say that in Luhmann's model, social systems are conceptualised as communicative systems or systems of meaning. Whilst there can be little doubt about the origin of communications, it is more difficult to identify the source of the crucially important system-integrating force of meaning. This takes us to the concepts of autopoiesis and self-referentiality.

6.3   Autopoiesis and self-referentiality

It is one of Luhmann's most fundamental assumptions that social systems constitute and maintain themselves, that is they themselves produce the structures of meaning and thus their difference from the environment. Unlike in the philo-sophical tradition, meaning in Luhmann's sense is not a metaphysical category, but it is system specific and has no validity beyond the system. Social systems can hence be described as meaning generating systems. This self-reliance of social systems regarding the production of their constitutive elements is captured in Luhmann's concept of *autopoiesis*. Meaning is not imported into the system from the outside, but what social systems need to maintain their boundaries and their dif-ference from their environment is generated in the system itself. Social systems are operationally closed, and owing to their autopoiesis, they achieve a high degree of autonomy *vis-à-vis* their environment. According to Luhmann, systems may be described as autopoietic systems,

> if they themselves produce and reproduce the elements they consist of by means of the elements of which they consist. Everything such elements use as a unit, that is their elements, their processes, their structures and they them-selves, is only determined in the system through such same units. Or, in other words: there is neither any input of unity into the system, nor any output of unity from the system.
>
> (Luhmann 1985: 403)

For communicative systems this means that meaningful communications, as their constitutive elements, are generated exclusively from meaningful communications. New communications may, of course, be based on events in the environment, but they become meaningful communications only through their connection to, or embeddedness into, the communicative context of the system. In other words, the constitutive parameters which define new communications as elements of a com-municative system, that is as meaningful, are exclusively internal categories. As Luhmann points out, meaning is the actualisation of 'expectational structures' (SS: 197). Every communicative context provides a plethora of further commu-nicative possibilities, which may be actualised by new communications. Out of these possibilities, every new communication actualises a highly restricted choice while excluding others. Fulfilling such communicative expectations, which emerge exclusively from the context, each new communication itself adds more to the range of communicative possibilities than can and will be actualised. Hence mean-ing can be described as 'the unity of actualization and virtualization, of re-actualization and re-virtualization, as a self-propelling process' (SS: 65).

Whilst the concept of autopoiesis places the emphasis on the system's repro-ductive self-reliance, that of *self-referentiality* captures the system's autonomy with regard to its internal operations. Meaning generating systems are closed systems in that 'meaning always refers to meaning and never reaches beyond the meaningful[2] to something else' (SS: 62). For this reason, social systems can 'never experience or act in a manner that is free from meaning'. As Luhmann insists, 'they can never

---

2 Official translation: '. . . and never reaches out of itself for something else.'

break open the reference from meaning to meaning' (SS: 62), that is they can never break free from self-referentiality. This phenomenon, that all operations performed by meaning-generating systems always refer and connect up to previous operations of the same system but never reach beyond its boundaries, follows logically from the process of coding which was mentioned above. Linguistic coding is not just the communicative duplication of external events and processes, but by means of this specific mechanism, 'the system also creates a negative version of meaning for itself, to which nothing in the environment corresponds, that is which can be controlled only through the system's self-computation[3]' (SS: 444f.).

In order to simplify this rather abstract idea, it is useful to think in terms of a triplication rather than a duplication. Firstly, there are non-communicative events and processes, to which the category of meaning cannot be applied at all. These events are neither meaningful nor meaningless. As soon as they are linguistically coded, that is subsumed under the category of meaning, they can be distinguished as either meaningful or meaningless, that is there is a further 'doubling of expressive possibilities by a yes/no difference' (ibid.). The negative side of this distinction is excluded from the system, but is still distinct from the environment in as much as it is defined in terms of the category of meaning which does not apply to the environment. From the environment's point of view, that is irrespective of the system, events cannot be described as the negative form of meaning. This is why Luhmann insists that this negative side does not correspond to anything in the environment. It is a creation of the system. So if the system refers with its operations to the meaningless, it still refers to itself and not to the environment.

Self-referentiality and operational closure, however, do not imply that social systems have to remain static and are unable to expand their boundaries. They can, and continuously do, respond to external events or processes. Although operationally closed, at least 'in principle, everything is accessible' to them (SS: 63); yet only in a form which they themselves construct under the category of meaning. 'A social system constructs its reality' (SS: 446), but there cannot be any proof that this construction 'reflects the world as it really is or describes it correctly' (ibid.). With regard to the further explorations below, it is hence important to note that the system's reactions to external stimuli are in no way determined by constellations or necessities of the environment. Every operation of a social system is entirely internally determined, that is self-referential. It responds to the necessities of the system itself and is blind to possible external necessities. These internal necessities are first and foremost the system's autopoiesis.

6.4   Temporalisation and differentiation

We finally have to deal with the concepts of temporalisation and differentiation, and can then try a first assessment of Luhmann's model. Social systems in Luhmann's sense emerge as soon as different communications are linked to each

---

3   Official translation: '. . . and which the system can control only by self-computation.'

other thus forming a meaningful sequence. The structures of meaning they produce are exclusive to this system, and distinguish it from its communicative and
extra communicative environment. Communications, however, are events which
are fixed in time and tied to specific contexts, that is neither they themselves, nor
the structures of meaning they generate survive much beyond the moment of
their creation. Hence, social systems in Luhmann's sense are not stable or lasting
structures, but cease to exist as soon as the flow of meaningful communications gets
interrupted. Luhmann speaks of the 'basal instability' (SS: 65) of all meaning systems, and the 'temporalization' (SS: 47) of their complexity:

> All elements pass away. They cannot endure as elements in time, and thus they
> must constantly be produced on the basis of whatever constellation of ele-
> ments is actual at any given moment. Reproduction thus does not mean simply
> repeatedly producing the same, but rather reflexive production, production
> out of products.
>
> (SS: 49)

Meaning that is not derived from metaphysics, but generated under conditions of
time cannot persist, because as the difference between the factual and the possible,
it emerges from, and remains tied to, a specific set of communicative possibilities
at a particular point of time. This set of possibilities is the result of prior communications and it changes with every new communication, thereby continuously
invalidating all old meaning. According to Luhmann, the 'instability of meaning
resides in the untenability of its core of actuality' (SS: 65). Meaning fades with the
fading of specific communicative contexts, that is constellations of possibilities.
Implicit in its ongoing disintegration and renewal is a constant shift of its focus.
The temporalisation of meaning forces 'a constant shifting of actuality' (SS: 63). As
temporalised complexity, 'meaning forces itself to change' (SS: 64). To the extent
that the meaning-system is constantly engaged in 'absorbing and processing its own
instability[4]' (SS: 65), it makes sense to reconsider the earlier definition of social systems according to which they have to be regarded as meaning *generating* systems. In
order to take account of the ongoing process that 'constantly shapes anew the
meaning-constitutive difference between actuality and potentiality' (ibid.), it also
makes sense to speak of meaning *processing* systems.

The temporalisation of meaning-processing systems, which implies the continuous shifting of the communicative focus and produces an abundance of
unactualised communicative options, is the reason why communicative systems
have the inbuilt capacity of diversifying themselves into multiple subsystems.
System differentiation is 'the repetition of system formation within systems' (SS:
18), whereby the embracing system then assumes the status of an 'internal environment' (ibid.) for the emerging subsystems. The differentiation of social systems
is triggered by the formation of new exclusive communicative codes which

---

4   Official translation: 'stability'.

establish boundaries of meaning between different communicative systems. Through processes of internal differentiation, the communicative operations performed by specific social systems become ever more specialised and deal with ever less likely constellations of events. As Luhmann points out, processes of differentiation increase the 'sensitivity to . . . what is capable of being connected internally' (SS: 183), that is they increase the system's performance in its field of specialisation, but at the same time, they increase the 'insensitivity to everything else' (ibid.). As any specialisation inevitably reduces the range of different aspects a particular system can handle, Luhmann notes 'an increase in dependence and independence at once' (ibid.). This dialectical process of increasing autonomy which at the same time means increasing reliance on the support or co-operation of other systems is particularly visible in contemporary societies where, according to Luhmann, communicative subsystems have evolved, or differentiated themselves, mainly along the lines of specific social functions.

Luhmann here develops the Weberian idea of functional differentiation, which is supposed to have divided modern societies into different contexts, each of which has assumed the status of an autonomous subsystem. On the one hand, internal differentiation increases the overall complexity of modern societies, but, on the other hand, 'it also enables new forms for reducing complexity' (SS: 191f.). To the extent that every subsystem focuses on special operations, one may say that it 'takes on . . . a part of the overall complexity' (SS: 192). The main societal subsystems which Luhmann describes are the economy, education, law, the sciences, politics, religion, the media and, as will be discussed below, protest movements. Echoing Weber's idea of different, system-specific rationalities, Luhmann suggests that each of these systems is structured by its own particular code of communication, and none of them is in any way privileged over the others. For the functioning of modern society, they are all equally indispensable in that each system performs tasks which cannot be performed anywhere else in society. None of the subsystems is in a position to replace any of the others. Through the formation of subsystems, each task within modern society can be completed at a level of sophistication and perfection which could otherwise not be achieved. Yet, as Luhmann emphasises, the process of functional differentiation is autonomous and automotive. It is neither driven by the aim of efficiency gains, nor controlled or co-ordinated from any superior point of view. For the argument further on this is an important point. Luhmann insists that 'like all formation of social systems, internal system formation occurs auto-catalytically, that is by self-selection'. And he goes on to say that 'internal system formation presupposes neither *activity* by the overall system nor its capability to act',[5] nor 'any overall plan' (SS: 190).

Societal *evolution* in Luhmann's sense is neither teleological nor continuous. Luhmann's evolutionary principle of 'self-conditioning selection' (SS: 433) distinguishes itself from its Darwinian predecessor in that Luhmann's selection 'is not simply selection of the appropriate system by the environment or, on the system's

---

5 Official translation: '. . . nor a capacity for dealing with that system, not to mention . . .'.

side, not simply the system's adaptation to the environment' (ibid.). In as much as in Luhmann's model societal evolution is 'directed only by the functional problems of the societal system itself' (SS: 193), it can be regarded as largely autonomous from the environment. Nevertheless, Luhmann insists that his 'sociocultural evolution is evolution in the strict sense, namely, the construction of highly improbable, unplanned complexity' (SS: 434). Compared to Darwinian evolution, Luhmann's socio-cultural evolution implies 'an enormous increase in speed' (ibid.). There is no need to wait for new generations and mutating organisms. Processes of subsystem formation can occur with any frequency, at any point in time, in any section of the communicative system. Given the contingency of internal differentiation and the exclusive focus of each system on its own autopoiesis, it follows logically that to Luhmann, any evolutionary 'orientation to human beings' or their perceived needs must appear as 'an ideology' (SS: 193).

6.5   Operation and observation

Functional differentiation and the emergence of multiple function-centred codes implies that a formerly monocentric world, or to be more precise, a *world-view* that was oriented towards the transcendental subject and integrated by its rationality, becomes polycentric. Luhmann explicitly abandons 'the traditional constitution of the world around a *center* or a *subject*'. In his model, 'the center is replaced by . . . system/environment differences that . . . constitute the world' (SS: 208). And as there are multiple system–environment differences, 'every difference becomes the center of the world'. 'In this sense', Luhmann explains, 'the world has multiple centers'. But contrary to the common criticism raised against postmodernist approaches, this multicentrism does not mean plunging into the abyss of normative relativism. Such relativism does not occur because, from its particular perspective, each system '*integrates* all the system/environment differences that a system finds in itself and its environment' (SS: 208; my emphasis). In other words, within a particular system there is *no arbitrariness or value pluralism*. Every system claims totality, that is it offers a complete description of *the world* in its own particular code and does not tolerate any alternative views. In Luhmann's theory, the difference between his suggested *multicentrism*, on the one hand, and the *acentrism* or *subjective arbitrariness*, which could also be associated with the end of metaphysics, on the other, is fundamentally important. It marks a significant difference between postmodernist and systems-theoretical thinking. Although there is, for Luhmann, an unlimited number of potential centres – system–environment differences, on whose basis the world can be constructed – every system actualises only one of them, and no system can see beyond its own constitutive difference. An awareness of the own limitations and thus of the relativism of the own judgements is not built into the system. Such an awareness can only emerge from the distinction between *operation* and *observation*, which, in his later works, Luhmann also refers to as the difference between *first-order* and *second-order observation* (Luhmann 1989; 1993a).

As Luhmann suggests, any reproductive *operation* of the system is the *first-order observation* of processes or events in the environment which are coded so that they become processible within the system. An awareness, however, of the own coding procedures, that is mechanisms of operation, cannot be achieved from within the system. The own value system (code) cannot be questioned, and thus there is no room for relativism or arbitrariness. In order to identify and question the code of a specific system, a change of perspective is required, that is it is necessary to adopt an observing position. This establishes a difference between the observer and the observed – and thus creates the constellation of *second-order observation*. As Luhmann highlights, at the operative level, that is for the automotive reproduction of the system, this kind of observation is not at all necessary. The 'reproduction of the system can and will carry on without its unity being observed' (SS: 300). But '*action* [operation] *and observation do not necessarily exclude each other*' (ibid.). Luhmann suggests that particularly in social situations 'both almost necessarily facilitate each other because the requirements for communication rule out all participants' acting at the same time' (ibid.). Purely practical reasons, as well as the fact that the human mind is always much more complex than any specific communicative system to which a human being might contribute at a given point of time, imply that 'chances for action and observation constantly fluctuate; both occur together and collaborate as soon as observation is communicated' (ibid.).

Unlike *first-order observation* (reproductive operation), *second-order observation*, that is the observation of observation, allows us to see the world as polycentric. Second-order observation is possible only because the human being as such is not part of the system (which consists of communications), but part of the environment – or, with other communications, part of other systems. Internal differentiation is pre-requisite to the system acquiring the capacity of 'built-in reflection', which forces it 'to forgo absolutes' (SS: 485). Second-order observation can detect the limitations of the system, that is of first-order observation (reproductive operation). In other words, it can see that first-order observation reduces complexity. But second-order observation is itself subject to a different set of limitations because, as Luhmann insists, no observation is possible which does not reduce complexity. These second-order limitations may be made visible by further observations, but not without once again different limitations. Thus further observation may help to make visible the restrictedness of second-order observation, but it cannot claim more validity for its own judgements than it accredits to other second-order judgements. At the level of second-order observation, hierarchies of validity claims do not exist. Different second-order perspectives relativise each other, but do not take us any closer to 'apriority' (SS: 485). For this reason, Luhmann insists that, eventually, we have to take 'leave of ontological metaphysics' (ibid.). For any second-order observer, 'the world can only be perceived of as a construction, which emerges from the on-going observation of observations' (Luhmann 1990: 100). But, of course, understanding the world as a construction – or as multiple, mutually exclusive constructions presented by different second-order perspectives – does not mean completely denying the potential existence of an ontological reality (see Section 3.2). This is an important point to make. It only means that for human rationality this ontological level – if it exists – is not accessible.

6.6   **Provisional assessment**

To readers with no prior experience of systems-theoretical approaches and terminology, this reconstruction of the core elements of Luhmann's thinking may appear rather abstract and alienating. Admittedly, it is not immediately obvious how this theoretical framework might contribute to the analysis of ecological issues. But as I will demonstrate in the following chapters, Luhmann's model does indeed open a very innovative and revealing perspective on to ecological issues, and the last few sections have provided conceptual tools which are essential for the analysis of Luhmann's view of the eco-movement and of ecological discourse. However, before we narrow the focus once again to ecological matters, it might be useful to make some general comments on the specific way in which Luhmann fleshes out the communicative turn of social theory to which I pointed at the beginning of this chapter. One of the most striking points is surely Luhmann's radically new perspective on to the human being.

The main target of Luhmann's attempt to 'think everything anew', starting out from the concept of difference rather than that of unity, is, as we have seen, the traditional concept of the *subject*. The unity of the subject was a category which Kant had introduced by way of assuming, firstly, the transcendental unity of human perception and, secondly, the transcendental unity of reason. Although the Kantian model distinguished between *being* and *consciousness*, and insisted that no *noumena* (being) but only *phenomena* (consciousness) are accessible to human cognition, these fundamental assumptions secured the absolute reliability of human knowledge. They, firstly, implied the ultimate identity between the cognitive subject and the objects of its cognition, and, secondly, immunised rational cognition against the contingencies of space and time. Luhmann challenges the metaphysical foundation of the Kantian model and abandons both the Kantian transcendental subject as well as the traditional subject–object dichotomy. Whilst the subject is replaced by the concept of the system, the subject–object dualism gives way to that of the system and its environment.

On the face of it, this conceptual arrangement may look structurally similar to the Kantian model. But Luhmann does not simply substitute the old dualism for a new one. The concept of the system differs from that of the subject in that it is always plural, that is there are different types and a potentially unlimited number of systems which cannot be harmonised. Also, Luhmann introduces a categorical distinction between *operation* and *observation*. A *system* in his sense may keep stabilising and reproducing itself, but unlike the Kantian self-conscious subject, *it does not know what it is doing*. Its own operations remain opaque to the system itself. Operational self-referentiality must not be confused with Kantian self-consciousness. Unlike Habermas, for example, who criticises the idealist concept of the subject but does not fully depart from it, Luhmann has no further use for this category at all. He seeks to revise 'the overestimation implicit in the concept of the subject, namely, the thesis that consciousness is the subject of everything else' (SS: 178). Instead of the subject, the environment '*underlies* social systems, and *underlies* means only that there are preconditions for the differentiation of social systems (e.g., persons as bearers of consciousness) that are not differentiated with the system' (ibid.). In other words, there *are* prerequisites for the emergence of social systems, but unlike for the emergence of the idealist subject, there are no meta-physical assumptions.

Luhmann thus departs from the modernist tradition in a way that is significantly more radical than the bulk of postmodernist thinking. The central innovation of postmodernism is the principle of *plurality*, which takes the place of modernist *unity*. But postmodernists normally remain modernist in that they retain the (pluralised) subject, that is the individual, as the centre of their thinking. In contrast to this, Luhmann's model is genuinely *post*modernist in that it abandons both the principle of unity and the focus on the subject or individual. His replacement of the traditional idealised subject opens a new perspective on to human beings as well as their relationship towards their non-human environment. Human beings are no longer forced into the strait-jacket of the identical subject, but may unfold an unprecedented complexity and diversity. The devaluation of the subject thus means a revaluation of not harmonisable human individuality. In the language of early critical theory one might say, the abdication of the subject implies the decline of the prime instrument of subjective self- or identity-construction, identifying rationality, and thus the release of the non-identical. In particular, the transition from the subject–object paradigm to the system–environment paradigm allows Luhmann to see human beings as significantly more complex than was possible before:

> the distinction between system and environment offers the possibility of con-
> ceiving human beings as parts of the societal environment in a way that is both
> more complex and less restricting than if they had to be interpreted as parts
> of society, because in comparison with the system, the environment is the
> domain of distinction that shows greater complexity and less existing order.
> The human being is thus conceded greater freedom in relation to *his* environ-
> ment, especially freedom for irrational and immoral behavior.
>
> (SS: 212f.)

With regard to the explorations made further on, this increase in freedom is an important point to note. One may, of course, argue that the transition from the ide-alised subject to the concrete human being, which resides in the environment of the social system rather than in its centre, implies a radical devaluation of the human being. As a matter of fact, Luhmann explicitly points out that the human individual is 'no longer the measure of society' and that the whole tradition of 'humanism cannot continue' (SS: 213). At the same time, however, Luhmann strictly denies that in his model 'the human being is estimated as less important than traditionally' (SS: 212). He can convincingly argue this point because his concept of the environment-related system does not establish any hierarchy between the two sides of the distinction. As was outlined above, systems and their environments are closely tied to each other and cannot exist without their respective counterpart. Undeniably, Luhmann's focus of interest is on the system, yet as he himself concedes, the environment 'may contain many things' without which the system cannot emerge in the first place, and which are therefore 'more important for the system than the parts of the system itself' (ibid.). Rather than the *devaluation* of the human being, Luhmann's project may be described as its *renaturalisation*. Whilst 'humanism retreated from nature to mind' (ibid.), Luhmann regards 'observation, description or knowledge', once again, as '*natural* operations' which no longer pre-suppose any 'privileged *metaphysical* subjective position' (SS: 178).

The tradition of European humanism renders it difficult to accept the socio-logical decentring of the human being and the thesis of the abdication of the idealised modernist subject. By relocating the human individual from the centre into the environment of the social system, Luhmann seems to be radicalising what the Marxist tradition describes as *alienation*: it is now no longer just *economic rationality* that disregards the human being, but *all forms* of rationality (codes) in general. Luhmann has always been aware that his model provokes the charge of being anti-humanist. But he deliberately departs from the humanist tradition acknowledging that – coming back to Gray's words quoted in Section 2.3 – this tradition has become 'peculiarly ill-suited to the realities and dilemmas' of contemporary soci-ety. Of course, trying to devise a post-humanist model of sociological description and analysis must not be confused with abandoning humanist ideals as a basis for political demands and concrete policy making. And from the ecological point of view, the fundamental revision of the humanist tradition might actually be regarded as a necessary precondition for the long demanded radical change in the human–nature relationship. Ecologists have always criticised both the anthro-pocentrism of modernist thinking and the modernist subject's instrumental rationality, which is responsible for the systematic domination and exploitation of the non-human environment. In this sense, the French structuralists had already indicated that the end of the humanist tradition and the decentring of the human being might open spaces for the revaluation of nature (Conley 1997). Arguing along very similar lines, ecological theorists like David Pepper (1993) or Jagtenberg and McKie (1997) have raised hopes for a 'post-modernist ecocentrism'. As I will demonstrate in the following chapters, such ecologist hopes are, unfortunately, completely unfounded. Nevertheless, the idea that the abolition of the Kantian subject might put an end to the competition between the modernist Self and nature (its Other) retains a certain attraction. In Luhmann's model, human beings and the so-called natural environment certainly find themselves on the same side of the equation, and the traditional cleavage between the two no longer attracts much attention.

In conclusion to this provisional assessment of Luhmann's systems-theoretical interpretation of the communicative change of paradigm, I want to highlight three other implications of his model which will become very important in the fol-lowing chapters. Firstly, the loss of the metaphysical point of view and the multiplication of human perspectives on the world obviously undermine the foundations for any social critique – including the ecological critique. Secondly, it is worth pointing out how Luhmann takes account of the perceived complexity and fragmentation of modern societies. His model not only offers an explanation for the emergence of a number of largely autonomous although interlinked subsystems, but also for the ubiquitous problems of co-ordination between the various subsystems. Thirdly, it is interesting to see how Luhmann gives substance to 'the fashionable label of the communication society'. Whilst the availability of new communication technologies seems to be a subordinate criterion, the communication society is primarily characterised: (a) by individual communications replacing human individuals as the constitutive elements of contemporary social systems; (b) by fragmentary and discursively constructed structures of meaning taking over the integrative function formerly fulfilled by generally shared social values in the traditional sense; and (c) by the achievement of an unprecedented level of flexibility and volatility. The integrative structures of meaning are in constant transition.

The decline of the individual, the dissolution of social values, and the loss of tradition and stability have always been lamented as the so-called *pathologies of modern society*. Ever since Durkheim and Weber these issues have been key themes in sociological analysis, and they also feature prominently in the work of Horkheimer, Adorno and Beck. But these *pathologies* are subjective experiences which are hard to prove and quantify. Luhmann's model helps greatly to explain what they mean, and in what respects such complaints are justifiable. It is, however, important to note that Luhmann not only theorises the *decline* of the individual, the *dissolution* of meaning and the *loss* of stability, but at the same time he actually *saves* all three categories beyond the abolition of metaphysics. His liberation of the human being through the abolition of the subject has been discussed above. The category of stability only disappears in its *static* variety, but *dynamic* stability is a key aim and element in the process of systemic autopoiesis and reproduction. And with regard to the oft-lamented loss of meaning, we can note that Luhmann saves the category of meaning by detaching it from its metaphysical origins and connecting it to communicative contexts rather than human subjects. Luhmann insists that 'there are no grounds for reacting . . . with cultural pessimism' (SS: 587f.). Even after the end of metaphysics, he notes, 'meaning is still the unavoidable form[6] of experience and action'. Without meaning 'society and every social system would simply cease to exist'. And the typically modernist complaint about the loss of meaning is not acceptable to Luhmann because it 'does not adequately indicate what it means, but exaggerates in order to pronounce society guilty' (ibid.).

---

6 Official translation: 'an unavoidable form'.

7   Ecological communication – Niklas Luhmann II

According to Luhmann, 'systems theory is a particularly impressive supertheory' (SS: 5). *Supertheories* in Luhmann's sense are qualified as such by their claim to *universality*. This does not, of course, mean that systems theory would claim to reveal the full and only truth. On the contrary, for an adequate understanding of Luhmann's model it is of the utmost significance that Luhmann himself regards other theoretical models as potentially equally valid and necessary. His theory is always aware of its own constructedness and limitations, that is it knows and admits that it can only offer insights from a restricted point of view. But what the claim to universality does mean is that at least from this particular perspective, systems theory can 'encompass all sociology's potential topics and, in this sense, . . . be a universal sociological theory' (SS: 15). It must, hence, also be possible to interpret political protest movements and the ecological critique of modern society within the framework of Luhmann's model. And, indeed, there are a number of pieces in which Luhmann deals with the social movement phenomenon from the 1970s to the present. The most important ones are, first of all, *Ecological Communication* (1986/1989; henceforth EC), then the chapter entitled 'Protest Movements' from *Risk: A Sociological Theory* (1991/1993b; henceforth PM), and several sections and passages in Luhmann's last work *Die Gesellschaft der Gesellschaft* (1998a; henceforth GG). Furthermore, there is a collection of essays and interviews dating from 1985 to 1995 which is called *Protest* (1996a; henceforth P). So Luhmann has written extensively about (eco-)political protests, but as Hellmann (1996a) correctly points out, he neither offers a fully developed and consistent social movements theory nor is he particularly sympathetic to the (ecological) protest movements. Perhaps for this reason, Luhmann's writings on this issue have so far been largely ignored. There is the widespread – and not totally unwarranted – view that 'this particular issue somehow refuses to fit into the perspective which the sociologist Luhmann normally takes to look at modern society' (Hellmann 1996a: 9). Nevertheless, with regard to the research tasks that emerged from the analysis of Beck's eco-theoretical model (see the end of Chapter 5), Luhmann's thinking offers extremely valuable insights. And in a number of respects, Luhmann's approach is – although there are also substantial differences – thoroughly comparable to my own approach is this book.

In *Ecological Communication*, Luhmann's perspective is not determined by ecological interests. Instead, the emphasis is – as for me – on the shortcomings of contemporary sociology, for which the ecological discussion 'began – like so many others, unexpectedly – and caught it, as it were, unprepared theoretically' (EC: 1). *Ecological Communication* applies the systems-theoretical approach with analytical and *deconstructive* rather than, in the ecologist sense, *constructive* intentions. The primary objective is not 'to provide a solution to the problem of ecological adaptation of the system of society, but instead to see what contours the problem takes on when it is formulated with the help of this theory' (EC: 7). Luhmann anticipates that this theory-oriented approach will be criticised for its 'lack of *practical reference*' and for not providing 'prescriptions for others to use' (EC: xviii), but he believes that not much is to be gained if ecologists 'hastily take action on the basis of unfermented assumptions'[1] (ibid.). Throughout *Ecological Communication*, Luhmann therefore remains very reluctant to acknowledge the existence of an environmental problem as defined by ecologists, and he is eager to retain a critical distance from the ecologist perspective.

The general undertone in the book is that the ecologist issue was forced upon Luhmann, but that he is not really prepared to discuss it in any detail. In particular, he is not prepared to discuss it on the terms set by ecologists themselves. On the one hand, Luhmann seems to feel that he cannot ignore an issue which, particularly in the year of Chernobyl, had become a big focal point of both the media and the public debate. Indeed, such neglect would have called his claim to the universality of his theory into question. On the other hand, Luhmann sees no need to address an issue just because certain sectors of society have framed it as a major problem and installed it as a mainstream concern. Luhmann feels that he will not be given the chance to conceptualise ecological issues in his own terms, that is to look at them from a non-ecologist perspective. He seems to fear that pressures for *ecological correctness* will distort his analysis and pre-empt any discussion that deviates from the established patterns. Reluctantly, he does then accept the challenge, but already, before embarking on this project, he states that, ultimately, 'ecological and the systems-theoretical formulations of the question are mutually exclusive'[2] (EC: 150). According to Luhmann, the fundamental difference between the ecological and systems-theoretical approaches is that ecologists start out from the assumption of a single, all-embracing systematic coherence, and discuss the relationship between civilisation and its so-called natural environment under the premise of their *unity*. Contrary to this, systems theorists start out from the opposite assumption of *diversity*, and focus on the mechanisms by which certain systems generate and reproduce their difference, their distinctive identity and their internal cohesion (EC: 6, 150).

There are three fundamental questions which accompany and guide Luhmann's eco-sociological investigations: The first one is the above-mentioned question of 'what contours the environmental problem takes on when it is formulated with the

---

1 Official translation: '. . . making such a hasty use of incomplete ideas'.
2 Official translation: '. . . the ecological problematic cuts across the systems-theoretical problematic'.

help of systems theory'. This is an *eco*-theoretical question and experiment which looks for new and perhaps more revealing ways of conceptualising the ecological problem. Secondly, Luhmann asks: 'Can modern society adjust itself to the exposure to ecological dangers?' (EC: xvii). This is the subtitle of the German version of *Ecological Communication*. It is a *social*-theoretical investigation which focuses on the structures and flexibility of contemporary society. And, thirdly, Luhmann wonders: 'How can one genuinely believe that a new ethics might lead to an ecologically adequate behaviour without colliding with other requirements on all sides?' (P: 48). This question has two different dimensions. On the one hand, it is a *discourse*-theoretical questions that asks for the internal structure and validation mechanisms of ecological communication. On the other hand, it is an eco-critical question shedding doubts on the belief in a new eco-ethics as an instrument of eco-political change.

7.1   A revised concept of the environment

As a starting point for his eco-sociological investigations, Luhmann tries to sketch out a concept of the environment which does not bear any normative connotations and which, above all, bears no direct relationship to any traditional concept of nature or the natural. One might say that Luhmann tries to liberate the concept of the environment from the ecologist siege (GG: 128f.). He achieves this by defining the environment purely *ex negativo*, whilst a positive definition is only given for the system which constitutes itself according to its own rules (code). As I outlined in Section 6.1, the system and its environment emerge at the same time, in parallel to each other, with the system defining its own boundaries and the environment emerging by means of exclusion from the system (EC: 6). Since the environment is defined as 'whatever lies outside the boundary' (ibid.), Luhmann describes it as merely 'a system-relative situation' (SS: 181). In other words, the environment can only be conceptualised from the perspective and in terms of the system. It has relevance only with regard to the system. It has no identity, meaning, or value of its own.

Luhmann's concept of the environment thus signifies a radical breach with the ecological tradition. Ecological theorists and eco-movement activists most commonly have an understanding of the environment which is induced by the science of ecology. The so-called natural environment is assumed to consist of a large number of more or less distinct eco-systems, which add up to the grand coherence of nature and contribute to nature's all-embracing systemic equilibrium. From the systems-theoretical point of view, however, the environment has no systematic coherence. Luhmann programmatically abandons the concept of a 'comprehensive ecosystem, that embraces nature and society' (P: 50), and he uses the term *ecology* as 'a concept for the analysis of interdependencies for which no comprehensive, externally limited system can be identified' (ibid.). He insists that 'the environment is not a system of its own, not even a unity that could effect anything' (EC: 6). It is no more than 'the totality of external circumstances', comprising 'whatever restricts the randomness of the morphogenesis of systems and exposes them[3] to evolutionary selection' (ibid.). In other words, the environment is no more than a meaningless and over-complex accumulation of relations. Unless radically simplified, these relations are in no respect meaningful. And only the reduction of complexity, which is the essence of systemic self-formation processes (see Chapter 6), allows for the development of meaningful relations. Of course, this does not preclude the system regarding its environment as a unity. But wherever the environment, despite its incoherence and its 'unlimited horizons', is referred to as such a unity, it has to be kept in mind that its unity 'is nothing more than a correlate of the unity of the system since everything that is a unity for the system is defined *by it* as a unity' (ibid.; my emphasis).

This revised concept of the environment has important implications. Firstly, the traditional notion of environmental protection becomes completely meaningless. On the basis of Luhmann's approach, it is neither possible to conceptualise the object of such protection, nor would it make sense at all to protect the meaningless over-complexity. Secondly, the concept of the environment is radically pluralised 'because *the* environment' was only 'the correlate of *the* system' (EC: 135). The assumption, however, that the process of functional differentiation leads to the formation of a virtually unlimited number of social systems implies the existence of an equally unlimited number of distinct, although of course partially overlapping, environments. As Luhmann points out, 'every system excludes only itself[4] from its environment', and 'therefore the environment of each system is different' (SS: 181). Efforts of environmental protection can hence – if they make sense at all – only be directed towards particular exclusive environments, but never towards *the* environment as an all-inclusive entity. And the most such efforts can try to achieve is to stabilise particular exclusive social systems, but never society or even humanity at large. Thirdly, each of these multiple environments now includes both the extra-societal natural environment in the traditional sense as well as substantial parts of the civilisatory world, whereby no distinction is made between their 'natural' and 'civilisatory' components. Whilst for traditional understanding the environment was the *Other*, the extra-social physical environment providing the framework for and the conditions of the possibility of human life and civilisation, Luhmann's concept of the environment includes both the so-called natural foundations of life as well as those preconditions for the functioning of a specific social system which are located inside the civilisatory world. Of course, any system remains dependent on its surrounding environment, yet the dividing line between the system and its environment is no longer the dubious nature–culture divide, but the line established by the system's exclusive rules of autopoiesis.

Luhmann's concept of the environment may legitimately be regarded as a *post-natural* concept of the environment, that is as a concept that reflects what I described as the *abolition of nature* (see Chapter 3). Firstly, the idea that the 'environment is only a negative correlate of the system', which 'is not a unity capable of

3   Official translation: 'not even a unified effect. . . . the morphogenesis of the system and exposes it to'.
4   Official translation: 'removes itself'.

operations' and which 'cannot perceive, have dealings with, or influence the system' (SS: 181), takes away the subject status that was accredited to nature in the traditional sense. Secondly, Luhmann's understanding of the environment disregards the traditional distinction between natural and cultural. It takes full account of the changes which Beck tries to capture with his concept of *reflexivity*, that is that the main thrust of the process of modernisation is no longer the subjugation (systematic integration) of a previously extra-societal nature, but the transformation of civilisatory structures which were established by earlier phases of modernisation (see Section 5.2). Thirdly, Luhmann's new definition of the environment differs from the traditional understanding in that it comprises both physical as well as discursive, that is material as well as non-material, components. Luhmann has no use for the traditional notion of the natural environment as the totality of the physical conditions providing the material basis for social processes.

In two respects, Luhmann's redefinition of the system–environment dualism may be described as not just *post-natural* but actually *post-ecologist*: Firstly, ecological questions in Luhmann's sense, that is the systems-theoretical analysis of the relationship between particular systems and their respective environments, has no moral dimension or implication. Secondly, following the abolition of the traditional distinction between the societal system and the system of the natural environment, the ecologist question for the physical relationship between the two systems no longer arises. Both the question of nature's normative value as well as the question of inter-systemic material flows or metabolisms were based on the assumption of a singular nature–society dualism. From a Luhmannite perspective, however, they either dissolve or have to be radically reformulated. This is what Luhmann means when he points out that the ecological and systems-theoretical perspectives are not easily compatible. As Luhmann's social systems are purely communicative systems, while the totality of physical and material conditions – and thus most ecological issues in the traditional sense – are (amongst other elements) all part of the environment (which is not under consideration), one could either say that Luhmann's model is blind to ecological issues in the ecologist sense, or that by reshuffling the basic parameters of analysis, Luhmann reveals the contingency of the ecologist perspective. These observations will have to be developed in more detail at a later stage. Given these *post-natural* and *post-ecologist* qualities, Luhmann's revised concept of the environment promises to be an interesting and useful tool for the analysis of contemporary environmental politics, which is, as I argued in Chapter 3, a politics after the abolition of nature and beyond the singular ecologist dualism.

7.2   A revised understanding of the environmental problem

Luhmann's revised concept of the environment has important implications for the understanding of the environmental problem. As I pointed out above, Luhmann wants to explore what contours this problem takes on when seen from a systems-theoretical point of view. In response to this question we can firstly note that from a Luhmannite perspective, concepts like *environmental deterioration*, *degradation* or *destruction* no longer make sense. As Luhmann's *systems-theoretical* model has no space for the *subject-theoretical* concept of *nature*, the ecologist diagnosis (problem) that nature is under threat or being destroyed can hardly be formulated, and there is no room for the ecological imperative to save or protect nature. Secondly, the post-natural pluralisation of *the* environment invariably implies the pluralisation of *the* environmental problem in the sense that different systems will, obviously, experience different phenomena in their respective environments as problematic. Whilst environmental problems have traditionally been conceptualised as threats to *civilisation at large*, they are now only problematic for particular subsystems. Phenomenon X might present a fundamental threat to the survival of system A, but be unproblematic – or even a vital precondition – for the smooth functioning of system B. Thirdly, the notion of the environmental problem becomes narrower, but at the same time wider. It becomes narrower in so far as it only includes those environmental phenomena in the traditional sense which pass the filter of a particular system's code. It becomes wider because environmental problems may now emerge from both the *internal* environment (other social systems) as well as the *external* environment (nature in the traditional sense). Fourthly, in a way that seems similar to the approach taken by Beck (see Section 5.3), environmental problems now have to be regarded as always and exclusively *societal* problems. If the environment is not accredited the status of a system, 'not even a unity that could effect anything', it would be nonsensical to assume it could have any problem. Problems can only emerge where the achievement of defined goals comes under threat. Social systems have a problem when their stability and reproduction, that is their autopoiesis, is irritated. Luhmann's environment, however, for its lack of an identifiable structure, can neither be disturbed nor irritated. Hence, when referring to what is commonly understood as an *environmental* problem, Luhmann insists 'that this is a phenomenon that is exclusively internal to society' (EC: 28).

The crucial point, however, where Luhmann goes a significant step beyond Beck's *societalisation* of the environmental problem is his suggestion that environmental problems are under no circumstances 'a matter of allegedly[5] objective facts' (EC: 28). As I outlined in Chapter 5, Beck points towards the social constructedness of ecological problems and their dependence on cultural norms and patterns of perception, but ultimately he continues to believe in the objective and extra-societal material reality of environmental problems. Contrary to this approach, Luhmann suggests that the 'allegedly objective facts' remain completely irrelevant. As Luhmann argues, it may very well be true that

> oil-supplies are decreasing, that the temperature of rivers is increasing, that forests are being defoliated or that the skies and the seas are being polluted. All this may or may not be the case. But as physical, chemical or biological facts they create no social resonance as long as they are not the subject of communication. Fish or humans may die because swimming in the seas and rivers has

5 Official translation: 'blatantly'.

become unhealthy. The oil-pumps may run dry and the average climatic temperatures may rise or fall. As long as this is not the subject of communication it has no social effect.

(EC: 28f.)

So phenomena of environmental change or particular conditions in the physical environment can never acquire the status of environmental problems, unless they become the subject of communications. But even that is only a necessary, but not in itself a sufficient condition. They, secondly, have to be coded in such a way that they happen to make sense within a specific communicative (social) system, but do not fulfil its structures of expectation. In other words, the respective communications have to link into an existing communicative system and disturb its established routines of self-reproduction. From the perspective of a particular social system, this means that most changes occurring in the environment will not at all be taken notice of. And if they are taken notice of, the so-called *environmental* problems thus appear not only as *societal* problems, but more precisely as *communicative* problems. They are problematic not as objective physical phenomena and not because they have a physical impact on physical systems, but in as much as they irritate the structures governing particular social systems and force these systems to adapt themselves. Luhmann thus confirms the thesis that environmental problems are social constructions, and by conceptualising them as *communicative* construction, he even radicalises it.

An important implication of this systems-theoretical variety of the *societalisation* of environmental problems is that environmental problems in Luhmann's sense are always and necessarily self-generated. Once again there seems to be a parallel to Beck, whose model of the risk society emphasised that the ecological risks and hazards contemporary society has to confront are self-induced. But contrary to Beck, who is thinking of concrete physical conditions in the environment which have – deliberately or as unintended side-effects – been brought about by human action, the central point for Luhmann is that social (communicative) systems are operationally closed, that is that they can only respond to communications and only be disturbed by communications. And as the system alone can generate communications, it follows logically that it can only be disturbed by itself, but not directly by the environment. The communicative turn, which Luhmann, like Habermas, makes the very basis of his social theory, thus results in the de-ontologisation of environmental problems. Further specifying the above definition, environmental problems may therefore be described not just as communicative problems, but more precisely as *problematic communications*. So with regard to his question about 'what contours the environmental problem takes on when it is formulated with the help of systems theory', Luhmann comes to the conclusion that, ultimately, environmental problems are problematic to the extent that they threaten, or at least challenge, established norms of communication, that is structures of *meaning* (EC: 28). In an unexpected way this result confirms and radicalises the thesis that *meaning* and *identity* are at the heart of environmental problems. From a systems-theoretical perspective, environmental problems are the violation of communicative expectations (norms) which are basically contingent, but derive a certain claim to validity from the fact that they are established, that is that their reproduction implies stability and continuity.

Within traditional ecological discourse, Luhmann's reconceptualisation of environmental problems as 'irritations' or as 'distorting noise' (EC: 1) that interferes with autopoiesis-oriented communication must appear as even more bizarre than the social constructionist views which were discussed in Chapter 3. Luhmann's model not only questions the substantive reality of environmental problems, but it also sheds doubts on the relevance of the social values and norms of perception which ecological constructionists regard as the crucial criterion deciding about the acceptability of phenomena of environmental change. Instead of the needs, values, meaning and identity of human individuals and communities, systemic norms and requirements shift into the centre of attention. At first sight, one might of course get the impression that there is not that much of a difference between Luhmann's model of 'irritation' and the traditional understanding of environmental problems. Anything which the traditional perspective would describe as an environmental danger, one might think, will certainly be translated into communications and thus force the system to take notice of the problem and deal with it. But this is not the case. At the risk of overstating the point, I will repeat why it is not.

Firstly, empirical phenomena of (societal or environmental) change do not necessarily translate into communications. Strict criteria of selection decide what becomes an issue for societal discourse and what does not. Secondly, those phenomena of change which are picked up by societal communication, may appear as an irritation to one system without appearing as such from a different system's perspective. As different social systems are constituted by different codes, their respective environments are not congruent, and neither are the parameters turning a merely irrelevant environmental phenomenon into an environmental problem. And, thirdly, whilst environmental problems in the traditional sense gain their problem status through their relationship to the specific needs and values (identity) of human individuals, Luhmann's criterion is the requirements (meaning, identity) of social systems which consist of communications, but relegate human individuals into their environment (see Sections 6.2 and 6.5). Thus, in several respects, Luhmann's reconceptualisation of the environment and the environmental problem breaks with traditional communication about the environment. But it opens a new perspective on both the anatomy of what is commonly referred to as the environmental challenge and the mechanisms shaping modern society's response to phenomena of environmental change.

7.3   Confronting environmental problems

Of course, Luhmann's reconceptualisation of the environment and the environmental problem does not mean to deny that society as a whole is exposed to phenomena of change in the physical environment which affect, in one way or another, all function systems. Such phenomena would be environmental problems in the traditional sense, and the question arises how contemporary society can respond to such changes in the physical conditions. The standard way in which ecologists approach this question is to demand that society develops a (bad) environmental conscience, 'accuses itself as a risk society' (Beck) and adopts a completely new attitude towards the so-called natural environment. In other words, ecologists commonly rephrase the question and ask how contemporary society *ought to* respond rather than analysing its factually available structural possibilities. Contrary to this traditional approach, Luhmann is firmly convinced that 'the solution to the (ecological) problem cannot be found in new value-conceptions, a new morality or the academic elaboration of an environmental ethics'[6] (EC: xvii). For Luhmann, the ecologists' 'aggressive, self-righteous way of turning ecological problems into moral questions' (P: 48) is unacceptable. He regards this approach as 'a symptom of a fundamental deficit in terms of theory' (ibid.). Like all social movements in general, so Luhmann argues, the ecology movement, in particular, sets out to criticise societal developments 'without ever analysing the all-important system structures' (EC: 5), and especially without ever achieving a decent 'understanding of the theoretical structure of the ecological question' (ibid.) itself.

Luhmann suggests that when trying to attune itself to environmental challenges of the above kind, contemporary society is confronted with two major difficulties. The first one is related to the task of formulating the problem; the second one to the task of devising strategies for its solution. Luhmann's acentric or polycentric model of late modern society implies that even where society is challenged as a whole, its response can only be 'formulated within the individual functional systems and cannot be steered from a centre' (P: 54). The autonomy of the subsystems, the indispensability of every function system and the lack of an all-integrating rationality, lead – as we know from the discussion of Beck – to conflicts between competing views about both the nature of the problem and the options for its solution. But whilst Beck believes in the possibility of an ecological consensus, Luhmann suggests that under the conditions of functional differentiation, 'the idea that rational consensus ought to be attained is quickly trivialized' (EC: 27). In Luhmann's view, such a consensus is an ideal that can only be promoted by those who mistake their own personal perspective for the generalisable truth, and who forget that 'everybody is prepared to make concessions only in accordance with their own understanding of the problem'[7] (ibid.).

Given the lack of an authority that could decide about conflicting validity claims, a consensual and co-ordinated approach does not seem possible. Modern society has no means of generating a reliable definition of the problem or co-ordinating the way in which it responds. As Luhmann argues, the first and most important imperative for every function system is its own autopoiesis. And when

---

6 Official translation: 'that the solution to this problem can be found in new ideas about values, a new morality or an academic elaboration of an environmental ethics'.

7 Official translation: 'Those who think they know that this is going to be a protracted enterprise use this idea and test their willingness to make concessions according to their own judgement.'

they respond to what they perceive as irritations, the systems follow just this imperative. Every system sees a problem to the extent that its own structures are threatened, and it reacts in such way as is required to restabilise itself. Ever since functional differentiation has become the structural principle of modern society, so Luhmann argues, 'a plurality of functionally specified codes has steered resonance to the environment', and these multiple codes 'lack integration to the extent[8] that a positive valuation in one code . . . does not automatically entail a positive valuation in the other codes' (EC: 43). Hence the way in which one system reacts may reinforce the reaction of a different system, but it may also neutralise it.

Particular reactions of one system may even themselves appear as environmental problems to another system. Given the differentiated structure of modern society and the assumption that society as a whole cannot respond to external challenges in any other way but through its 'function systems according to specific codes and programs' (EC: 50), Luhmann comes to the conclusion that *modern society cannot adjust itself* to the exposure to threats and dangers in the ecologist sense. Undoubtedly individual social systems will adapt themselves to the changing external circumstances, but this is a normal process which happens irrespective of the societal perception of so-called environmental problems. Social systems, as Luhmann understands them, are never in stagnation, but in the process of their own reproduction, they constantly generate self-irritations and adapt their structures accordingly. Beyond this ongoing process of regeneration at the subsystem level, however, contemporary society as a whole has no means of devising and implementing co-ordinated strategies to confront the so-called environmental challenge.

7.4   Ecological communication as a function system

This seems to be a rather pessimistic view, although in a number of respects it confirms the findings of Chapter 5, where we discussed the pluralisation of rationality and social problem perceptions, and rejected Beck's unfounded ecological optimism. However, Luhmann's conclusions are only pessimistic if we accept the unquestioned assumption that ecological risks and hazards really are inescapable physical realities, and that it really is necessary for society to react as a whole and in a co-ordinated way. In other words, they are only pessimistic if we rely on the traditional understanding of the environment and the environmental problem. But within the framework of Luhmann's theory, environmental issues can be dealt with in two different ways. Accepting the traditional formulation of the ecological problem, Luhmann firstly explores how – or whether at all – contemporary society can manage such a challenge. For this purpose he requires a theory of the structure and functioning of modern society, and we have seen where his social-theoretical model takes him. The second way of applying Luhmann's theory to ecological issues is to focus not on modern society's ability or inability to confront

---

8   Official translation: 'only to the extent'.

environmental problems in the ecologist sense, but to focus instead on the discourse where environmental problems are framed and promoted in this ecologist sense. Rather than providing a critique of modern society, this leads to a critique of the ecological discourse. This approach goes significantly beyond Beck's analysis. In a way, one might even say that it goes beyond Luhmann himself, for in *Ecological Communication*, Luhmann only sketches this approach, and in order to develop it to its full extent, I have to apply Luhmann's scattered comments on new social movements and protest communication in general to the particular case of *ecological* protest and communication. In certain respects, this takes us beyond what Luhmann explicitly states. But the focus on the internal structures of the ecologist discourse is undoubtedly fully in the spirit of his analysis. Characteristically, the third of his above-quoted guiding questions starts with the words: 'How can one genuinely believe that . . . ?', that is Luhmann is interested to find out by what (unreflected) mechanisms ecological communication becomes meaningful and secures normative validity.

For the purpose of exploring the internal structure of ecological communication and the mechanisms that make ecological judgements meaningful and authoritative, ecological communication has to be regarded as a social system in its own right. So far, ecological communications have been regarded as parts of the various existing function systems. Yet under this premise, it remains somewhat unclear how we can at all speak about ecological communication. If, as Luhmann seems to suggest, ecological communication occurs exclusively within the various function systems, this confirms the idea of the above-mentioned *disintegration of the ecological issue* (see Sections 2.1 and 5.6), but it raises the question of how it can be distinguished at all from the dominant kind of communication within the respective system. In other words: what is the specific difference between ecological communication and political, legal, economic, and such like communication? It follows that although practical responses to phenomena of physical environmental change may be formulated within society's function systems, there must also be an independent ecological discourse which is the *original home* of ecological communication and which gives it its specific character and identity. Luhmann is not entirely clear to what extent he is prepared to regard ecological communication as an autonomous system, but he certainly identifies and criticises central characteristics of this communication, which would seem to imply that it has system status.

If ecological communication can be regarded as an independent social system in Luhmann's sense, it must be possible to specify a function which is fulfilled exclusively by this system, which cannot be taken over by any other system, and which is indispensable for the smooth functioning of modern society. The availability or non-availability of such an essential function may be regarded as an indicator for the legitimacy and necessity of the ecological critique. In *Social Systems*, Luhmann suggests that the specific function of ecological communication, and political protest movements in general, could be to enhance the reflexivity of modern society. He points out that functional differentiation and the emergence of mutually exclusive codes can lead to problems of co-ordination between different societal subsystems, as well as between society at large and its environment. Such problems can threaten the autopoietic reproduction of individual subsystems as well as the whole of modern society, yet there is no mechanism through which society can deal with such problems. Under 'normal' conditions, social structures are reproduced 'according to prescription, that is on the basis of structures of expectation' (SS: 402). However, Luhmann suggests that this automatism may run into evolutionary cul-de-sacs, and he therefore sees a need for an 'immune system' that 'secures autopoiesis' (SS: 403).

In a way that resembles Habermas's conceptualisation of the social movements as an *early warning system* (Habermas 1981), Luhmann therefore suggests that (eco-) political protest movements can fulfil this role. In other words, he shares the idea that social movements stabilise rather than challenge established societal structures. But he points out that the *immune system* is not a mechanism of 're-establishing the status quo ante* (SS: 369). It also cannot perform what Beck describes as reflexive modernisation. What Luhmann's *immune system* preserves or restores is not any concrete material conditions, but only the *continuation of autopoiesis*. In order to 'rescue communication's self-reproduction', communications of (ecological) protest 'tend to abandon structures' (SS: 403), thereby opening up perspectives for new sequences of communication. In this activity, this *immune system* is not guided by any superior knowledge. It tries to rescue autopoiesis 'not by doing it better, but rather by doing it differently' (PM: 143). As Luhmann points out, its attempts 'may, but need not, result in a better adaptation of the societal system to its environment. In the long run, only evolution can tell' (SS: 403).

In *Protest Movements*, Luhmann elaborates on the idea that social movements pick up issues which emerge as side-effects of functional differentiation, but which are systematically ignored by all the different function systems. Here he points out that the communication of (ecological) protest 'espouses subject matter that none of the function systems, neither politics nor the economy, neither religion nor education, neither science nor law would acknowledge as its own' (PM: 142). Once again he emphasises that ecological and other protest communication 'compensates for modern society's manifest inadequacies in reflection' (PM: 143). It thus seems that ecological communication does indeed fulfil an exclusive function that is vital for the smooth functioning of modern society. However, the 'subject matter' it embraces is not *eo ipso* problematic. If ecological communication can be regarded as a social system in Luhmann's sense, it is a self-referential system, that is it does not address extra-communicative realities, but it only refers to its own problem constructions. Like any self-referential system, ecological communication *'operates without communication with the environment'* (SS: 403), that is completely from within its own self-constructed communicative universe and without any kind of superior knowledge of developmental goals or the means to promote them.

As Luhmann points out, (ecological) protest movements construct their problems from their particular point of view and impose them upon other parts of society where – within their partial rationalities – the respective subject matter had previously not been perceived as a problem. So, unless the eco-movements can legitimately claim some superior kind of rationality, the question arises why society should take the problems they raise (construct) any more seriously than those raised by any other system. As a matter of fact, Luhmann points out that the emergence of conflicts between different system rationalities does not automatically imply 'that society must solve problems of this kind in order to survive' (SS: 477). According to Luhmann's model, 'evolution is all that is needed for survival' (ibid.), and thus the necessity and legitimacy of ecological communication is called into radical doubt.

This idea of the self-referentiality of ecological communication needs further explanation. It is an important element in Luhmann's interpretation and critique of the ecological discourse. As Luhmann suggests, ecological communication does not just construct the problems it raises, but beyond this, it actually also constructs the society–environment dualism to which these problems relate. The task and project of ecological communication is to look at society as a whole and highlight cases of malco-ordination between different societal subsystems as well as between society at large and its extra-societal environment. For this purpose, ecological communication needs to adopt a superior point of view from which it can observe society as a whole and its relationship to the external environment. But, in reality, such a point of view from outside both society and its environment is, of course, not available. And ecological communication therefore has to rely upon the *simulation* of a superior perspective. Already, in *Social Systems*, Luhmann notes that strictly speaking, there can never be a 'societal subsystem for perceiving environmental interdependencies', and that 'such a subsystem cannot come about by functional differentiation because it would mean that society would occur a second time within itself' (SS: 477). He explains this idea further in *Protest Movements*, where he suggests that in order 'to be able to think about itself', society 'needs an internal boundary' (PM: 140). As any observer of society is invariably at the same time part of the observed (society), 'the only possibility is that of an imaginary projection with which a self-description can claim for itself a fictitious external standpoint' (ibid.). This implies that society's self-observation is built upon 'the paradox of the unity of inside and outside', and in order to secure validity for its critical judgements, it needs to 'find a form that annuls this paradox' (ibid.).

The problem of the *paradox* and the mechanisms of its *invisibilisation* will be followed up in the next section. At this stage, it is first of all important to understand the strategy ecological communication generally has to adopt if it wants to undertake a criticism of society at large. Protest movements invariably remain part of society, but they draw an internal boundary, thereby duplicating society within itself and pretending to be standing outside. 'Thus they protest inside society *as if* they were doing so from without' (PM: 139; my emphasis). But they cannot go beyond this *as if*. Both their society–environment dualism as well as the problem perceptions they relate to this dualism remain their specific constructions, and this, obviously, sheds doubts upon the validity and necessity of the kind of reflexivity they provide. Ultimately, their descriptions of society and their judgements about societal problems are no more reliable than those made from any other perspective. Ecological communication attempts to transcend the partial rationality of specific function systems and to fulfil its reflective function *within* society by distinguishing itself *from* society. But this project remains paradoxical. Luhmann therefore comes to the conclusion that ultimately (ecological) 'protest movements do not fully qualify as a function system arrangement' (P: 179). But it is still very useful to regard ecological communication as such a function system because this allows us to observe ecological communication from the perspective of other social systems, and thereby make visible the blind spot of its specific code. As Luhmann points out, this 'is precisely what second-order observation makes clear' (EC: 27).

7.5   The code of the eco-movement

Ecological communication voices criticism and demands decisions. It is evident – and has been pointed out repeatedly in earlier chapters – that 'to require decisions means to appeal to values, explicitly or implicitly' (EC: 112). In Luhmann's model, these underlying values decide about the affinity of different communications and sort them into discrete communicative systems. These values are a constitutive part of ecological communication, and they must refer us back to its basic *code*. Once we have identified a code for ecological communication, we can observe how it erects its 'order of values' (ibid.), its '*totalizing construction*' that makes a 'claim to universality' (EC: 38). By means of second-order observation we can then analyse how ecological communication secures its own meaningfulness. We can test the consistency of the ecological argument and the validity of its critical judgements about modern society. Luhmann himself does not explicitly specify a code for the ecological discourse. However, its code seems to follow logically from what ecological protest or criticism seeks to preserve or restore: *nature*, or in more contemporary terms, *sustainability*. Undoubtedly, both would qualify as a code in Luhmann's sense. If we assume that the most fundamental distinction of ecological communication is the distinction *natural–unnatural* or *sustainable–unsustainable*, all statements which are intended to be a contribution to the ecological discourse must be derived from and reducible to this distinction. In terms of Luhmann's discourse-theoretical analysis, it does not really matter which of the two alternatives we prefer. For the moment, I will go along with Goodin's (1992) suggestion that *naturalness* is the most fundamental value of the ecological discourse (see Section 2.1); not least because the analysis of early critical theory has revealed a fundamental human interest in nature (see Section 4.4), which has not yet been matched by any intrinsic reason why we should be interested in sustainability.

Ecological communication in this sense then has to be considered as first-order observation. Whatever issue ecological communication picks up is subsumed under the category of *naturalness*. For ecological communication, everything is necessarily either *natural* or *unnatural*. Like all social systems, the ecological discourse 'claims universal validity and excludes further possibilities' (EC: 36). And like any first-order observation, ecological communication 'can see only what it can see', but 'it cannot see what it can not see'[9] (EC: 23). As a matter of fact, ecological communication

---

9   Official translation: 'It cannot see what it cannot.'

cannot even see that there is something it cannot see, that is that its own perspective is restricted. 'For the system this [the own restrictedness] is something concealed *behind* the horizon, that, for it, has no *behind*' (ibid.). Ecological communication therefore claims absolute validity for its judgements about the relationship between society and the natural environment. Elaborating on what was said above (and more explicitly in Section 6.3) we may say that by applying the category of naturalness, ecological communication is generating its own representation of the world, and is no longer talking about *a priori* reality, that is reality irrespective of all human perception and conceptualisation. Within this self-constructed world, ecological communication distinguishes between the *natural* and the *unnatural*, whereby each of the two sides merely reflects the other. So, when talking about the natural or the unnatural, about the system or the environment, ecological communication is never talking about *a priori* reality, but always about itself. Its judgements may therefore claim absolute validity, but only within the universe it constructed (for) itself. With its own operations, ecological communication can never reach beyond its own system. This is the essence of what Luhmann calls operational closure and self-referentiality.

As first-order observation, ecological communication may reflect upon (its self-generated image of) society and its environment, but it cannot reflect about itself, that is it cannot reflect on the conditionality of its own operations. Only second-order observation (from a sociological perspective, for example), which observes ecological communication on the basis of a different code, reveals – of course at the cost of introducing its own blind spots – that something is 'behind' the horizon of naturalness, and thereby exposes the contingency of first-order ecological observation. In Luhmann's terms, ecological communication 'invisibilises' this contingency by applying its code to everything except its own distinction between natural and unnatural. This distinction itself is the unquestioned precondition of all operations within ecological discourse. It is the non-negotiable fundamentalism of ecologist thinking (see Section 1.2) and the reason why this thinking will never get beyond the status of 'truncated modernity' in Beck's sense (see Section 5.2). The distinction between natural and unnatural presupposes the superior, predefined validity of the criterion of naturalness. If applied to itself, the ecological code generates either tautological or paradoxical judgements. If one were to ask whether the criterion of naturalness is natural (tautology) or unnatural (paradox), this would make the whole ecological construction of the world collapse.

Obviously, this would be no different if we replaced the distinction of natural and unnatural with the allegedly more concrete pair, sustainable and unsustainable. Within the system of ecological communication, however, it is (fortunately) not possible to even pose this question anyway, because this would imply that this communication itself (the question) would be at the same time *part of* the ecological discourse (applying the code) and *outside* of it. In the previous section this was referred to as 'the paradox of the unity of inside and outside' (PM: 140). In *Ecological Communication*, Luhmann highlights once again that 'every attempt within the system to make the unity of the system the object of a system operation encounters a paradox because this operation must exclude and include itself' (EC:

113). The impossibility of such an operation secures the validity of first-order ecological observation and judgements. Whenever the ecological code is called into question, it can only happen from the perspective of other social systems. But such second-order observation cannot invalidate the critical judgements made by ecological communication. All it can do – on the basis of a code that is itself contingent – is demonstrate that the ecological code is contingent, and that the judgements ecological communication produces are no more valid than contrary judgements which may be produced from a different perspective and on the basis of a different code.

What do we gain from these rather abstract reflections? We, firstly, understand how in ecological (and any other) judgements, absolute validity coincides with total contingency. This contributes to explaining why the societal process of formulating an ecological diagnosis keeps paralysing itself. Secondly, having exposed the self-referentiality of the ecological code, we can see that, as well as why, this code is not suitable for generating practical directives. We are thus moving towards an explanation of why ecological communication does not easily translate into ecological behaviour and factual ecological improvement. Ecological communication voices radical criticism and makes demands for fundamental changes, but cannot produce guidelines for action. As Luhmann points out, it raises problems but is structurally unable to suggest solutions – which are hence expected to come from elsewhere (see Section 7.3). The reason behind this incapability is that ecological communication has no more than a code. However, a code can never give an answer to the question: what should I do? As codes are generally 'at the same time tautological and paradoxical', 'they allow everything and nothing' (P: 55). All the ecological code on its own can suggest is: do what is natural, and avoid what is unnatural! Or if we want to use the dualism of sustainable–unsustainable, this formula can be adjusted accordingly. Any attempt, however, to spell out what this implies in practical terms will remain circular.

This has already been indicated in the context of Beck's model. In his analytically less succinct way, Beck refers to this problem as the *naturalistic fallacy* (Beck 1995a, ch. 2) of the eco-movement and ecological thought. As I quoted in Section 5.5, he notes that the ecological critique 'attempts to use nature as a normative standard against its own destruction' and thus 'fall(s) prey to a self-deception' (1988: 62; also see Giddens 1994: 11). Luhmann's analysis demonstrates that this 'self-deception' is necessary and unavoidable for the ecological critique to 'invisibilise' its own contingency, but without further specification the distinction between natural and unnatural stays meaningless. In itself it is an empty schematism, it cannot generate any criteria for what in practical terms actually *is* natural (or sustainable). As Luhmann points out, 'the code's values are not criteria', in other words, they have to be supplemented by something else. Luhmann therefore differentiates between 'the level of coding and the level on which *the conditions of the suitability of operations* are fixed and, if necessary, varied' (EC: 44f., my emphasis). This second level is the level of what Luhmann calls the *programme*. In order to become meaningful the code depends on external input which is provided by this programme. Only these programmes can 'de-tautologise and de-paradoxise the codes' (P: 56). Making reference to the systems of law and science, Luhmann explains that the distinction between *code* and *programme* 'is required because the code does not specify what is justice and injustice, what is true or false'. It is 'because a code is circular, tautological, that is without contents, that further criteria are needed' (P: 177).

If applied to the system of ecological communication, Luhmann's analysis in terms of codes and programmes allows us to draw further conclusions about the validity of the ecological critique of society and the political demands which may be derived from it. The ecological code, we said, is available as the dualism of *natural* and *unnatural* – or, in its more contemporary form, *sustainable–unsustainable*. This code, however, is not just contingent, that is its judgements are no more authoritative than those based on any other code, but this code remains an empty formalism as long as it is not supplemented by a programme, that is by 'criteria for correct operations' (EC: 40). Only this programme brings contents into the formalism of naturalness, that is substantive criteria for ecologically correct behaviour. These criteria, however, which make ecological communication practically meaningful, are flexible and can be changed. As Luhmann points out, only the code of a system has to remain stable, thereby guaranteeing that the system is operationally closed. The programme, however, may regularly be redefined in order to ensure that the system remains open and can respond to its environment. So while the social system of ecological communication remains stable and constantly reproduces itself, its content and its practical imperatives are always in flux. Shifting his codes into immediate proximity to Horkheimer and Adorno's purely formalistic instrumental reason – which is 'neutral in regard to ends' and can 'thus be attached to all ends' (see Section 4.4) – Luhmann even suggests that, 'in principle', the code 'can outlast the change . . . of all criteria' (ibid.).

From an eco-sociological point of view this analysis in terms of ecological codes and programmes is highly attractive because it provides room for the emergence of multiple ecological discourses based on different, and changing, conceptualisations of nature, the natural and the ecologically necessary. From the ecologist point of view, however, Luhmann's model must appear as completely unacceptable because it undermines the normative validity of the ecological critique and ecological imperatives. Ecologists would certainly insist that they are diagnosing objectively existing problems and risks, and that their ecological imperatives must not be ignored. But Luhmann clearly demonstrates that the ecological code in itself cannot secure this claim to absolute validity and that it also cannot generate any practical rules of concrete ecological behaviour. We thus need to explore how else ecologists may try to fill their 'empty schematism' with normatively valid content. Substantive criteria can, for example, be scientifically constructed, democratically negotiated, religiously believed, passed on by tradition, or – under the cover of culturally determined notions of the natural – they can simply remain unspecified, which does not, of course, imply that no such criteria are in operation. In all these cases, however, the substantive criteria for ecological correctness are ultimately contingent and thus confirm Luhmann's analysis. From this contingency there is probably no escape, and the question is therefore not so much where ecological communication finds its normatively valid contents, but how it manages to conceal the fact that it does not have any.

7.6   Eco-ethics and the communication of *Angst*

Luhmann's suggestion that the ecological critique of society lacks 'normative meaning[10] for which one could at least assume, if not attain, a thoroughgoing consensus' (EC: 127) does not preclude that ecological reformists may devise concrete policies which are designed to respond to particular circumstances in particular places at particular points of time. But invariably, such concrete policies are based on contingent assumptions and are, therefore, without any protection, exposed to criticism from radical ecologists, other reformist strands, and – if under the conditions of ubiquitous green commitment there still is such a thing – the anti-ecological opposition. As a matter of fact, even the reformists themselves will find it difficult to spell out in positive terms why they want to implement their particular policies, that is what they ultimately want to achieve and how this can be justified. Invariably, their argument soon becomes circular. However, Luhmann argues that ecological communication can disguise its lack of positive meaning by the choice of topics it deals with. It compensates for its inability to make normatively valid judgements about society and its relationship to the so-called natural environment by focusing on issues of *Angst*. Luhmann suggests that in order 'to replace the difference of norm and deviation', 'anxiety (*Angst*) is chosen as a theme'. In his view, 'anxiety, then, becomes the functional equivalent for the bestowal of normative meaning[11]; and a valid one since anxiety . . . cannot be regulated away by any of the function systems' (ibid.).

As I indicated in Section 1.2, *Angst* is not accessible to rational discussion. The experience of *Angst* cannot be contested from the perspective of any social system. One might therefore say that 'the communication of *Angst* has the advantage of always being authentic' (P: 62). For the ecology movement, so Luhmann suggests, the communication of *Angst* has the particular benefit that it allows it to assume a position which is 'within society', but at the same time 'outside the functional systems' (ibid.). The communication of *Angst* sets the perspective of the individual against that of the function systems. It reveals a view on to the function systems which is not available from any other perspective. Hence the discourse of *Angst* believes that it can claim for its judgements that extra bit of insight and legitimacy which elevates its communications beyond the contingency of all judgements made from within any of the function systems. With this extra bit of legitimacy – which is ultimately derived from the assumed superiority of the human individual over the societal function system – the concept of *Angst* forms the transition from contingent communications about the environment to a normative eco-ethics.

As Luhmann puts it, *Angst* 'infuses ecological communication with morality'

---

10   Official translation: 'normative sense'.
11   Official translation: 'sense'.

(EC: 130). Yet as we know from the discussions in Section 5.5, all that is achievable on the basis of *Angst* is, at best, 'a common interest in the alleviation of anxiety' (EC: 127). Provided there is agreement about the sources of *Angst*, one might be able to establish Becksian *imperatives of avoidance*. But such imperatives cannot even specify in concrete terms what we should *not do*, let alone generate any positive guidelines for what we *should do*. Luhmann therefore speaks of a 'preventative consensus' that implies no more than 'an abstract agreement about preventing all possible damage' (EC: 74). In any case, under the conditions of functionally differentiated society, *Angst* will, according to Luhmann, normally remain without significant practical consequences. It is an individual-related by-product of autopoietic system-differentiation and reproduction. Yet in Luhmann's model, functionally differentiated modern society has manoeuvred the human individual into the systems' environment. Whilst societal development is largely determined by the necessities and automatisms of system-autopoiesis and reproduction, the needs and feelings of human individuals play a rather subordinate role.

Luhmann's marginalisation of the human individual is probably exaggerated, but in a number of respects his analysis is surprisingly similar to that of Beck. Beck's 'consensus of defence', his 'imperatives of avoidance', his 'non-substantive norms of societal self-critique' and his 'morality beyond morality' all have their equivalents in Luhmann's model. Beck's connection between *Angst* (risk) and ethics strongly resembles Luhmann's treatment of the issue. But whilst Beck regards these elements as particular strenghts of the ecologist critique (see Section 5.5), Luhmann portrays them as weaknesses which threaten the viability of the ecologist project. Whilst Beck assumes that *Angst* and the consensus of defence provide a favourable framework – a 'Red Cross consciousness' (1998a: 156f.) – for society's moral rejuvenation and self-ecologisation, Luhmann is convinced that ecological challenges – if they can be mastered at all – can most certainly not be confronted by means of ethical renewal. In accordance with his shift of emphasis from the human subject (individual) to the function system, he insists 'that resonance to the exposure to ecological danger is created essentially through . . . (the) function systems and cannot be, or at most only secondarily, a matter of morality' (EC: 48). The factual failure of eco-ethics and the experience that ecological progress never goes beyond marginal and incremental adjustments certainly support Luhmann's rather than Beck's view. Luhmann also avoids Beck's mistake of reintroducing – via the ecological consensus – the abolished unity of reason. In one respect, however, Luhmann's analysis of *Angst* needs further elaboration.

Luhmann suggests that *Angst* 'offers a substitute when normative principles can no longer be communicated convincingly' (P: 62). Referring to Kant, he describes *Angst* as the 'successor of the old *a priori* of reason' (P: 246) and suggests that it 'resists any kind of critique of pure reason' (EC: 128). Luhmann sees *Angst* as 'the modern apriorism – not empirical but transcendental; the principle that never fails when all other principles do' (ibid.). Indeed, the function of Kant's pure reason had been to provide a substitute for substantive metaphysical values and a transcendental source of meaning. And undoubtedly, this is exactly what ecologists need in order to make their schematism of *natural* and *unnatural* meaningful. But

Angst cannot convincingly be conceptualised as the functional equivalent of pure reason. Contrary to what Luhmann seems to suggest, eco-ethics does not rely on *Angst instead of* pure reason, but on *Angst and* pure reason, whereby the latter is, arguably, even the more important element. Ecological ethics seeks to solve the problem of its contents not through the concept of *Angst*, but, fully in line with the Kantian tradition, through the assumption that the ecologically correct, that is the morally good, is equivalent to the ultimately rational, valid and sustainable, as opposed to the short-term, tempting or profitable. Of course, this leaves eco-ethics with the same two problems which Kant had already had to confront when he was trying to fill his *categorical imperative* with meaning: Firstly, an incentive has to be nominated which is sufficiently strong to induce ecologically (morally) sound behaviour even though it does not seem to pay off immediately, that is as long as ecological destruction goes on elsewhere. This is where the concept of *Angst* has its systematic place. Secondly, and this is the more crucial point, even by presupposing the metaphysical congruence of the morally good and the *a priori* rational, Kant did not manage to infuse his categorical imperative with positive values allowing us to formulate concrete imperatives. Kant finally had to admit that we only know the good because it is 'inscribed in the soul of man in the plainest and most legible characters' (Kant 1793/1991: 71), and he thus introduced what Luhmann calls the *programme*.

What this demonstrates is that ecological communication will – in the same way that Kant did – necessarily fail if it relies on the congruence of the ecologically good and the 'really' rational as the source of contents for its formalism. In other words, the closer analysis of Luhmann's allusions to Kant reveals that not even through its focus on issues of *Angst* will ecological communication be able to conceal that its code remains empty, or that any meaning inserted into it is contingent. Sticking to the words of Kant, we can thus say that ecological *programmes*, that is the substantive criteria of ecological correctness, are not legitimated in any other way but through their being 'inscribed in the plainest and most legible characters in the souls' of the ecologically enlightened. And since for an ecological ethics the rationally inaccessible *Angst* is not the source of contents but merely the incentive for ecological behaviour, the ecological 'morality that propagates anxiety-related distinctions' turns out to be much less resistant against 'theoretical analyses' than Luhmann seems to suggest (EC: 130).

7.7   Conclusions

Luhmann's overall evaluation of the ecological crisis and the related protest movements remains ambiguous. Confirming Habermas's reservations towards the ecology movement, he points out that 'neither he [Habermas] nor I [Luhmann] can come to the conclusion that nature is a *thing out there* which is in need of help' (P: 70). Nevertheless, he acknowledges that (ecological) protest movements address problems which have so far not been dealt with appropriately. He recognises that they 'put issues on the public agenda, try to cut through bureaucratic devastation or at least make it visible, and above all: that they enhance the understanding of the extent to which modern society is a society which is built upon risk' (P: 77f.). Yet Luhmann rejects 'the blasé moral self-righteousness observed in the *Green* movement' (EC: 126), and he discards the belief that 'caring about the environment could justify carelessness in the talk about it' (EC: xviii). According to Luhmann, 'indifference in the choice of words and a lack of sensitivity for theoretical decisions of grave consequence belong to the most noticeable characteristics'[12] (ibid.) of the (eco-)politically committed social movement literature (also GG: 128ff.). But he refuses 'to believe that strong commitment is *necessarily* characterised by scanty thinking' (P: 63; my emphasis). Whilst first-order ecological communication may be forgiven for being theoretically 'cheap and insufficient' (ibid.), Luhmann insists that particularly at the level of (second-order) eco-sociological theory 'we can do better' (ibid.).

In Luhmann's view, the critique presented by the (ecological) social movements is ultimately a critique of functional differentiation. This critique, however, he argues, is intrinsically contradictory and at least potentially dangerous. It is intrinsically contradictory because any rational critique of rational (social) systems only becomes possible through the process of functional differentiation, which allows the critical observer to look at a particular social system by assuming a point of view from within another social system. Every act of observation and critique thus reproduces and continues what it claims to resist, namely functional differentiation. In Luhmann's view, more careful theoretical enquiry could have taught ecologists that they cannot do things 'better' but only 'differently', and that therefore 'there is no reason to believe that protest movements know more about the environment' or make 'more valid judgements than other systems within society' (P: 214). For functional differentiation, he insists, 'there is no alternative – unless one would want to revert to segmentary differentiation . . . or a political-bureaucratic hierarchy of society' (P: 76). Ultimately, 'the alternative movement is hence without an alternative' (ibid.) and offers 'nothing more than a resigned comment on decline in the manner of Adorno or Gehlen' (EC: 126).

Of course Luhmann would not contest that every social system has to respond to changing conditions in its environment. The eco-movement, however – and this is what Luhmann himself considers as his 'main argument' in *Ecological Communication* – 'creates too little as well as too much resonance' (EC: xvii) to environmental change. It generates *too little* resonance particularly because its fundamentalist strands fail to recognise that in functionally differentiated societies, 'events in the environment can only set a system vibrating under the particular conditions of its own frequencies' (P: 49). Luhmann therefore demands that the subject matter ecologists seek to address be expressed in the codes of the various societal function systems so that these may respond 'in accordance with the(ir) particular structures' (ibid.). The ecologist critique of society generates *too much* resonance because, according to Luhmann's model, the specifically ecologist problem for-

---

12 Official translation: '. . . and absence of interest in significant theoretical decisions are two of the most noticeable characteristics'.

mulation is only the construction of one particular system, which erroneously believes itself to be superior to all others. Ecological communication forgets that its 'controversy is and remains a controversy of the protest movements' (P: 211). The environmental problem ecologists urge society to address 'is not content that is imported into the system from the environment; it is a construct of the system itself, the grounds for which are then assigned to the environment' (P:127). But as Luhmann fears, the excessive resonance the ecological critique generates may well 'damage or even destroy' important elements of contemporary society (P: 49). Luhmann therefore describes his own project of deconstructing the ecologist project and perspective as the attempt to 'reduce the probability' of 'unnecessary anxiety' (P: 73) and 'useless excitement' (EC: xviii).

As Luhmann points out, the further course of functional differentiation is not foreseeable. Functional differentiation will undoubtedly continue, and with it the emergence of ever new problems of malco-ordination. In Luhmann's view, this development may 'be observed and analysed'; the problems it generates 'can be understood and described as a structural property of modern society, but they cannot be anticipated' (EC: 119). Hence Luhmann sees little chance of ecological communication changing the direction of society's future development. He concedes that 'it is not certain that things will continue as in the past, but very different, and in particular quickly different, they will only become by means of changes which are commonly described as catastrophes' (P: 59). Once again, the course of development over the past three decades seems to confirm his views. Nevertheless, Luhmann's above-quoted consolation that society does not necessarily have to 'solve problems of this kind in order to survive', because 'evolution is all that is needed for survival' (SS: 477) is somewhat dubious. The implications of this evolution are not specified. Luhmann does not seem to care much about the question of *whose* survival this evolution secures, and *under what circumstances* life may continue. These implications, however, can and have to be spelled out. And from an ecologist point of view, they will be evaluated in a quite different way than from a post-ecologist perspective. These questions will have to be addressed in the following chapters.

Part IV
Post-ecologism

8   Ecology without identity

After the extensive analysis of Luhmann's model it is time to review where a systems-theoretical approach takes us regarding the analysis of contemporary eco-politics and the project of constructing a theory of post-ecologism. It has been suggested that Luhmann's theory merely 'reformulates in its own jargon what others have analysed and described a long time ago' (Rucht and Roth 1992: 32). Neckel and Wolf (1994) believe that the attractiveness of Luhmann's model boils down to 'the fascination of amorality', which they consider as characteristic for 'the new individualism of the middle classes' and the 'postmodern *Zeitgeist*' of disoriented 'left-wing intellectuals' (92ff.). Ulrich Beck suggests that Luhmann's thinking fails to recognise that in contemporary society, 'questions of functional differentiation' are increasingly replaced by 'questions of *functional coordination*' (1997a: 27), and that the 'logic of differentiation' therefore needs to be replaced by a more contemporary 'logic of mediation' (ibid.: 112). Undoubtedly, all these views contain an element of truth, but such generalising rejections of the systems-theoretical model do not do justice to Luhmann's enormous theoretical efforts, and they fail to capture the fundamentally new elements in his thinking. Luhmann's theory can, of course, be criticised in a number of respects, some of which will be addressed below. But this should not distract us from the fact that it provides most valuable cues for a theory of contemporary eco-politics.

Early critical theory and Beck's updated version of it were primarily helpful for *reconstructing*, that is understanding, what traditional ecologism is all about. Critical theory explained that the ecological problem (the destruction of nature) is essentially a problem of the modernist subject, and that the ecological imperative to save nature boils down to the imperative to save the subject. Critical theory also raised some questions about the viability of the ecologist project, that is it pointed beyond traditional-style ecological thought. But Horkheimer, Adorno and Beck are undoubtedly committed agents of nature, the subject and modernist thinking in general, and thus any deconstructive implications have the status of *loose ends* within their theories. To the extent that contemporary society and the way it conducts its ecological politics have developed beyond the modernist constellations, critical theory has become inadequate as a theoretical framework for its conceptualisation and interpretation. In contrast to this, Luhmann's emphasis is clearly on *deconstructing* ecologism. In many respects he confirms and radicalises doubts which had first emerged in the context of our preliminary investigations into the *crisis of the ecological crisis*, and which were then consolidated during the discussion of critical theory. Luhmann suggests that contemporary society is structurally unable to solve the so-called ecological problem, but he also demonstrates that society *does not really have to solve it*, anyway, because this problem is no more than a specifically ecologist construction. He supports this claim by revealing the contingencies of the ecologist perspective and the mechanisms ecological communication uses in order to secure normative validity for its problem perceptions and remedial imperatives.

But what Luhmann achieves is significantly more than just the deconstruction of ecologism. He suggests a social-theoretical model which is no longer centred around the modernist subject, and which leaves the whole of the humanist Enlightenment tradition behind. He thus provides the framework for a new analysis of contemporary society's politics of nature. As I have pointed out in several sections, established ecological thought 'in all its standard varieties . . . is a species of Enlightenment humanism' (Gray 1997: 162). But, arguably, 'the humanist commitments of standard green thinking belong to those parts of modern culture that no longer track our world' (ibid.: x). For the analysis of contemporary society and its eco-politics, we require a post-humanist model of contemporary society – and this is exactly what Luhmann provides. In other words, after *deconstructing* the ecologist perspective, Luhmann's thinking also becomes *constructive*: it actively contributes to the construction of a theory of post-ecologist politics. Unlike its ecologist predecessors, such a theory does not seek to provide ecological activists – or those who are urged to become active – with more convincing arguments for the severity of the environmental crisis, with more attractive ecological utopias and with more effective incentives for ecological behaviour. A theory of post-ecologist politics is not an ecological ideology (see Section 2.1). It no longer focuses on what *ought to* happen – for ecological or whatever other reasons. Instead, its aim is to capture and explain a political reality, that is a factually happening politics of nature, which is clearly no longer – if actual politics ever has been – determined by ecologist principles and which can therefore not adequately be described by ecologist theories.

In a somewhat paradoxical expression, the eco-political reality which the theory of post-ecologist politics aims to capture could be described as *ecology without identity*. In the previous chapters I argued that ecologist thought and the ecologist politics of nature were essentially a theory and a politics of the modernist subject and its identity. In contrast to this, the post-ecologist *ecology without identity* has shed the typically ecologist 'commitment to Enlightenment humanism'. It is a politics of nature that does not centre around the modernist subject and its identity, and that is also not steered and controlled by the modernist identical subject. As a matter of fact, it is not really identifiable as ecological politics at all (that is it does not have its own identity) because it is defined in the categories of society's various function systems and carried out through them. In other words, the theory of post-ecologist politics seeks to capture a condition where the *ecological* issue has been broken down into other issues, a condition where *the ecological issue has disintegrated* (see Sections 2.1 and 5.6). Unfortunately, Luhmann himself – although he provides the theoretical tools – is not particularly interested in developing a full-blown theory of post-ecologist politics. He does not enquire how else – if not according to ecologist criteria – contemporary society may practically organise its politics of nature. He sees no need for this because, as I pointed out before, he believes that ecological and systems-theoretical questions are mutually exclusive. But it seems evident that even the kind of society Luhmann describes will have to deal with certain issues ecologists would have categorised as ecological issues. In the following sections the task will therefore be to spell out the characteristics and practical implications of a post-ecologist politics of nature. I will begin by once again reviewing a set of fundamental ideas which were first introduced in the preliminary chapters, which were then gradually developed throughout the discussion of our three theoretical models, and which can now be presented as the central parameters shaping contemporary eco-politics. They represent the core-ingredients of the theory of post-ecologist politics.

8.1 Core ingredients

The most fundamental idea of the theory of post-ecologism is undoubtedly the one of the *abolition of nature* which was introduced in Chapter 3 and has accompanied us ever since. Horkheimer and Adorno's model provided the first theoretical basis for this idea, and Beck helped us to fully theorise the collapse of the modernist singular nature as well as the emergence of multiple and competing concepts of nature and the natural. In contemporary social theory and environmental sociology, the thesis of the abolition of nature is by and large uncontested. As it has already been discussed *in extenso*, there is no need for further explanations. But with a view to post-ecologist theory formation, it is still interesting to note how differently Beck and Luhmann handle this idea. In accordance with Beck's demand that a contemporary social and ecological theory needs to abandon the modernist dualism of nature and society, Luhmann chooses an ostentatively non-modernist point of departure. Strictly speaking, he therefore does not really need to *abolish* nature at all because he does not introduce the category in the first place. As we noted in Section 6.1, his theory is based on the idea of difference rather than unity. He therefore neither assumes the unity of nature, nor that of society. His sociological model replaces singular nature by an unlimited number of environments, and the unity of society by an equally unlimited number of social systems. When it comes to theorising the post-natural condition, Luhmann's model is therefore much more robust than Beck's. Whilst Beck's *nature-society*, that is his amalgamation of the two modernist antipodes (see Section 5.2), comes close to forming once again a single unified whole and is thus in danger of reproducing the single dualism of modernity, Luhmann introduces a virtually unlimited number of dualisms which can neither be reduced to each other nor replaced by each other. Whilst Beck gets caught up in contradictions between his thesis of the abolition of nature and his theory of reflexive modernisation (see Sections 5.5 and 5.6), Luhmann's much more radical approach helps him to avoid such inconsistencies. Luhmann's model thus offers the more convincing explanation for the findings of environmental sociologists who have documented the existence of multiple and competing concepts of nature and the natural (see Chapter 3). Contemporary society and its politics of nature are clearly no longer – if they ever were – based on the traditional (ecologist) idea of a singular nature, and a theory of post-ecologist politics needs to take this into account.

Immediately implicit in the idea of the abolition of nature is that of the abdication of the subject. Already, Horkheimer and Adorno had conceptualised singular nature and the identical subject as two sides of the same modernist construction. It is therefore no surprise that in social theory the decline of one goes along with that of the other, and that the abdication of the modernist subject thus becomes the second fundamental ingredient of post-ecologist thought. Of course, this suggestion that the identical subject is no more than 'a historically limited mode of self-interpretation' which has 'a beginning in time and space and may have an end' (Taylor 1989: 111) is very well known from a range of critical approaches to modernist thinking, as well as from the postmodernist literature. But in the eco-theoretical context it warrants some further discussion. As I demonstrated in Chapter 4, Horkheimer and Adorno had anticipated the collapse of the modernist subject, yet only Luhmann is prepared to draw the sociological consequences. Whilst the sociological tradition had regarded the idealist construct of the autonomous, unified self or subject as 'our inner truth' rather than 'our last illusion' (Rose 1996: 5), and made it the centre, the purpose and the normative standard of modern society, Luhmann convincingly argues that the idealist interpretation of the individual is now due for revision, and that even in a revised conceptualisation, the individual is no longer suitable as the central category of sociological analysis. He suggests that in functionally differentiated societies, the individual plays a rather subordinate role. As I outlined in Chapter 6, Luhmann regards human individuals as part of the environment of social systems, but never as their centre. With their communications they participate in multiple social systems, yet the rules of participation are determined exclusively by these systems. With their actions human individuals are the agents of societal change, yet the purposes these actions pursue are systemic requirements rather than those freely chosen by autonomous individuals. In other words, although as generators of communications and performers of physical actions human individuals contribute to societal development and historical progress, they are neither in control of this process nor its purpose. For this reason, so Luhmann argues, the self-interpretation of the human individual as the autonomous and unified self or subject has become historically outdated, and an adequate theory of contemporary society has to revise 'the overestimation implicit in the concept of the subject' (SS: 178).

For a theory of contemporary eco-politics, Luhmann's fundamental distinction between society and the individual and the decision to look at society from a perspective that is no longer subject-centred mark a radical innovation. Traditional ecologist theories – even where they presented themselves as holistic or eco-centric – have always been centred around and geared towards the idea of the autonomous individual. They have always been committed to the humanist tradition. As I demonstrated in the previous chapters, the so-called ecological problem was actually the problem of the specifically modernist conceptualisation of the individual, and this autonomous individual was also regarded as the starting point of any conceivable solution. Therefore, ecologists were trying to provide individuals with rational arguments, attractive utopias and effective incentives. But from a post-ecologist perspective, it seems evident that ecologists were trying to tackle the problem from the wrong end. They failed to realise that the problem is not that individuals lack genuine commitment or sufficient motivation, but that the allegedly autonomous individual, whatever its concerns, beliefs and intentions, is neither the purpose of societal development nor in control of it. In adopting the idealist utopia of the autonomous subject, ecologists simply overestimated the relevance and capacities of the human individual. An adequate analysis of contemporary eco-politics has to abandon the idealised conceptualisation of the individual and the unrealistic expectations connected to it.

For ecologists, and from any other modernist point of view, this abdication of the modernist subject is a difficult suggestion to accept. Firstly, there are strong moral objections against this thesis, for the entire humanist tradition was based on the idea(l) of the autonomous individual, whose collapse would thus imply the end of European humanism (see Section 6.6). Secondly, empirical experience seems to provide strong evidence against this social theoretical suggestion. With regard to the first point, however, it is important to keep in mind that there is a categorical difference between demanding a post-humanist framework for the description and analysis of contemporary (eco-)politics, on the one hand, and abandoning humanist goals and values as the basis of political demands and agendas, on the other. With regard to the second point, it is indeed true that the contemporary culture of individualism and the unprecedented celebration of the ego seem to be in direct contradiction to the thesis of the end of the subject. The ubiquitous rhetoric of individual empowerment and self-responsibility, as well as the new belief in public involvement and public accountability, seem to indicate the contemporary rediscovery, rather than the decline, of the individual as both the goal and agency of societal development. This rhetoric, however, is not only clearly ideological, underpinning the political agenda of social elites trying to shed the burden of, and responsibility for, the less privileged and successful. But closer investigation also reveals that the contemporary celebration of the self may well be seen as evidence *for* rather than *against* the abdication of the individual.

The striking inflation of the ego can be interpreted as a reaction of defence against the decline of the autonomous Self, which triggers an increased need for Self-assertion and desire for Self-experience (see Section 2.2). Symbolic participation, the rise of the polling culture, ever-improved communication technologies, constant reassurances that decision makers *do listen* and individuals *do matter*, and so on, may all be said to reflect the pathological desire of the dying Self to be reassured of its existence and ongoing significance. Products which the advertising industry charges, not with specific identities, but with identity as such (e.g. 'Me and my Magnum!', the ice-lolly 'Ego', L'Oréal cosmetics 'Because I'm worth it!', etc.) promise to reconstruct the damaged Self. But what the culture of marketing, opinion polls and public accountability nourishes must not be confused with the identical subject or the autonomous individual in the idealist sense. This carefully cultivated ego is merely the valued customer or voter. Unlike its idealist predecessor, it is not the embodiment of absolute values and intrinsic purposes, but constituted from largely contingent patterns of behaviour and habits of consumption which public relations and marketing departments are eager to stabilise into calculable consumer profiles. To a certain extent this consumer ego is in control of its financial spending power, but this does not reinstate the individual as the purpose and agency of societal development. Despite all protestations to the contrary, it is therefore probably correct to assume that the idealist subject and the autonomous individual have indeed abdicated. For the analysis of contemporary society and eco-politics, more appropriate categories have to be found. And as Luhmann correctly indicates (see Section 6.6), this actually means the liberation of the contemporary individual from a quite unpleasant idealist strait-jacket. Beyond the identical subject, the contemporary individual can unfold a completely unprecedented level of complexity.

Apart from the abolition of nature and the abdication of the modernist subject, the third central constituent of a post-ecologist approach is the end of eco-ethics. Ecologists believed that categorically valid ecological imperatives (ecological *morality*) or a set of rationally justifiable ecological values (ecological *rationality*) would provide them with a normative basis for a radical critique and reorganisation of contemporary society. Yet in practical terms, both the eco-morality and the ecological rationality failed. Our discussion of early critical theory and Beck's ecologised version gave some indication why they were bound to fail. Luhmann's model then provided the full explanation why the eco-critical project can never be successful. As regards ecological rationality, he points out that 'an ultimate foundation of rationality [is] unattainable' (EC: 83). The transition from the monocentric to a polycentric world-view implies that there is no point of view from which society as a whole and its relationship towards its so-called natural environment could be looked at. It is therefore not possible to establish an all-embracing code that integrates all the individual system-codes and that is in exactly this sense truly ecological. Ecological rationalities will thus necessarily remain multiple and conflicting. If, however, ecologists take refuge in simply *assuming* a highest ecological good or value and thus establish an ecological *morality*, they are, firstly, left with the problem of having to provide a normative foundation for their essentially arbitrary decision and, secondly, with the problem of having to translate empirically empty ecological imperatives into concrete guidelines for action. This immediately implies that a normatively valid ecological critique of society will never be possible, and that the eco-political practices of contemporary society will never be guided by a singular eco-ethics. A theory of post-ecologist politics has to take this into account. It can neither describe factually ocurring actions or patterns of (non-) behaviour in terms of moral criteria, nor can it formulate any eco-ethical imperatives.

This post-ecologist refutation of eco-ethics and the ecological rationality helps to avoid the theoretical inconsistencies of Beck's attempt to establish a normative basis for his idea of society's ecological self-critique. But from an empirical point of view, there once again seems to be substantial evidence against the end of eco-ethics. In contemporary society (eco-)political correctness, that is compliance with established normative standards, plays an unprecedented role. More than ever, political leaders, economic decision makers and public figures in general find their statements and behaviour being monitored by a disapproving public and media, which relentlessly apply strict moral standards. However, in the same way that the conspicuously inflated consumer ego *proves* rather than *disproves* the decline of the idealist subject, this, in some respects unprecedented, pressure for ethical correct-ness may be interpreted as evidence *for* rather than *against* the decline of morality in the ecologist sense. In a societal context (political economy of uncertainty), where a reliable moral foundation and orientation is urgently required but hard to come by, the insistence on (eco-)political correctness may be seen as the simulation of morality and the reassurance that moral values do exist and are being obeyed. Closer investigation, however, quickly reveals that this contemporary (eco-)ethical correctness is categorically different from the morality ecologists sought to establish.

Morality in the traditional and ecologist sense meant a code of absolute values and imperatives. As we have seen, ecological thought failed to identify and imple-ment such absolute values and imperatives. In a drive for *customer care, public accountability, consumer protection* and the like, the polling culture therefore seeks to fill the empty shell of (ecological) morality with contents. Substantive values which eco-logical thought itself failed to generate and implement, and which – to come back to the Kantian phrase (see Section 7.6) – were also not 'inscribed in the soul of man in the plainest and most legible characters', are now supposed to be derived or col-lected from the empirical *status quo*. In other words, an empirically derived code of values replaces the *a priori* ideals of an eco-ethics. Of course, the best the polling cul-ture may hope to detect by means of empirical surveys is the contingent habits and preferences of particular focus groups. And the social function of any empirically derived code of conduct is of course quite different from that of the aspired eco-logical morality: Whilst the eco-morality was supposed to implement – if necessary at the price of radical social change – categorically valid ecological values and necessities which have so far been neglected, an empirically derived code of ethical correctness can only stabilise and reproduce the societal structures on which it is based. In accordance with the prophecies of early critical theory and Luhmann's thesis of autopoiesis, systemic self-reproduction thus becomes the highest value. This obviously implies the unconditional surrender of an ecological ethics in the tradi-tional sense, even though there may be an unprecedented abundance of moral criticism and communication. A theory of post-ecologist politics thus has to explore the mechanisms which determine a post-eco-ethical politics of nature.

So the post-ecologist politics of nature has now been characterised as post-natural, post-subjective and post-moral. It can fourthly be described as *post-problematic*, which means that a post-ecologist politics of nature is no longer cen-tred around the specific problems and concerns that determined ecologist thinking and politics. From a post-ecologist perspective, these specifically ecologist problems and concerns do not need any further attention because they have genuinely dissolved. Throughout this book, I have been trying to identify what exactly ecological concern is concerned about, and what exactly is problematic in the ecological problem. Ecologists believe that the problems they address are empirically measurable physical realities, that is they are objectively problematic for every member of society and even humanity at large. Yet in the course of the argument, it gradually emerged that the *a priori* physical conditions are never *eo ipso* problematic, and that the ecologist problems and concerns are essentially contingent constructions. Horkheimer and Adorno's model suggested that the modernist subject and its identity needs are at the very centre of human concern for nature. This subject was portrayed as a cultural construction of Enlightenment thinking, and so concern for nature appeared as equally constructed. By pointing towards the significance of cultural values and socially mediated patterns of perception which decide about the acceptability or non-acceptability of phenomena of environmental change, Beck's model confirmed and further developed the idea of the social constructedness of ecological problems. Yet Beck never explores what exactly these cultural parameters are. Also, contradicting his own theory, Beck eventually falls back into the mode of conceptualising ecological problems as absolute physical realities.

But on the basis of Luhmann's model, it finally became clear that ecological problems, in the ecologist sense, are the construction of a discourse which is determined by the fundamental assumption of *unity and the grand systematic coherence* of the universe. Luhmann thus offers two important points of clarification: Firstly, he confirms that change in the physical environment is never in itself problematic, but its problem status always depends on normative standards which are discursively attached to the physical realities. Secondly, the cultural parameters Beck fails to explore are the parameters of modernism itself. As regards the validity of the ecologist problem-perceptions, we can therefore say that they can claim absolute validity only as long as the modernist parameters themselves have absolute validity. Yet as soon as alternative world-views, that is possibilities of second-order observation, emerge, it becomes visible that the modernist system of ecological communication only 'constructs the issue' and 'invents the respective history in order to avoid appearing as the inventor of the problem' (Luhmann 1996a: 210). It then becomes transparent that what ecologists present as the ecological problem is not an existential problem for society or even humanity, but only for the assumptions and ideals of modernity, most importantly, the modernist identical subject which, as we know from Horkheimer and Adorno, is the very foundation of the modernist belief system.

As Luhmann suggests, contemporary society has clearly reached this stage of development where alternative ways of thinking challenge the modernist belief system. The confidence in absolute truth and the singular systematic coherence of the universe has collapsed. The established certainties of modernity are dissolving, and the 'entire political and social lexicon . . . must be rewritten' (Beck 1997a: 7). Contemporary individuals have accepted that different perspectives construct different realities, and they have learnt to live with multiple truths. The modernist world-view has been superseded or at least complemented by a range of other possible perspectives, and the identical subject has abdicated as both the ideal for individual self-construction and as the centre of sociological analysis. The specifically ecologist problem, which was not an objective physical reality but, first and foremost, an identity problem of the modernist subject, has thus genuinely disappeared. Of course, contemporary society still has to deal with issues like the management of biodiversity, rising population figures, the distribution of material resources and social opportunities and so on, but it no longer has to deal with the specifically ecologist problem.

The important point to note here is that this specifically ecologist problem and the environment-related issues society still has to deal with are not the same thing. The concrete issues which are still on the agenda can be dealt with through the various functional subsystems of society. The specifically ecologist problem, however, can not be broken down into smaller, more manageable tasks. By its very nature, it is a macro-level problem which cannot be reformulated at the micro level. It is the issue of unity, the all-embracing systematic coherence which is required by the modernist subject. Trying to break this issue down into smaller units would be a contradiction in terms. The specifically ecologist problem is a question of *the principles* according to which concrete issues are framed and handled, but not of any physical or material issues themselves. In other words, the specifically ecologist problem is an issue of *form* rather than *substance*. And if – due to the abdication of the modernist subject and its *totality perspective* – the agent of the ecologist principles disappears, that is if the ecologist macro-problem dissolves, society no longer has to deal with its remaining concrete tasks in specifically ecologist ways. Contemporary society then becomes free to explore completely new patterns of framing and solving its environment-related problems. We can therefore say that society's on-going politics of nature is *post-problematic* in that it is no longer determined by specifically ecologist problems, concerns and standards. Whilst its ecologist predecessor was centred around the problems and needs of the modernist subject, a post-ecologist politics of nature is primarily determined by the problems and needs of specific function systems. Whilst ecologist politics sought to create and stabilise society as a singular rational systematic coherence, post-ecologist politics is committed to partial rationalities and particular exclusive interests.

8.2   Post-ecologist explanations

From an ecologist point of view, the eco-political theory that emerges from Luhmann's post-humanist model of contemporary society is not particularly appealing. But an adequate analysis of contemporary eco-politics cannot ignore the, in the above sense, post-natural, post-subjective, post-moral and post-problematic constellations and elements in contemporary society's eco-political practice. Ecologist theories will necessarily fail to capture these elements, and therefore a post-ecologist theory is indispensable. Of course, there are a number of respects in which contemporary eco-politics is still ecologist rather than post-ecologist. Therefore, a post-ecologist perspective on its own would not be fully sufficient. Nevertheless, Luhmann's model and the theory of post-ecologist politics to which it gives rise are extremely useful because they provide convincing explanations for a range of phenomena which have so far remained unexplained. As we noted in Chapter 2, contemporary eco-politics is characterised by ubiquitous green commitment, but the social and political structures, whose removal had once been perceived as an essential precondition for avoiding the ecological catastrophe, have easily survived several decades of environmental campaigning. As a matter of fact, they have stabilised to such an extent that even political elites and business leaders – once the arch enemies of ecologists – can now nonchalantly echo the ecologist demand for a *radical change of attitude* and behaviour towards the environment.

Contemporary eco-politics consists of a flood of regulations and activities at all societal levels which are poorly co-ordinated and hardly motivated by a shared view of the ecologically necessary and desirable. The course of eco-politics is driven by continuously changing strategic and political alliances, many of which would have been inconceivable until quite recently and involve actors with rather dubious ecological credentials. The political mobilisation of environmental concern has become completely unpredictable. Highly specialised knowledge generated in scientific institutions is the basis of pragmatic responses which reflect both the limitations of scientific research as well as economic, social and political restrictions to the implementation of scientifically defined necessities. Contradictory opinions not just about global phenomena like ozone depletion or climatic change, but even about local issues like waste management, energy provision, road construction, or air quality translate into multiple and often conflicting problem perceptions and views about what measures should best be taken and who should actually take them. The rhetoric of *ecological modernisation* (see Chapter 10) spreads ecological optimism and reassures us that ecological issues are being dealt with. But even though ecological considerations have undeniably become part of social and economic policy making, this has not yet led to a state of civilisation which ecologists could genuinely describe as ecologically more benign than at any earlier point in time. On the contrary, while *old problems* like the decline of indigenous forests, the destruction of natural habitats, the loss of biodiversity, the shortage of fresh water, and such like, persist and are becoming ever more urgent, a set of *new problems* – with as yet unforeseeable implications – is only just being added as bio-technological research is beginning to bear fruit and to be commercially implemented.

The post-ecologist explanation for the impressive immunity of the capitalist growth economy against the ecological critique is a combination of three elements. Luhmann's theory of contemporary society firstly suggests that social systems are always primarily concerned with their own reproduction. At any given point in time, their first priority is their immediate continuation. In economic terms this means immediate growth and profit. Considerations like possible external side-effects of this systemic self-reproduction or the question of the sustainability of particular reproductive strategies into the future play a subordinate role. In other words, the ecological critique goes largely unheard because the economic system is structurally uninterested in the issues ecologists raise and structurally unable to respond to them. As for all social systems, the most relevant dimension of time for the economy is the present. And potentially emerging problems are being addressed as and when they actually become imminent.

Secondly, the stability of the capitalist growth economy may be explained by Luhmann's idea that social systems are, although operationally closed, open to their environment and fully capable of adapting themselves to external necessities. They have a considerable capacity of reflexivity in Beck's sense. Contrary to Beck's suggestions, however, this reflexivity only affects the level of the *programme* (see Section 7.5), whilst the *basic code* and structure remain unchanged. As the increasing reliance on market instruments as a tool for ecological reform clearly demonstrates, the economic system can take account of changing circumstances in its material environment, and it can also accommodate changing social perceptions of the ecologically valuable and desirable. But for the economy to respond, the material conditions and social value preferences have to be translated into the economic code of profit or loss. This implies that the capitalist growth economy, although it may well acquire the image of *ecological correctness* (see Chapter 10), will always retain its basic structural principles.

Thirdly, the fact that ecologist concerns have rather limited resonance in the economic system may be interpreted as the implicit awareness that these concerns have much less stable and reliable foundations than ecologists tend to assume. The temporalisation of environmental concerns (see Section 2.2), as well as the permanent societal review of the underlying normative assumptions, often leads to the *dissolution* of the concerns without any major changes being introduced. For this suggestion, the current discussion about the introduction of GM-foods is a good case in point. Normalisation, habituation, adaptation of social attitudes to (bio-) technological innovations and changing external circumstances are most powerful mechanisms which ecologists tend to underestimate, but on which the economy (GM-industry) can firmly rely.

The fact that even top business leaders can now afford to pay lip service to the necessity of radical ecological change could firstly be explained by the fact that ecological questions have by and large now been reformulated in economic terms. This view would imply that ecological concerns are now *genuinely* being taken into account. The term *lip service* would thus not really be appropriate any more because there would not be a discrepancy between the public statements of economic leaders and their actual beliefs. But as I pointed out in the last section, these economic problems which now *are* being addressed are categorically different from the original ecologist concerns which have actually not been captured in the process of the attempted reformulation of the ecological problem, and which are thus – unless they have dissolved – still being ignored. The eco-speak of political and economic elites may therefore, somewhat cynically, also be interpreted as their implicit realisation that radical ecologist demands may well be parroted without the fear of detrimental consequences because factually such beliefs and demands have very little impact on the development of social systems like the economy, anyway.

In the previous chapters I demonstrated that ecological problems and concerns are basically concerns individuals have *qua* individuals in the idealist sense. Luhmann, however demonstrates that for the functioning of contemporary society the idealist notion of the individual and the concerns related to it are largely irrelevant. As I outlined above, he suggests that societal development is predominantly determined by system requirements, whilst the concerns, convictions and intentions individuals may have *qua* identical subjects, that is as a system or unity of their own, find little or no representation. If the function systems perceive them at all, they have the status of external *irritations* which may, if anything, trigger minor adjustments to the systems' internal procedures. Obviously, the neo-liberal policy of deregulation and giving free reign to the mechanisms of the market further promotes the marginalisation of the idealist autonomous individual and ensures that economic development is not disturbed or restricted by extra-economic factors. In such a context, political and economic elites may rest assured that propagating ecological beliefs with anti-growth, anti-consumption and anti-profit overtones will not negatively affect economic and political profit margins. On the contrary, there is plenty of evidence that as long as they reproduce the currently valid standards of (eco-)political correctness, such statements can be employed as an effective marketing strategy which enhances their public image and increases economic or political returns.

Going on from the ecological beliefs and good intentions of political and business elites, Luhmann's model and the theory of post-ecologist politics can also explain, why in general even genuine and widespread green commitment does not easily translate into factual ecological progress. Luhmann, firstly, demonstrates how ecological committedness can have very different phenotypes. His thesis of the system-specific formulation of both environmental problems as well as the respective responses, and his theory of society's incapability of devising co-ordinated strategies for managing ecological threats provide a plausible explanation why significant ecological improvement is factually so difficult to achieve. On a much more fundamental level, however, he, secondly, demonstrates that committedness on the side of individuals is generally not the pathway towards system change. As I indicated above, it was a fundamental error of traditional ecologist thought that it relied on the individual and its consciousness as the starting point for the ecological transformation of society. The project of changing society by means of a new ecological morality was bound to fail not just because ecological moralities and rationalities will always remain multiple and contradicting (see above), but also because increasingly complex life-world contexts make ever more excessive demands on individuals, and render the belief in an ecological morality ever more unsuitable. Empirically, individual behaviour is determined by multiple and conflicting pressures, loyalties and commitments, which Luhmann conceptualises as the rules of participation dictated by the various social systems. As these pressures increase, there is ever less scope for the individual to act autonomously and in accordance with the requirements of any hypothetical eco-ethics.

Given the necessity for every individual to play to the rules of the multiple systems on which it depends, it becomes ever more dubious whether the individual can realistically be expected to prioritise the (somewhat unspecific) interests of nature and future generations, and whether it can really be criticised for failing to do so. Given the increasing fragmentation of the singular identity or, put positively, the unprecedented complexity of contemporary individuals, it is no surprise that ecological behaviour is factually always determined by a patchwork ethics which cannot even achieve consistency at the level of the individual, not to mention society at large. Luhmann is therefore right in suggesting that the demand for an eco-ethics is 'equally feeble and irresponsible' (Luhmann 1987: 132). It is 'feeble' because it fails to take account of the complex structure of modern society; and it is 'irresponsible' because it causes pressures and anxieties, and produces ecological hopes at a stage of societal development where its normative validity has been called into radical doubt and where its structural inadequacy to ecological threats has been clearly demonstrated. From an ecological point of view, one might even argue that by continuing to channel political energies into a project (an eco-ethics) whose futility and inadequacy has been clearly revealed, ecologists themselves contribute to the continuation of the very societal practices which they describe as ecologically ruinous.

As regards the mysterious relationship between physical environmental change and the social response it triggers, Luhmann theorises the autonomy of two different levels at which environmental problems are socially constructed: firstly, he sees them as communicative problems rather than a physical reality; and, secondly, he sees them as problems of consciousness, that is even as *psychological* rather than discursive realities. It was outlined above that for Luhmann, physical phenomena do not gain the status of a problem unless they are transformed into coded communications. But beyond what was outlined in Chapter 7, it is interesting to note that according to Luhmann these communications 'can *only* be induced by consciousness' (Luhmann 1988b: 893). Consciousness, so Luhmann explains, is a system in its own right, which 'belongs to the environment of the societal system'. Whatever it produces is 'a psychical, not a social fact' (EC: 29). It is important to note that for Luhmann, 'processes of consciousness *are not* communications', but merely 'the production of ideas by ideas' (ibid.). Hence an environmental problem does not exist unless it is: (a) 'perceived, measured, made conscious'; and (b) 'then the attempt is stimulated to communicate about it in accordance with the rules of communication' (ibid.). What is particularly interesting is that here Luhmann obviously reintroduces the level of the individual, which is otherwise excluded from his thinking.

As Luhmann points out, systems of consciousness and communicative systems are closely connected to each other, but they are, nevertheless, autonomous from each other. Their mutual autonomy implies an additional level of contingency because 'the relation of conscious systems and social systems has to reckon with a resonance threshold that selects in a very rigorous way' (EC: 29). Luhmann thus helps to explain why the social perception of environmental change is so highly selective and why the social response it triggers is so unpredictable. He demonstrates that for the analysis of contemporary eco-politics, we have to distinguish three largely autonomous levels: (i) physical environmental change; (ii) concerns emerging in systems of consciousness; and (iii) problems framed in particular function systems. In accordance with his disinterest in the individual and the remains or successor of the modernist subject, Luhmann does not clarify what norms and criteria determine the operations of systems of consciousness. Also, the relationship and co-operation between systems of consciousness and systems of communication remains, somewhat disappointingly, unexplored. At least for the modernist individual, however, critical theory's analysis of the unified subject and its identity needs can step into this gap. For the postmodernist individual, these criteria still need to be explored.

Finally, we may look once again at the phenomenon of the new ecological optimism which Beck's ecologist theory could not explain in any satisfactory way, but which obviously takes the wind from the sails of the eco-movement (see Section 2.2). On the basis of the two assumptions that: (i) the ecological problem is ultimately an identity problem of the modernist subject; and that (ii) this modernist subject has abdicated both as the dominant pattern of individual identity construction and the centre of (eco-)sociological analysis, contemporary (post-ecologist) eco-politics was described above as *post-problematic*. What this meant to say is that with the abdication of the identical subject, the specifically ecologist problem, that is the identity problem, has genuinely disappeared. Whilst with regard to the management of the physical environment there remain a plethora of legal questions, economic questions, health questions, distributive questions and so on, the specifically ecologist problem, which was the demand for unity, systematic integration and all-embracing coherence has genuinely dissolved. This dissolution of the ecologist problem and the fact that the remaining problems all seem to be much more manageable is the post-ecologist explanation for the new ecological optimism. In other words, this new optimism does not emerge from any factual improvement in the physical environment, but exclusively from the fact that contemporary individuals and contemporary societies have a different perspective onto the physical world, which implies that they have adopted different patterns of framing their environmental problems and different patterns of managing their environment-related affairs. Ironically, the old ecologist demand for a *radical change of attitude* towards the environment has thus been fulfilled – in a rather unexpected way though.

Taking up the idea I sketched in Section 3.3, we may therefore say that the eco-movement, rather than being the vanguard of a radically different ecological society, is fighting a rearguard battle. It is trying to impose a specifically modernist problem construction on to a society which is phasing out its modernist principles of operation. It defends the modernist identical subject and the modernist notion of a singular nature *vis-à-vis* a singular society at a point of time when these conceptualisations have become obsolete. In other words, it aims to preserve the modernist singular dualism at a stage when it has clearly exceeded its life-expectancy. The pace at which the new ecological optimism spreads and the extent to which ecologist warnings fail to raise concerns may be taken as indicators of the extent to which contemporary society has already adopted postmodernist (and post-ecologist) *modi operandi*. But the interpretation of the eco-movement as a rearguard battle does not mean to reinforce suggestions that ecologist thinking is reactionary or even fascist (e.g. Bramwell 1989, Jahn and Wehling 1990). As a strongly emancipatory movement, it is firmly tied into the enlightenment tradition (Eckersley 1992; Hayward 1995; Gray 1997). It is a movement in defence of the basic principles and values of modernity (see Chapters 4 and 5). And exactly because the eco-movement sought to safeguard these values and principles, it is wrong to regard it as fighting for *the radically different*. As a matter of fact, it was fighting for *much more of the same*, and this only appears as radically different from societal reality in the sense that the values and ideals of modernity had never really been implemented. So contrary to the ecologist interpretation of the eco-movement as the vanguard of a new ecological and for the first time really *modern* age, the theory of post-ecologism suggests that the social function of the eco-movement is to organise the civilised retreat of the modernist belief system. Ecologism is an *endgame* (Gray). As I indicated above, the eco-movement and eco-logical communication are the societal institution which administers the decline of modernist and ecologist ideals, and thus smoothes the transition to postmodern and post-ecologist practices. Moving beyond the post-ecologist explanations which have been offered so far, we now need to describe in positive terms what post-ecologism factually implies, what criteria determine a post-ecologist politics of nature and along what lines contemporary society's eco-political practice might develop in the future.

8.3 Post-ecologist perspectives

As I indicated above, the abolition of nature, the deconstruction of ecologism, the dissolution of the ecologist problem and so on do not mean that the politics of nature become irrelevant. Only ecologists believed that after ecologism there would be nothing but the apocalypse. As Gray puts it, 'the belief that the failure of Enlightenment projects of human emancipation heralds the wholesale collapse of society is itself an Enlightenment superstition' (1997: 175). The modernist con-ceptualisation of nature might have become inappropriate, but the finiteness of resources, the growth of the global population and the emissions this population generates – in short the preservation and social distribution of the so-called *natural foundations of life* – remain important issues and make a politics of nature as indis-pensable as ever. Beyond this, there are also the issues of meaning and the problems of normative disorientation in the *political economy of uncertainty* (Giddens 1994; Beck 1997a; Baumann 1999). Human beings might no longer conceive of themselves as identical subjects, yet they will certainly want to have a sense of meaningfulness, and they will require normative standards on the basis of which they may organise their private lives and social interaction. Technological progress and the process of social individualisation keep expanding the sphere where indi-vidual and societal decisions are required, yet the ongoing dissolution of traditional values and the so-called grand narratives keep dissolving all criteria by which such decisions may be taken. In this vacuum of values, nature and natural-ness will retain their attractiveness as normative standards (see Chapter 3). Hence, in this normative sense, too, the politics of nature will probably remain as impor-tant as ever. So, even after the dissolution of the specifically ecologist problem and the abdication of the ecologist paradigm, there are still important tasks which a post-ecologist politics of nature will have to fulfil.

With regard to the so-called natural foundations of life, we first of all have to acknowledge that life in contemporary societies depends to an ever larger extent on foundations which have never been natural in the first place. Especially after the abolition or radical pluralisation of nature, it no longer makes sense to distinguish *natural* foundations of life from the wide range of *man-made* foundations which are equally indispensable. Furthermore, we have to broaden the understanding of the so-called natural foundations of life in such a way that they include not just *material*, but also *non-material* elements. These non-material foundations become particularly important if we are talking about more than mere physical survival, and it is evident that they, in particular, are *cultural* rather than *natural*. For these reasons, the task of a post-ecologist politics may more appropriately be described as the management of *opportunities* of life rather than of its natural foundations in the ecologist sense. With regard to these opportunities of life, we can then note that the problem is not so much their general non-availability, but rather their non-availability to growing strata of particular societies or of mankind at large. This is not a problem in itself, but only to the extent that an uneven distribution of opportunities of life and the exclusion of certain parts of society (humanity) is *perceived as normatively problematic*.

From the ecologist point of view, social inequality and exclusion did, indeed, appear as problematic. The reasons for this have been outlined in the previous chapters, and the political demand which resulted from this was an agenda of self-restriction for the rich (countries) and social redistribution to the poor (countries). Universal egalitarianism and social inclusion were the underlying principles. In contemporary society, however, social and political practice indicate that the patterns of perception have changed. The ideas of scaling down and vertical redistribution have been largely abandoned. The official farewell to the ideal of full-(time-) employment, the privatisation of the welfare state (health care, pensions, education) and the rapidly increasing inequalities in the social distribution of material and non-material wealth provide clear evidence that even at national level, the ideals of social equality and inclusion are giving way to mechanisms of exclusion (e.g. Levitas 1998; Byrne 1999; Gregg and Wadsworth 1999; Young 1999; Beck 2000b). Whilst the ecologist world-view had considered both society (humanity) and nature as undivided and indivisible unities, contemporary society has accepted the division of humanity along the lines of economic criteria. Mechanisms restricting access to goods and services, which certain parts of society define as ecologically sensitive, to the financially solvent are widely accepted and celebrated as so-called eco-taxes. And as the process of commodification has permeated not just every area of society, but even the human body, human health and human reproduction, right down to the level of genetic material, social exclusion by economic criteria becomes more effective, comprehensive and permanent than has ever been conceivable so far. We may therefore legitimately say that whilst ecologist thinking was determined by the principles of unity and inclusion, a post-ecologist politics of nature is determined by the principles of differentiation and exclusion.

Of course the suggestion that social differentiation and exclusion is not just an unintended side-effect of certain societal developments, but actually a constitutive element of contemporary society's politics of nature will once again raise objections of the kind that were discussed above: firstly, this suggestion will be rejected as immoral and politically incorrect; secondly, empirical evidence seems to suggest that political agendas factually centre around policies of social inclusion rather than exclusion. On the moral argument I have commented at several earlier stages in this book. Some additional remarks will follow further below. As regards the empirical argument, it is indeed correct that particularly in the context of economic globalisation, which has contributed significantly to the concentration of wealth in the hands of relatively small social elites and the emergence of considerable poverty even in traditionally rich countries, the issue of social exclusion is high on both the academic and political agendas. Politicians, in particular, constantly reassure us that they continue to regard social inclusion as a key objective. But once again, there is a fundamental difference between inclusiveness in the ecologist sense and social inclusion in the contemporary sense. Firstly, the ecologist notion of inclusiveness was holistic. Transcending the contemporary ideal of *social* inclusion, it involved both nature and society. It thus implied the idea of human self-restriction for the benefit of nature. Secondly, the ecologist notion of inclusiveness clearly implied the ideals of liberty, equality, justice and solidarity, which aimed to secure an equal social distribution of both resources and restrictions, goods and bads.

Contrary to this, contemporary policies of social inclusion do not at all aim to secure the same level of participation for every individual. The point is not to share environmental resources, material wealth, social opportunities and civilisatory risks equally among all members of society (humanity). On the contrary, it has become painfully clear that the standards of living achieved by the elites cannot be generalised. And as the option of scaling down is completely out of the question, the only way of maintaining and further increasing these standards is to restrict the number of those who may enjoy them. Social exclusion thus becomes an ecological necessity. But, of course, social exclusion and poverty also represent a considerable risk, both in terms of their detrimental effect on the physical environment and in terms of the direct threat and disturbance they imply for the good life of the elites. This raises (once again) the crucial question of how the marginalised majority (national as well as international) may be kept occupied and under control. In a seemingly paradoxical way, the most effective method of preserving and reserving limited resources and social opportunities for the established elites, and at the same time minimising the negative impact of social exclusion, is to promote low-level social inclusion. But in contrast to the ecologist ideal of inclusiveness, the objective of contemporary policies of social inclusion is really to perpetuate the principle of social exclusion, which appears as an ecological necessity and which is a core characteristic of a post-ecologist politics of nature. Against this background, post-ecologism appears as the return to a premodern, a pre-revolutionary and pre-Enlightenment normality. 'The lot of humankind everywhere has always been to live under the harrow'; 'there is no reason why this normal human condition should not recur in a late modern context of high-tech weaponry and mass communications' (Gray 1997: 174). This seems to confirm Horkheimer and Adorno's suspicion that 'mankind, instead of entering into a truly human condition, is sinking into a new kind of barbarism' (DE: xi; also see Beck 1997a: 53).

As regards the normative dimension of a post-ecologist politics of nature, we may distinguish between the societal and the individual need for normative standards. With a view to the societal level, the problem is once again not the general non-availability of efficient decision-making criteria, but rather the non-acceptability of the established practices. As I outlined above, economic considerations have come to determine all areas of social interaction. The criteria of competitiveness, affordability and profitability effectively decide most social affairs. As a matter of fact, they have become so powerful that they seriously challenge Luhmann's thesis of the existence of multiple, equally important and irreplaceable functional codes (rationalities). Yet although the necessities of the market are increasingly accepted as quasi-metaphysical imperatives, and although economic instruments are widely regarded as highly efficient, there are, occasionally, still moral concerns about the social implications of this regime. Such concerns, however, are probably a transitory phenomenon. Already, McKibben has suspected that 'the only ones in need of consolation will be those of us who were born in the transitional decades, too early to adapt completely to a brave new ethos' (1990: 199).

Processes of social marginalisation and exclusion raise concern only as long as there are remains of the belief in (the necessity of) the grand rational coherence, that is in total egalitarian inclusion. They can be criticised only as long as there are normative criteria on the basis of which the idea of total inclusion can be shown to be rationally or morally superior. Yet as we have seen, the belief in the grand coherence of rationality is in decline, and morality is giving way to flexible and rather patchworked codes of political correctness. Invariably, this leads to a situation where no criteria are available by which a political practice governed predominantly by the (highly efficient) principles of economic profitability or financial solvency could be criticised with any authority. As long as there are effective means for keeping the marginalised under control, we can therefore safely assume that the post-ecologist politics of exclusion is not going to be challenged in any serious way, and that the metaphysics of profitability will provide permanent and efficient answers to the societal need for normative criteria.

With a view to the individual, its sense of meaningfulness and its need for criteria to manage the ever-increasing decidability of life, there are two points which need to be discussed. Firstly, we need to reconsider Beck's thesis of the *reinvention of politics* (see Chapter 5); and secondly, we have to ask to what extent the contemporary individual really still *requires* normative standards in the traditional sense. Beck is certainly right in pointing out that for the contemporary individual, ever less is decided by nature and tradition, whilst ever more depends on personal choice and responsible decision, that is on *life-politics*. But the question arises how much scope for negotiation and decision, that is need for normative criteria, there realistically is. Beck's universal decidability (politics) is located in a systems-determined context which severely restricts the factually available options. Contrary to Beck's optimism that individuals and communities may now be in a position freely to negotiate what they want to consider as *natural* or in what kind of environment they want to live, the metaphysics of the market effectively deprives decision makers, from the individual right up to international organisations, of their power and reduces them to executors of the economically necessary (e.g. Albrow 1996, McMichael 1996; Baumann 1999). The enormous emancipatory potential emerging from the decline of natural and traditional predetermination is thus largely absorbed by the dynamics of competitiveness and profitability, which do not leave much space for the experience of normative disorientation.

The second of the above points takes us back to the changing patterns of identity formation: whilst the idealist identical subject required absolute normative criteria in order to fulfil its ideal of overall consistency, the postmodern individual *naturally* (habitually) applies different criteria to decision making in different contexts of life. As I outlined above, the ideal of the unified subject with a singular identity, which has probably never been more than a cultural ideal, has proven impractical, and has been replaced by multiple context-oriented identities. To a large extent these identities are determined by the respective system-requirements. But wherever these contexts do leave room for choice and decision, the absence of binding and reliable values is compensated for by the installation of momentary desires or pleasures as the ultimate guideline for making the right choice from the range of available options. Within a societal framework that constantly increases the individual's self-responsibility and reduces its social accountability, this principle of choice appears fully appropriate.

So in terms of their decision-making requirements, the contemporary individual is indeed much less dependent on nature as an absolute normative standard than it would first have appeared. And in terms of its requirements of meaning, the fragmented individual no longer depends on the universal or transcendental context either. Böhme is therefore probably right in suggesting that the ecologist interest in nature is anachronistic, 'a transitional stage, perhaps a hesitation or an inconsistency' (1992: 183). Certainly, meaning continues to be indispensable, and, of course, it continues to emerge from distinctions. The continued significance of the category of meaning and the mechanisms of its generation have been demonstrated on the basis of Luhmann's model (see Chapter 6). But whilst the identical subject derived its (metaphysical) meaning from its distinction from nature, and depended on the assumption that the universe comprises no more than this one single dualism, fragmented identities can – and actually have to – derive their meaning from multiple distinctions and dualisms. In the same way in which the modernist identical subject depended on the external boundary, that is the exclusion (and subjugation) of nature (see Chapter 4), the postmodernist multiple subject may therefore be said to depend on multiple internal, that is inner-societal boundaries generating partial meaning for partial identities. After the abolition of nature as the singular external Other of society, the contemporary fragmented identity depends on the installation of multiple internal Others. In other words, social differentiation and exclusion, which was once morally unacceptable, has become a structural necessity for the contemporary individual. Factually, this has, of course, always been the case. But what is new is the open and exclusive reliance on this pattern of identity construction, which is no longer controlled by moral imperatives and counterbalanced by the ideal of a self-sufficient and autonomous identity. Once again we are reminded of the above-quoted fears of a new barbarism.

This analysis of the post-ecologist politics of nature in terms of inclusion and exclusion may be further developed by considering not just the relationship between presently existing individuals or societies, but by widening the perspective to the relationship between contemporary and future generations. The ecologist ideal and demand of inclusiveness certainly implied both these dimensions, and post-ecologist politics abandons the principle of inclusiveness in both senses. Post-ecologist politics may be defined as the continuation of the established western civilisatory and developmental model beyond the point where it has become clear that this model is neither suitable for implementation around the globe, nor sustainable into the future. But the specifically post-ecologist point about this societal practice is that this seemingly irresponsible and dangerous continuation is actually no longer perceived as problematic. As we have seen, the post-ecologist response to the non-generalisability of the western civilisatory model to mankind at large is the naturalisation of social exclusion. Without either sinister intentions or moral uneasiness, post-ecologist politics restricts access to the opportunities of life, nationally and internationally, to the emerging global middle class (Sachs 1997). The post-ecologist response to the unsustainability of the western civilisatory model into the future is a radical revaluation of the ecologist dimensions of time. Whilst ecologism was completely preoccupied with the long-term future, but had a rather negative relationship to the immediate present, the exact opposite may be considered as characteristic for post-ecologism. Whilst for ecologists, the present was primarily a bone of contention and an object of critique situated between the pre-alienated – and therefore better – past and the utopian reconciled future, the post-ecologist point of view fully rehabilitates the present and radically devalues (excludes) the future and the past.

The post-ecologist devaluation of the past is reflected in contemporary society's disregard for traditions and established social practices, which are subjected to ever shorter cycles of reorganisation. Innovation, modernisation and flexibility have adopted the status of intrinsic values. Of course, there is a lot of talk about stability, continuity and conservation, but, factually, committedness to nature (the natural), tradition, cultural heritage and so on is largely restricted to carefully managed theme parks and storage places for potentially valuable genetic material. The post-ecologist devaluation of the future is not a question of immorality or culpable neglect, but under the conditions of contemporary society, concern and provision for the future are factually becoming ever more pointless because the evolutionary process and the acceleration of change continuously shift the parameters and invalidate all criteria of planning. The process which Luhmann describes as the *increasing temporalisation of autopoiesis* (see Chapter 6), creates systems whose constitutive elements are ever more ephemeral (EC: 13). With the increasing degree of societal differentiation and complexity, the future becomes ever less predictable and the immediate present ever more important as the only reliable point of reference. Total flexibility and adaptability have become essential virtues. Constantly changing constellations and necessities give rise to an educational culture of *life-long learning* or re-education.

Of course, individuals and societies can never abandon their attempts to anticipate the future and make appropriate provisions, yet the perspective invariably becomes ever less long-term, and as I argued above, *momentary* necessities, desires and pleasures become ever more significant. This strong orientation towards the present is reflected in all areas of contemporary society. Political culture, the media, the economy, and even social movements (see Section 2.2) have all been permeated by the principle of instantaneity. The marketing culture generally aims to minimise the temporal distance between the emergence of feelings or needs and their compensation or gratification. In those areas where individual behaviour is not entirely determined by external necessities, the goal is to mobilise the forces of the present moment – emotions and instincts – before rational consideration may delay or even overrule the economically more desirable pre-rational impulse.

The liberating effect of this post-ecologist revaluation of the ecologist dimensions of time is evident. Ecologists were obsessed with – and tied by – the ideas of stability, security and rational controllability. They felt committed to the past and wanted to foresee and manage even the distant future. They believed they could halt, or at least control, evolution and plan for eternity. In line with Kantian ethics, they subjected themselves to categorical moral imperatives which weighed heavily on them and effectively crippled their expectations of earthly happiness. The post-ecologist focus on the present, however, removes the ecologist imperatives of conservation, preservation and precaution. It replaces them with the paradigm of construction. It makes unlimited room for the momentary realisation of the self, which has no stability or identity, but is involved in a process of permanent construction and reconstruction. In the enjoyment culture, or to use Schulze's (1993) term, the *adventure society*, the primary mode of such self-construction is probably the *exciting experience*, the personal *adventure* in which the individual seeks to encounter its own identity, which lasts, of course, no longer than the adventure itself. In line with the thesis that ecologists have always underestimated the identity-related dimension of the eco-movement (and overestimated the unmediated significance of the physical environment), even direct ecological action probably has to be interpreted as such a self-centred adventure rather than a contribution to the restoration of certain physical conditions or their preservation for the future (see Section 2.2). With the abdication of the modernist nature–society dualism and the ecologist paradigm of alienation and reconciliation, both the past and the future become fully accessible as a quarry for the construction of the present. This is evidenced by the atemporality of postmodernist modes of existence and self-construction, which draw liberally on the most diverse periods of human civilisation in order to construct an elusive contemporarity.

For the theoretical purposes of this study, we now have a sufficiently detailed outline of the implications of a post-ecologist politics of nature, and we have identified the central differences between ecologist and post-ecologist patterns of thinking. Post-ecologism, I suggested, is *ecology without identity*, both in the sense that the formerly central issues of identity no longer play a major role and in the sense that post-ecologism is no longer identifiable as an independent discourse and policy. Post-ecologism is post-natural, post-subjective, post-ethical and post-problematic. It has abandoned the ideals of unity and inclusiveness, and replaced them by plurality and differentiation. It is strongly individualistic and self-centred. It places the emphasis on on-going construction and innovation rather than consolidation and preservation. It celebrates the present and revels in momentary pleasures and excitement. And although the future may hold unforeseeable risks, post-ecologism has a fundamentally positive attitude and perspective. It has transcended the paradigm of loss and completed the *mourning process of modernity*.

In conclusion to this section, two most significant points ought to be emphasised once again, even though they have been mentioned several times before: Firstly, post-ecologist politics is neither an option contemporary society may choose or avoid, nor a prophecy about a future it may have to expect. Of course, the theory of post-ecologism also aims to anticipate the direction of future societal development, but, first and foremost, it is a model that seeks to conceptualise and interpret what is happening in the present, that is geared towards the currently ongoing politics of nature. Secondly, and closely related, post-ecologism must not be understood as something categorically new or unexpected. Surely, compared to the thinking of ecologism, post-ecologist thinking marks a paradigm shift. But in many respects post-ecologism can be described as the return to a pre-ecologist normality, or simply as the realisation that contemporary society's politics of nature has actually never been ecologist and that it also never will be ecologist. This statement must under no circumstances be confused with a justification of the *status quo* or the attempt to provide post-ecologist practices with any kind of normative legitimation. It is no more than the observation that the process of modernisation has undermined the very foundations of ecologist thinking long before it could really be implemented politically. Ecologism was an intellectual construct that was based on certain cultural assumptions. The theory of post-ecologism is the attempt to update these assumptions and to observe how this affects the constitutive elements of the ecologist paradigm of thought.

9 Avoiding ecologist fallacies

The theory of post-ecologist politics is a theoretical model for the interpretation of contemporary eco-politics that has to compete with other such models. Post-ecologist thinking may help to reveal the unquestioned assumptions which provided the basis of ecologist thinking, but like any theoretical model it necessarily makes its own assumptions which are no less speculative than those of ecologism. The post-ecologist approach may hence be criticised from a range of different – including ecologist – perspectives. Before I move on to providing a post-ecologist interpretation of how contemporary societies practically cope with the decline of the ecologist paradigm and the advance of non-ecologist patterns of thinking and policy making (see Chapter 10), it therefore seems appropriate to try and anticipate some objections ecologists may want to raise against the post-ecologist model. A good indication of the criticism the theory of post-ecologism will have to confront may be obtained from the eco-sociological criticism levelled against Luhmann's social theory on which the thinking of post-ecologism strongly relies. At least in his own country the enormous innovative potential of Luhmann's theory and its impressive diagnostic capacities have been widely acknowledged. Jürgen Habermas believes Luhmann's theory to be 'second to none today[1] when it comes to its power of conceptualisation, its theoretical imaginativeness and its capacity for processing information' (Habermas 1987b: 354). In the German original of *Ecological Politics in an Age of Risk*, Ulrich Beck, who is otherwise extremely critical of Luhmann's approach (e.g. Beck 1997a: 24ff.) concedes that his 'insights into the systemic self-blockade of a preventive approach towards ecological threats are enlightening and realistic' (Beck 1988: 169).[2] However, in the sociological literature critical views and serious reservations about Luhmann's theory have always outweighed the positive appreciations.

Particularly the idea that Luhmann's thinking 'has no critical potential what-so-ever' has become 'part of an unquestioned consensus in the current sociological discourse' (Kneer 1996: 390). Long before Luhmann presented a comprehensive

---

1 Official translation: 'today incomparable'.
2 The English translation unfortunately omits a long passage [pp. 165–76] in which Beck discusses Luhmann's *Ecological Communication*.

and systematic version of his theory, Habermas had already, as early as 1971, criticised his project for approaching contemporary society exclusively with 'questions conforming to the principle of domination', and for presenting no more than an 'apologia of the *status quo* for the sake of its continuation' (Habermas 1971: 170). After the publication of *Social Systems*, Habermas reconfirmed his doubts, accusing Luhmann of abandoning 'together with the concept of reason' also 'the intention of the critique of reason', thus pushing 'the neoconservative affirmation of social modernity to a peak' (Habermas 1987b: 354). Variations on this Habermasian criticism are plentiful. They include ecologist varieties which amount to the reproach that Luhmann's model – and thus probably also the theory of post-ecologism – is immoral, anti-ecological, overly pessimistic and cynical (e.g. Gerhards 1984; Beck 1988; Görg 1992; Metzner 1993; for more differentiated views e.g. Breuer 1995; Hellmann 1996; Kneer 1996). A closer look at these allegations will help to avoid ecologist fallacies and provide a further opportunity for consolidating the theory of post-ecologist politics.

9.1   Is post-ecologism uncritical?

In the western tradition any sociological or political theory that fails to formulate concrete demands about how contemporary society ought to be improved almost automatically attracts the criticism of being conservative and affirmative, that is approving of the socio-political *status quo*. In this respect the theory of post-ecologism will undoubtedly share the fate of Luhmann's model, and although Luhmann himself strictly rejects any allegations of his theory being conservative and an 'uncritical hymn on the achievements of functional differentiation' (Rucht and Roth 1992: 30), it will be difficult to defend his thinking – and that of post-ecologism – against such allegations. As I indicated in Chapter 6, Luhmann explicitly makes the abdication of the critical paradigm and *The End of Critical Sociology* (Luhmann 1991) the starting point for his own project. The very first sentence of *Social Systems* states that contemporary 'sociology is stuck in a theory crisis' (SS: xlv). And as Luhmann explains, a main reason for this crisis is that the 'critical intellectual gesture', although it has 'gone limp' and is today merely 'remembered with more or less admonitory overtones', has still 'not really been replaced' by a more adequate sociological model (SS: 6). In *Ecological Communication* Luhmann reconfirms that 'the theoretical background' for a sociology that 'presented itself as opposition or as *critical theory*' has 'long since disappeared' (EC: 3f.). So there can be no doubt at all that Luhmann refuses to continue the traditional critical project, and it seems that he has to accept the reproach of being affirmative. As regards the theory of post-ecologist politics, one might say that in the same sense that Luhmann's systems-theoretical thinking is directed against established social-theoretical approaches, post-ecologist thinking is directed against established eco-theoretical approaches. Both theories abandon the 'critical differentiation between truth and ideology' and dissolve the distinction 'between legitimate and illegitimate value-systems' (Gerhards 1984: 70/72). Neither of them present any theory of social change. In accordance with the (deeply modernist) logic that there is no third alternative to being either in agreement or in opposition to the established system, both theories will therefore find it equally difficult to avoid giving the impression that they aim 'to condition demands for social change along the lines of the *existing order*' and the 'prevalent system-rationality' (Metzner 1993: 182).

Nevertheless, the end of the critical paradigm and the sociological self-restriction to 'better description', 'better observation, and perhaps the moderation of unnecessary excitement' (Luhmann 1987: 37), neither imply direct approval of the *status quo*, nor that the critical perspective has to be completely abandoned. In order to capture the critical potential of Luhmann's theory, Kneer suggests that we 'replace the dichotomy of apologia/critique (or affirmation/criticism) with the distinction between criticism at the level of first-order observation and criticism at the level of second-order observation' (Kneer 1996: 391). Even if the transition from traditional (first-order) critical observation to system-theoretical second-order observation has rendered 'classic forms of sociological critique obsolete' (ibid.), so Kneer argues, the critical project can still be continued as second-order criticism. He identifies three different dimensions of the critique of contemporary society and is convinced that after the end of the critical paradigm, systems theory can 'take all three critical dimensions up' and 'reformulate them at the level of second-order criticism' (ibid.: 392). These dimensions are firstly, the 'exposure of unreflected, latent structures'; secondly, the 'development of alternative options of social development'; and thirdly, 'enlightenment about societal pathologies and anomies' (ibid.). If Kneer is right and the systems-theoretical approach can really be shown to be a second-order reformulation of the traditional critical project, this would be equally applicable to the theory of post-ecologist politics. One may of course wonder why systems-theoretical and post-ecologist thinking should at all be subjected to the imperative of adopting a critical stance, but as the *critical posture* is still the entry ticket into the contemporary (eco-) sociological debate, Kneer's suggestion would certainly increase the chances of both theories to be heard and taken seriously.

As regards the 'exposure of unreflected, latent structures', the explorations in Chapters 7 and 8 leave no doubt about the enlightening potential of Luhmann's model and the theory of post-ecologism which emerged from it. Referring back to the Wittgensteinian formulation quoted in Section 7.5, we can certainly note that systems-theoretical and post-ecologist second-order observation go far beyond traditional and ecologist first-order observation in that they can see structures which the latter cannot see. Second-order observation reveals the internal structure and mechanisms of traditional modernist – including ecologist – thinking, and opens a new perspective on established societal practices, including society's ongoing politics of nature. Beyond this, systems-theoretical and post-ecologist thinking can even make conclusions about their own structural limitations, although they can of course *not* see *what* they cannot see. With regard to 'alternative options of social development' the situation seems to be considerably more uncertain. Luhmann explains at great length that despite its potentially disastrous consequences, an alternative to functional differentiation is nowhere in sight, and that even the protest movements fully rely on this principle and help to reproduce it. In

ecological terms, Luhmann demonstrates how society cannot adjust itself to ecological threats, that no eco-ethics will ever bring societal evolution under rational
control, and that the future is effectively in the hands of fate. Against this background one may legitimately wonder whether systems theory really has any
potential for developing social alternatives, and the theory of post-ecologist politics
does not seem to be more imaginative either.

It was characteristic of the critical tradition that it immediately translated its
diagnoses of contemporary society into social utopias and connected far-reaching
hopes for (revolutionary) social change to these visions. This is not easily possible
for second-order observation because it extends its doubts to incorporate the 'critique of sociology's overestimation of its own theory-formation capacities' (Kneer
1996: 395). Prompted by the awareness of their own restrictedness and contingency, Luhmann's theory and the theory of post-ecologism refrain from outlining
societal alternatives and making prescriptions for political change. But one of their
most central messages is that the conditions and structures of contemporary society are highly contingent and could just as well be fundamentally different. So
Luhmann and post-ecologist theory would appear to be merely more modest than
the critical tradition, but not uncritical or even affirmative of the *status quo*.
Luhmann clearly demonstrates that things *could be* radically different. Contingency,
functional equivalence, temporalisation, and the extreme evolutionary improbability of the achieved level of differentiation, are central pillars of his theory.

The critical potential of his approach therefore 'lies in the fact that existing
arrangements are interpreted in a way which stresses their contingency'
(Grundmann 1990: 37f.). As Luhmann points out, ultimately even the principle of
functional differentiation itself is contingent. Admittedly, he is rather vague about
this idea, but in *Social Systems* he talks of the *ageing* of specific types of differentiation (SS: 379). He argues that the principle of functional differentiation was
historically preceded by other principles (segmentation and stratification; see SS:
187ff.), and he also considers the theoretical possibility of a future 'transition to
another form of societal differentiation' (SS: 377). Luhmann certainly gives no
reason to believe that the current state of societal evolution is likely to be a final
stage, and therefore his theory at least cannot be considered as affirmative or conservative in the traditional sense. If his model can be read as an apologia at all, it
surely 'refers to a system which is centrally characterised by rapid change and the
increase of contingency at all levels' (Breuer 1995: 116). As Breuer correctly points
out, 'the preservative intention of systems theory does not aim at concrete conditions existing here and now, be it power, property, education, or social institutions',
and in order to describe Luhmann's position as conservative, one therefore 'certainly needs to have a very peculiar notion of conservatism' (ibid.).

So Kneer is right in insisting that systems theory does, in principle, allow for
alternative routes of societal evolution and that it is not implicitly affirmative *vis-à-
vis* the societal *status quo*. As regards the theory of post-ecologist politics, this model
does not contain anything either to suggest that the established societal structures
should remain in place or that societal development will necessarily continue along
the established lines. On the contrary, a major aim of the theory of post-ecologism

is to highlight the arbitrariness and contingency not just of traditional ecologism, but of all naturalisations in general, including the currently dominant naturalisation of the market principles and the new polarisation of society along the lines of material wealth. It is correct to say that the theory of post-ecologism does not get involved with first-order ecological discourses. It does not focus on *eco-political* questions, that is on ecologically necessary socio-political changes and their implementation, but on *eco-theoretical* questions, particularly the question of how the dominant societal order and ecological communication continue to sustain and reproduce themselves despite, and beyond, their respective crises (see Chapter 2). But although the theory of post-ecologism itself does not have the tools to make normatively valid judgements or generate political imperatives, it can offer conceptualisations of contemporary eco-politics which can then be measured and judged from the perspective and by the standards of the established social systems. Indirectly, the theory of post-ecologism may thus make a very significant contribution to political change, and it most certainly provides important stimuli for environmental sociology.

In terms of the third dimension of social critique, that is the 'enlightenment about societal pathologies and anomies', Kneer insists that the systems-theoretical approach is 'far from giving away the possibility of identifying societal crises and pathologies' (1996: 396). He is right in emphasising that, whatever Luhmann's critics may propound, Luhmann does not draw a harmonious picture of modernity. On the contrary, he demonstrates how functionally differentiated societies generate problems of co-ordination which may well lead to 'catastrophic regressions' and to 'destructions of alarming proportions' (Luhmann 1993: 553). In Luhmann's view, there is no reason 'to assume that society will be able to continue to exist with the environment it creates' for itself (Luhmann 1988a: 169), and as the potentially catastrophic consequences of functional differentiation cannot even be foreseen and warded off, it is all the more obvious that 'a functionally differentiated society is anything but a harmonious society with inherent structures of stability' (Luhmann 1993: 573). Nevertheless, it remains dubious whether Luhmann really can critically diagnose *societal crises* and *pathologies*. If he wants to be consistent in his own theory, he can describe phenomena of social and environmental change, yet he does not have the intellectual tools to classify them as *pathologies* and *anomies*. These are normative categories tied and restricted to the modernist perspective of the identical subject, which Luhmann excludes from the analysis by his decision to base his sociological model on the idea of the communicative system. From the perspective of the function systems, however, the so-called *pathologies of modernity*, that is the suffering of the modern individual, is neither accessible nor important. All that is visible and that counts are the *irritations* of particular function systems (see Chapter 7). The exclusiveness and restricted validity of these problem perceptions, the blindness of Luhmann's model for the fate of the individual, and the lack of normative standards which are applicable to society as a whole shed doubts on Kneer's suggestion that from the perspective of second-order observation systems theory can continue to diagnose the crises and pathologies of contemporary society.

But it is worth pointing out that there is a significant difference between 'identifying societal crises and pathologies' and contributing to the 'enlightenment about societal pathologies and anomies'. Even though systems theory and the theory of post-ecologism can probably not achieve the former, there is no reason why they should not be very helpful with regard to the latter. The most valuable contribution they make to the 'enlightenment about societal pathologies and anomies' is that they reveal the constructedness and contingency of the *pathologies* and *crises* diagnosed from the perspective of traditional-style first-order critical observation. They expose the internal structure and the unquestioned assumptions of these diagnoses. And if beyond the second-order deconstruction of the first-order *pathologies of modernity*, Luhmann continues to speak, in a quite modernist and normative sense, of 'catastrophic regressions' and 'destructions of alarming proportions', this indicates a lack of consistency in Luhmann's thinking to which we will come back below. In its much more restricted area of applicability the theory of post-ecologism seeks to eliminate such inconsistencies by introducing its thesis of the dissolution of the ecologist problem.

So it seems that the traditional critical project can indeed be reformulated and continued at the level of second-order observation. Systems theory and the theory of post-ecologism can thus be defended against the accusation that they are uncritical or conservative. Certainly, they are not critical in the traditional first-order sense, but they are also not uncritical or affirmative of the societal *status quo*. Instead, they may be described as *post-critical* or *meta-critical*. As a matter of principle, however, the question arises why systems theory and the theory of post-ecologism should at all have to make the effort to prove their critical potential. Why do (eco-)sociological theories have to be critical? On what grounds are uncritical, or in the above sense post-critical, theories widely considered as less useful and legitimate than traditional critical theories? Traditional critical models are based on the modernist principle of unity. Irrespective of their substantive fundamentalisms, critical theories always defend, first and foremost, their assumption of systematic closure and universal coherence. Their concrete political demands emerge where societal reality is found to deviate from the principle of unity, and the primary aim of these demands is always to restore or achieve unity and systematic order. Theories which do not enforce unity thus appear as uncritical and affirmative. As a mechanism of self-protection, modernist thinking rejects such approaches, even though its own normative basis, that is the identical subject, has long disintegrated, and plurality and differentiation have been adopted as cultural ideals. We may thus conclude that the distinction between affirmation and critique, which Kneer seeks to save through his transition to second-order criticism, really ought to be given up altogether. The criteria of *affirmative* and *critical* represent a first-order code which is unsuitable for second-order models. It cannot be *applied by* post-critical theories because taking an affirmative or critical stance requires normative standards, which are not available to either systems theory or the theory of post-ecologism. It cannot be *applied to* post-critical models because their primary level of reference is not the allegedly objective world of empirical phenomena, but specific first-order conceptualisations and reality constructions.

Once the contingency and fundamental inappropriateness of the categories of affirmation and critique has thus been revealed, it may become possible to appreciate a certain *pacifying potential* which is undoubtedly inherent in both Luhmann's thinking and the theory of post-ecologism, and which may easily be mistaken for conservatism or political quietism. Luhmann repeatedly notes that he hopes to contribute to the 'avoidance of unnecessary excitement'. Going significantly beyond Luhmann, the theory of post-ecologism theorises how contemporary individuals and society manage to accept and naturalise social conditions and practices which, from a modernist perspective, appear as unacceptable and barbaric (see also Chapter 10). This is a most delicate issue. In the sociological tradition, any intellectual ventures pointing in this direction are immediately dismissed as neo-conservative and reactionary. Already, Hegel's philosophy, which was painfully aware of the insoluble problems and antagonisms of modern society and which, instead of raising unfounded hopes and further increasing the suffering of the individual, was looking for 'reconciliation with actuality' and sought to 'establish peace with the actual world' (*Philosophy of Right*; preface), had to confront such accusations. But, particularly if the modernist point of view, with its pretensions and problem perceptions, turns out to be a social construction which has been overtaken – and delegitimised – by the process of modernisation, the question arises whether the Hegelian project should not be resuscitated because it contains a significant amount of fundamental wisdom.

John Gray notes that, in contemporary society, the old modernist ideals are no longer 'a living faith', but merely 'a weak antidote to nihilism' (1997: 176). The humanist beliefs, he suggests, survive 'not as a living tradition, but as a deadweight on new thought' (ibid.: 170). If the modernist dream of the individual as the centre and purpose as well as the agency of societal development turns out to be unfounded; if, in other words, the process of modernisation has emancipated itself from its modernist nucleus and continues as a *denucleated modernity*, the stubborn insistence on modernist categories (naturalisations) may be said to cause unjustifiable suffering and disruption by making false promises and destroying existing postmodernist naturalisations, which are essential for making life a pleasant experience. Undeniably, there is only a very fine line – if any – between promoting political quietism and stirring up pointless and merely destructive anxieties. In many respects even the *most advanced* societies are still pre-modern rather than modern or even postmodern (Latour 1993; Beck 1997a). Failing to promote the modernist ideals would therefore mean accepting all kinds of pre-modern naturalisations which can make life an even more unpleasant experience. This is the old dialectic and dilemma of Enlightenment which has a kind of second-order reappearance. Nevertheless, social-theoretical thought has to both recognise the dangers, that is the exploitability of the human capacity of naturalisation, and appreciate this capacity as a precious gift. To even mention such considerations is, of course, a highly dangerous business; firstly, because it makes systems theory and post-ecologist thinking susceptible to neo-conservative appropriation, and, secondly, because any such remarks provide easy targets and welcome sound-bites for, in the traditional sense, *critical* book reviewers. Nevertheless, a serious debate on the question of whether post-ecologist thinking can be described as affirmative cannot exclude this aspect.

9.2   Is post-ecologism anti-ecological?

Post-ecologist thinking and politics may furthermore easily raise the impression of being anti-ecological. By and large, this criticism would just be a variation of the one discussed above, and the main arguments against this charge are already implicit in the above discussion. Nevertheless, it seems appropriate to address this allegation separately, for there are indeed a number of reasons why post-ecologism may appear as anti-ecological. First, post-ecologist thinking suggests that nature has been abolished, which seems to imply that the physical environment no longer needs any protection and may now be exploited and commodified without any restrictions. Second, there is the post-ecologist suggestion that concern for nature and ecological problems are *merely* identity issues, that is the theory of post-ecologism does not seem to recognise and take seriously the material problems and crises which are supposedly at the heart of ecological thinking. Third, the theory of post-ecologism suggests that the ecological problem has dissolved. In other words, what ecologists were most concerned about is for post-ecologists not just irrelevant, but actually non-existent. Fourth, the theory of post-ecologism seems to accept, or even approve of, social injustice and exclusion, and suggest that there is no point in worrying about the fate of future generations. It thus seems to snub the most fundamental moral values and humanistic foundations of ecological thinking. Fifth, the theory of post-ecologism regards the eco-movement as a rearguard battle, that is it seems to consider the eco-movement as a historical error and deny that huge ecological tasks are lying ahead of contemporary society. This list of anti-ecological indicators could be extended almost *ad libitum*. As a matter of fact, every definition of post-ecologism which has been suggested in the course of this book (and particularly in Chapter 8) may be turned against post-ecologism and used as evidence of its anti-ecological attitudes. Once again, a closer look at the eco-sociological debate about Luhmann's model may help to further develop these allegations and assess their validity.

The criticism of Luhmann's theory as anti-ecological is based on the argument that Luhmann completely fails to address the ecological crisis; firstly, because the very idea of *crises* (see Chapter 2) is necessarily alien to a theoretical model that relies on the principles of autopoiesis, self-referentiality and radical temporalisation (Habermas 1987b: 375; Görg 1992: 143) and, secondly, because his concept of the environment (see Section 7.1) is completely different from that used by ecologists (Beck 1988: 169f.; Rucht and Roth 1992; Metzner 1993: 171f.). According to Beck, Luhmann's suggestion that 'ecological threats are only selectively perceived by society and can hardly be processed at all' (Beck 1988: 169) amounts to a denial of their reality: 'they do not exist – at least not socially' (ibid.). He criticises Luhmann for mistaking the lack of institutional consciousness and responsiveness for the non-existence of ecological problems: 'by being institutionally eclipsed' ecological problems 'demonstrate their irreality' (ibid.). Beck concedes that the

societal response to ecological problems is limited by society's ecological recep-
tiveness and sensitivity, but referring to the radioactive cloud of Chernobyl, he
insists that the physical realities 'don't give a *nuclear* shit' about societal attitudes
(ibid.: 171).

Expressed in less colloquial terms, Beck's main argument against Luhmann is
that, quite irrespective of their being perceived and gaining communicative significance, environmental threats have objective physical reality and effects (see
Chapter 5) which, in his view, have to be the main point of reference for any serious ecological theory and politics. In other words, we are back to the
realism–constructionism controversy that was addressed in Chapter 3. From his
realist perspective, Beck argues that Luhmann's conceptualisation of ecological
problems as communicative problems and constructions amounts to 'a rather long-
winded pleading for an authoritarian *politics of mollification*' (1988.: 175). In his
view, Luhmann's communicative transformation of the environmental problem
necessarily leads to the unacceptable conclusion that 'only the *communication about*
ecological threats' is 'socially dangerous' (ibid.: 171), but not the physical conditions
themselves. Polemically, he suggests that 'Luhmann's systems-theoretical *solution* to
the ecological challenge' boils down to the 'silly and cynical' recommendation
that 'keeping your mouth shut protects against breathing poisonous fumes! Silence
detoxifies!' (ibid.).

Arguing along very similar lines, Metzner points out that Luhmann's theory
cannot 'do justice to the ecological problematique' as long as the crisis 'is completely stripped of its material or physical dimension', that is as long as it 'only
exists as a phenomenon purely internal to society' (Metzner 1993: 175). Like many
other contemporary commentators, Metzner tries to conceptualise the ecological
crisis in terms of the nature–society metabolism which does, indeed, not figure in
Luhmann's model. Echoing Beck's concerns, Metzner criticises Luhmann for framing ecological threats as *noise* or *irritations* generated by ecological communication,
that is for presenting 'the self-endangerment of society through the *basal anarchy* of
the protest movements' rather than the deteriorating physical environment as the
'true evil' (ibid.: 182). According to Metzner, Luhmann's social theoretical model
and his critique of ecological communication focus on the '*disposal of worries* instead
of genuinely attacking the problem' (ibid.: 203). Just as Beck takes refuge in
polemics, Metzner eventually finds consolation in the view that the material reality of environmental threats and their concrete social effects are 'equally certain to
explode Luhmann's theory, as the emission of 5 gigatonnes of CO_2 per year . . . is
heating up our atmosphere' (ibid.: 176). But to what extent are these charges justified? Does Luhmann – does post-ecologist thinking – really belittle or even deny
the existence of ecological threats beyond their communicative reality? Do they
declare the eco-movement as more dangerous than the ecological threats themselves? Will the physical realities before long invalidate Luhmann's theory and
thus at the same time also seal the fate of the theory of post-ecologism?

From the above elaborations, it should be sufficiently clear that neither
Luhmann nor the theory of post-ecologism which emerges from his model at any
point deny that the material conditions in the physical environment have most

significant implications and potentially fatal consequences for human beings, particular social systems and for society (humanity) at large. As a sociologist, Luhmann would be hardly worth mentioning if there really were any need for reminding him that 'the real effects' of the physical conditions and of environmental change 'do not depend on the communication about it' (Hinterberger et al. 1996: 199). But contrary to his critics, Luhmann – and the theory of post-ecologism – clearly distinguish between material conditions and empirically measurable environmental *change*, on the one hand, and environmental *problems*, on the other (see Sections 3.2, 7.2 and 8.2). Whilst the former are undoubtedly physical phenomena which exist irrespective of their societal perception and any communication about them, the latter are social constructions which have only discursive reality.

Problems do not exist *a priori*, but they are infringements of normative standards – in Luhmann's model, rules of communication – which themselves are never transcendental, but always socially negotiated. Unfortunately, Luhmann himself is not always very precise about this distinction. As I indicated in Section 8.2, he never fully explores its implications. But it should be clear that Luhmann cannot be accused of belittling or denying the significance of physical environmental change. The crucial point is that physical conditions, inter-systemic material flows or phenomena of physical environmental change are not at all his subject. The objective of his – and the post-ecologist – enquiry is rather to find out how society perceives and processes these physical conditions and this physical change. Particularly in *Ecological Communication*, Luhmann may be criticised for being terminologically unclear or even inconsistent: he sticks to the commonly used notions of ecological *threats* and *dangers*, and fails to clarify their exact relationship towards his 'irritations of established structures of meaning'. However, Beck, Metzner, Hinterberger and all those critics, who argue along the lines of their concerns, have to be criticised for failing to take account of the significant – one could even say the *all-important* – difference between physical environmental change and societal problem perceptions.

Once ecological problems are conceptually distinguished from material environmental conditions and phenomena of physical environmental change, it also becomes obvious that it does not make sense to say that those who communicate about environmental threats are more dangerous than the environmental threats themselves. In contrast to environmental change, environmental threats are only constructed in the process of ecological communication, which subjects intrinsically value-free material conditions to the specifically ecologist normative categories (see Section 7.5) and thus generates the ecologist world-view and problem perceptions. So it should go without saying that this communication is not *more* threatening, but *alone* threatening. In this sense, Luhmann notes that ecological protest refers to nothing but its own problem constructions (self-referentiality) and has to be understood as a communicative *self*-irritation (see Section 7.2). As regards the communicators, that is the human individuals who generate these threatening communications, it is important to remember that Luhmann sharply distinguishes between individuals on the one hand, and communications or communicative systems on the other. When he raises doubts about ecological communication (for its moralism and theoretical deficits), this can never mean criticising specific human individuals, or presenting certain social groups as a threat to society. For better or worse, the individual is not Luhmann's point of departure and reference. And in any case, Luhmann's concepts of *threat* and *irritation* are not meant to be normative concepts. In other words, if ecological communication is said to disturb the smooth functioning of other social systems, this must not be misread as *eo ipso* negative. On the contrary, Luhmann indicates that this disturbance can fulfil important functions (see Section 7.4).

In this context it is finally worth reiterating a point that was made Section 3.3, where I emphasised that it is a fatal error to consider environmental problems as 'less real' and 'less important' just because they are discursive constructions rather than *a priori* material realities. Criticising Luhmann – and the theory of post-ecologism – for '*reducing* today's central conflict to the communication of *Angst*' (Rucht and Roth 1992: 27; my emphases) implies a number of significant misunderstandings. Such criticism, firstly, fails to take into account that anxiety, whatever its source and legitimation, is very real for those who experience it, and constitutes a point of reference in the process of democratic policy making which is arguably even more important than the so-called scientific realities. Secondly, *Angst* would normally – though not necessarily – be attached to a set of concrete physical conditions which are perceived and evaluated in certain (ecologist) ways. In other words, the communication of *Angst* would normally have a clear physical dimension, and it is in this sense, too, fundamentally wrong to say that Luhmann's theory has lost touch with reality and is 'above the clouds' (ibid.: 31). Thirdly, Luhmann's model conceptualises the communication of *Angst* not as *inferior* or *irrational*, but simply as a specific kind of system-rationality that competes with other system codes. On the basis of our investigations in Sections 1.2 and 7.6, *Angst* could at best be described as *trans*-rational or *post*-rational, but Luhmann's model does not provide the tools for disqualifying the communication of *Angst* as less valuable, legitimate, or realistic than any other form of communication. Despite Luhmann's reservations about the arguably unnecessary anxiety caused by the communication of protest, it is fundamentally misguided to accuse Luhmann of contesting the legitimacy and rationality of the social movements. It is certainly correct to highlight Luhmann's peculiar disinterest in the fate of concrete human individuals and his failure to address the needs of the remains of the idealist subject (see next section). But the criticism that Luhmann denies the legitimacy of ecologist problem perceptions, or belittles the significance of the issues ecologists concerned themselves with is inadequate.

So we may come to the conclusion that even though Luhmann does indeed not have much use for the ecologist concept of *crisis* (e.g. SS: 477; EC: 112), and even though he indeed rejects the ecologist notion of the natural environment as an *ecosystem* (e.g. P: 50; see Sections 6.1 and 7.1), the criticism of his theory as anti-ecological is fundamentally flawed. It fails to recognise Luhmann's change of paradigm (see Chapter 6) and continues to argue in categories which are not applicable to Luhmann's thinking. In as much as Luhmann never leaves any doubt that ecological questions are categorically different from and incompatible with systems-theoretical questions (see Chapter 7), his theory can neither be described as *anti*-ecological, nor for that matter as *pro*-ecological. Luhmann does not accept the fundamental assumptions of the ecologist discourse. He abandons the modernist (and ecologist) division line between the system of nature and the system of society, and replaces these two assumed entities (and their singular dualism) by the assumption of an unlimited number of communicative systems. In line with the post-ecologist research agenda outlined in Section 3.3, he, furthermore, abandons the ecologist distinction between material/objective/valid on the one hand, and immaterial/subjective/invalid on the other. He understands (ecological) problems not primarily as physical realities but conceptualises them as normative issues, that is as violations of established cultural (communicative) rules – which do not, of course, exist in a vacuum, but are directly related to the material world. Given this rearrangement of the most fundamental parameters, the categories of *ecological* or *anti-ecological* are simply no longer applicable. If anything, Luhmann's model can be described as *non*-ecological. And if it makes a conscious effort to follow up those specific issues (or their constituents) which from an ecologist perspective would have been framed and categorised as *ecological* issues, it may, as I did above, be described as *post*-ecologist.

As regards the theory of post-ecologism, much of what was said to defend Luhmann's model against the charge of being anti-ecological is equally applicable to post-ecologist thinking. The major difference between Luhmann's theory and the theory of post-ecologist politics is that the latter seeks to compensate for the deficits of the former, that is it explores what Luhmann's model implies for contemporary society's concrete politics (of nature). Without changing Luhmann's basic parameters, the theory of post-ecologist politics shifts the emphasis back to concrete human individuals and their material conditions and normative needs. Whilst Luhmann – despite distinguishing systems of consciousness from systems of communication (see Section 8.2) – somewhat unsatisfactorily only focuses on ecological problems as communicative problems, the theory of post-ecologism goes the step beyond the communicative systems and relates ecological problems back to the level of consciousness and the identity needs of human individuals. But in doing so, post-ecologist thinking retains Luhmann's fundamental decision to conceptualise ecological problems as normative rather than material issues. And to the extent that it rejects the traditional set-up in which ecological problems are framed primarily as questions of the society–nature metabolism, the theory of post-ecologism will therefore probably have to share the charge of being anti-ecological. But ecologist thinking originally certainly comprised both the material and the normative dimensions (see Chapters 4 and 5). It was only because ecologists were implicitly aware that following up the normative dimension would lead into insoluble problems that they increasingly neglected the issues of meaning and identity, and focused instead on the material dimension where they thought they were treading on safer ground. The discourse of sustainability, natural capital, inter-systemic material or energy flows (metabolisms), and such like, hoped to be able to displace and avoid normative issues (see Section 1.3). But the systematic neglect of the normative and identity-related dimension in ecological thought takes its toll. And if attempts to reinstate this neglected dimension are immediately rejected as anti-ecological, this provides evidence of a profound deformation of eco-political theory.

As a matter of fact, the accusation that systems-theory and the theory of post-ecologism are anti-ecological and have lost touch with societal reality may well be turned against ecologist thinking itself. In the life-world of contemporary individuals the narrow questions to which the ecologist perspective has been reduced, that is absolute resource scarcity, nature–society metabolisms, biodiversity, ecological sustainability and so on are actually not that relevant. Contrary to what concepts like the one of the risk society suggest, 'real scarcity' and 'direct physical threats' are not 'primary points of reference' for the typical contemporary individual (Schulze 1993: 22). Particularly in the western affluent societies, identity issues, that is questions of self-construction and self-experience, take the central place formerly occupied by immediate material needs. Undoubtedly, questions of finiteness and limited resources do come into consideration. But in contemporary society, these issues enter the personal life-world primarily as issues of finite *financial* resources, and beyond this relative finiteness, absolute ecological limits play a rather subordinate role. For the analysis of contemporary society's politics of nature – particularly if this politics depends on majority consent – it is therefore fundamentally important to shift the emphasis from what, according to the ecologist perspective, *ought to be* the primary criterion back to what arguably *really is* the primary criterion, even if this may trigger the charge of anti-ecological attitudes.

The demand for ecological correctness which is implicit in such charges distorts the analysis of how contemporary society really frames and handles issues and concerns which, as ecologists dogmatically insist, ought to be framed as ecological issues. The theory of post-ecologist politics neither denies that contemporary society has to manage concrete tasks related to the material world, nor that there are certain societal developments which ecologists interpret as ecological problems, achievements, or setbacks. But its central objective is to make a categorically new analytical start and avoid the specifically ecologist prejudice and preoccupations. Obviously, by sketching and applying its own normative criteria, the theory of post-ecologist politics introduces its own prejudice and preoccupations. But to the extent that these are really different from the former, that is to the extent that post-ecologist thinking succeeds in avoiding the specifically ecologist criteria, the charge of its being anti-ecologist is not tenable.

9.3   Is post-ecologism pessimistic or cynical?

We finally have to address the question whether post-ecologist thinking and politics are pessimistic or cynical. I pointed out above that in certain respects, contemporary society's politics of nature might be described as the return to premodern principles, and we also spoke of the arrival of a 'new barbarism'. Such suggestions seem to place post-ecologist thinking into the tradition of cultural pessimism. This impression is reconfirmed by the fact that neither Luhmann's model nor the theory of post-ecologist politics seem to take much notice of the potential sources of ecological optimism. Neither of them seem to acknowledge that substantial ecological progress has already been made: Undeniably, DDT has come out of use, coal-fired power stations have been fitted with filters, petrol is now unleaded, many rivers are cleaner than they were a few decades ago, substantial amounts of waste are being recycled, etc., etc. But instead of taking these achievements as an incentive and encouragement for further and more ambitious projects, Luhmann seems to insist that society cannot attune itself to ecological threats, and the theory of post-ecologism seems to be saying that there is not much point in *even trying* to make provisions for an ecologically better future because the acceleration of social change keeps shifting the goal posts and constantly reshuffles all parameters. Against this background it seems legitimate to criticise Luhmann and post-ecologist thinking for being unduly pessimistic. And if they suggest that huge droughts, famines, floods and so on, although they threaten thousands or even millions of livelihoods, do not necessarily have to be conceptualised as a problem (see Chapters 7 and 8), it also seems adequate to describe these models as cynical.

As regards the theory of post-ecologist politics, it may be emphasised once again that this theory does not suggest, demand, recommend or criticise anything, but rather than making normative judgements about what – for whatever reasons – ought to be the case, it merely seeks to describe what factually is the case. Hence neither pessimism nor cynicism seem to be within its range. As regards Luhmann's theory, it is worth pointing out that Luhmann himself does not believe his thinking to be pessimistic, and cynicism is even more alien to him. In Luhmann's view, contemporary society is by no means doomed to lethargy or paralysis. On the contrary, he believes that it 'could become active to an extent which is virtually unlimited' (P: 73). The main obstacle to societal reform, Luhmann argues, is not that there is nothing that could be done, but the problem is 'the non-exploitation of available options' (ibid.). Although he believes that for contemporary differentiated societies the grand ideologies have become structurally inadequate, and that increasingly complex and fragmented societies cannot act or react in a centrally planned and co-ordinated way, Luhmann still believes that there is plenty of scope for implementing more effective concrete policies. He does not see why societal reform and improvement should necessarily depend on central planning and grand utopias. As long as the various functional subsystems can formulate and implement their particular policies and strategies, there is, according to Luhmann, no need at all for a 'central idea of improvement' (ibid.). He therefore does not see any reason for pessimism and resignation.

But after the extensive analysis of Luhmann's model, this optimism does not come across as particularly convincing. Luhmann presents a meticulously elaborated analysis showing why modern society *does* not and *can* not ward off ecological threats. Time and again he points out that there is no practical alternative to functional differentiation, which appears to be the very root of society's dilemma. Given the increasing differentiation and fragmentation of society, it becomes ever more dubious why sociology should at all try to provide 'better observation and description'. If comprehensive solutions cannot be found anyway, it might, after all, be better not to know the true extent of the dilemma in the first place. Not knowing at least preserves the principle of hope. Luhmann, on the other hand, could hardly be more efficient in destroying hope. Correctly, Metzner points out that Luhmann's message 'could be reduced to the fatalistic formula that intellectuals, although they can penetrate everything, can change nothing, whilst the functional subsystems of society . . . could change everything, but understand nothing' (Metzner 1993: 203). Luhmann may be right to criticise the eco-movement and ecological thought for failing to reflect on their own limitations. With regard to both their ecological diagnoses as well as their suggested remedies, he may be right to insist on 'better observation'. Yet to the extent that Luhmann keeps emphasising the extreme evolutionary improbability of the achieved level of differentiation, the rapid build-up of potentially fatal problems, and the likelihood of an ecological collapse or catastrophe, while at the same time pointing towards – even insisting on – the structural inability of modern society to confront these problems, his theory remains – despite all protestations to the opposite – pessimistic and cynical.

But for what reasons does Luhmann's thinking come across as pessimistic or cynical even though Luhmann himself reassures us that it is not meant to be? With a view to the theory of post-ecologism, this disparity between Luhmann's own perception and the impression his reasoning makes on his readers is worth exploring. Luhmann's central thesis is that society is structurally unable to act in a co-ordinated and purposeful way, that is in accordance with an overall rationality. He can be criticised as pessimistic or cynical only if there is a perceived need for society to act in such a way, and if he himself concedes such a need. This need, however, only exists if society as a whole is confronted with problems which require such a co-ordinated approach. Ecological threats seem to be a good case in point, and indeed Luhmann himself keeps talking about the ecological crisis. He seems to believe in its reality and urgency, and demands that it be taken seriously. Yet, trying to think in Luhmannite categories, one begins to wonder how Luhmann thinks he can come to his ecological diagnosis. As a matter of fact, his theory does not really leave him any central point of view from which he could describe societal conditions or developments as problematic or catastrophic in the traditional absolute sense. As I have demonstrated in the previous chapter, Luhmann's radical constructivism leads directly, and invariably, to the dissolution of the ecological problem in the ecologist sense. Luhmann's model dissolves the traditional environmental problem into multiple discursive problem constructions and individual problem perceptions. Accordingly, there is no need at all for society as a whole to become active in a co-ordinated way, but what is required are appropriate responses at the level of particular social systems or human individuals. Against this background it seems that it is wrong to criticise Luhmann for being cynical. Instead, he might be criticised for being inconsistent. He continues to talk about ecological problems as if they were still *out there* waiting for society to respond to them, although his own theory conceptualises them in a completely different way.

By talking about ecological problems and crises in the traditional sense, Luhmann endorses a particular – the ecologist – mode of problem construction and reproduces the old modernist dualism. If his model appears pessimistic or cynical, this impression emerges from a theoretical inconsistency which the theory of post-ecologism tries to avoid. As I outlined above, post-ecologist thinking suggests that the ecologist problem has genuinely dissolved and that by changing the patterns of identity formation and self-construction, that is by rearranging the parameters which determine the perspective onto the world, contemporary society and its individuals have attuned themselves very successfully to the so-called environmental challenge. Post-ecologist thinking is therefore even less pessimistic or cynical than Luhmann's model. Nevertheless, it will not easily be able to rid itself from this negative smack. It has the specific aim of bridging the gap between ecologist and non-ecologist thinking. It seeks to follow up how the issues ecologists framed as ecological issues develop beyond the abdication of the ecologist paradigm. In other words, the theory of post-ecologist politics aims to think, at the same time, in two paradigms which are actually mutually exclusive. It aims to conceptualise the simultaneity of the ecologist and non-ecologist perspectives onto the world. Luhmann himself indicates that after the abolition of nature, the modernist subject and the ecologist paradigm, at least 'for some time, we have to reckon with a certain *simultaneity of the non-simultaneous*'[3] (EC: 4). For the theory of post-ecologist politics, this simultaneity implies that it will always be perceived as pessimistic. But on the other hand, post-ecologist thinking would not make sense, and could not be described as such, if this simultaneity of the two perspectives ceased to exist. If the post-ecologist perspective were to be no longer counterbalanced by its ecologist counterpart, it would adopt the status of a *universal delusive context* or a *second nature* in Horkheimer and Adorno's sense (see Chapter 4). It would lose its identity (see Chapter 8), and contemporary society's politics of nature could no longer be described as post-ecologist.

So we may come to the conclusion that the theory of post-ecologist politics is neither affirmative, nor anti-ecological, nor really pessimistic and cynical. It tries to be more consistent than Luhmann's model, and it tries to take account of the fact that even if, philosophically, the modernist idea of the identical subject and the critical paradigm have abdicated, we cannot simply assume that, in a life-world sense, the experience of Max Weber's *pathologies of modernity* immediately disappears. As Habermas points out, Luhmann's systems functionalism 'tacitly sets a seal on *the end of the individual*' (1987b: 353) and simply presupposes that the individual and its lifeworld have 'disintegrated without remainder into the functionally specialized subsystems' (ibid.: 358). But the transition from the paradigm of the individual to that of the system is not that easy: the individual's *'perceptions of crises in the lifeworld'* cannot simply be translated 'without remainder into *systems-related problems of steering'* (ibid.: 363). Even if, as I quoted above, the modernist interest in nature is becoming increasingly anachronistic, that is even if in contemporary society it is no more than 'a transitional stage, perhaps a hesitation or an inconsistency' (Böhme 1992: 183), an adequate social and ecological theory has to take account of the

---

3   Official translation: '...the *simultaneity of the non-simultaneous* still had to be reckoned with for a long time.'

remains of the modernist constructions, and it has to spell out the concrete social implications of the newly emerging patterns of looking at (or constructing) the world. Luhmann's systems-oriented perspective necessarily 'remains unaware of the social costs arising on the side of the life world when systems are breaking away from it' (Gerhards 1984: 92). It therefore needs to be 'extended by the perspective of a life world analysis' (ibid.: 93). At least with regard to ecological matters, this is exactly what the theory of post-ecologist politics seeks to achieve.

10 Managing the transition to post-ecologist politics

In the previous chapters I outlined the key parameters of post-ecologist thinking and politics, and I tried to anticipate the most important ecologist objections against the post-ecologist model. In order to complete the theory of post-ecologist politics, I finally need to explore how contemporary society practically manages its transition to a politics of nature which – from the ecologist perspective – can only be described as completely unacceptable or even barbaric. As I pointed out above, post-ecologist politics is not an option or a prophecy, but a political reality, an ongoing societal practice. The *transition* to post-ecologist politics must therefore not simply be understood as the introduction of a new (post-ecologist) type of environment-related policies, but first and foremost as the psychological process (at the individual as well as the societal level) of coping with the decline of the modernist and ecologist ideals, and naturalising social attitudes and societal structures which have so far widely been regarded as unacceptable. Even though ecologist values and beliefs have factually never been more than regulative *ideals*, their abdication marks a significant cultural shift, and the adoption of new normative standards and new ways of perceiving social relations can only be a gradual process. *Managing* the transition to post-ecologist politics therefore also means framing and interpreting ongoing post-ecologist developments and eco-political practices in such a way that they become socially acceptable. Beyond that, managing the transition towards a post-ecologist politics implies finding means to control ecologist reflexes of rejection and defence against the post-ecologist tide.

In this concluding chapter I want to suggest that the societal strategy that fulfils this function and facilitates contemporary society's transition from the ecologist to the post-ecologist paradigm is the discourse of *ecological modernisation*. Since the Brundtland Report (1987) and the UNCED conference in Rio, 1992, the discourse of ecological modernisation has clearly dominated the environmental debate and environmental policy making in all major industrialised countries. This discourse acknowledges that in ecological matters, the late 1980s or early 1990s marked a paradigm shift which implied the abdication of the radical ideology of ecologism. In a sense, it may therefore also be described as *post*-ecologist. Yet contrary to the comprehensive theory developed in the previous chapters, the discourse of ecological modernisation frames contemporary society's ongoing politics of nature in such a way that the core elements of ecologist thinking – the ecological diagnosis and ideals – appear to have been preserved, whilst only the strategy for the implementation of these ideals has been modernised. In the recent literature there are several attempts to clarify the meaning of *ecological modernisation*, to spell out different perspectives of society's ecologisation, and to assess the appropriateness of the ecological modernisation approach (e.g. Weale 1992; Hajer 1995, 1996; Mol 1995, 1996; Christoff 1996; Blowers 1997; Dryzek 1997; Gouldson and Murphy 1997; Neale 1997; Reitan 1998; Rutherford 1999).

Environmental sociologists have even developed an *ecological modernisation theory* which claims the status of an independent eco-theoretical model (Mol 1996, 1998) and aims to guide and interpret the efforts and activities which are commonly described as the ecological modernisation of late industrial societies. But despite all this, there is still considerable uncertainty about what exactly these efforts achieve, what problem-perceptions they actually respond to and whether they will really take late modern societies any closer to the realisation of ecological ideals. This is not the place for a discussion of specific policies of ecological modernisation nor for a detailed analysis of ecological modernisation theory. But at the end of this book I want to interpret the whole discourse of ecological modernisation from the perspective of post-ecologist thinking. What this means is that the point here is not to provide arguments for or against the ecological suitability of the theory and practice of ecological modernisation, but to interpret this whole discourse within the framework of a much more comprehensive theory than is normally done in the ecological modernisation literature. As a second-order theory, the theory of post-ecologist politics can reveal insights about the discourse of ecological modernisation which are not available from any first-order (ecological) perspective. The post-ecologist perspective exposes the unquestioned assumptions of the proponents as well as the critics of ecological modernisation. It thus challenges both the optimistic belief in this strategy as well as the ecologist objections it has attracted. From a post-ecologist point of view, the discourse of ecological modernisation, which almost hegemonically dominates the contemporary debate on environmental issues, appears in a radically new light.

10.1 Ecological modernisation and ecological modernisation theory

Ecological modernisation is an unspecific label that has been used in several different ways. In the widest sense, it covers all reformist environmental efforts since the 1970s, which have otherwise also been described as 'environmentalist' (Dobson 1995). More specifically, the concept is used to refer to the pragmatic, policy-oriented and anti-ideological approach to environmental issues that superseded the anti-modernist as well as the leftist-revolutionary (ecologist) approaches typical of the 1970s and early 1980s (Weale 1992; Prittwitz 1993a; Hajer 1995; Mol 1995; Spaargaren 1997). If there is any truth in the suggestion that, historically, the ecological discourse has developed from *conservationism* through *environmentalism* to *ecologism* (Rucht 1989), ecological modernisation might be regarded as the latest stage in the evolution of ecological ideologies. Amongst the most important characteristics of the ecological modernisation approach are its incrementalism, its reliance on economic instruments and its confidence in mechanisms of self-regulation. Its emergence signalled the end of 'the sharp antagonistic debates between the state and the environmental movement' (Hajer 1995: 28f.). Given that the achievements of the welfare state seemed to depend on the continuation of the established economic model, and that processes of globalisation rendered the principles of growth and competitiveness ever more inescapable, the ecologist demand to turn away from the path of techno-economic progress and expansion no longer appeared as a realistic option.

Ecological modernisation therefore aims to turn quantitative growth into qualitative growth. At the macro-economic level, it seeks to shift the emphasis away from energy- and resource-intensive industries towards service- and knowledge-intensive industries. At the micro-economic level, it aims for an efficiency revolution through the intelligent implementation of new, clean technologies and production methods. The change of strategy from the 'flight from technology' to 'a technological attack' (Jänicke 1993: 18) obviously meant 'the acceleration of technological progress', but it was assumed that it would be possible to promote economic growth and technological progress, and still accomplish the 'change in the direction of development' (ibid.) which ecologists have always demanded. This U-turn was meant to be achieved by the emergence and implementation of a new *ecological rationality* that would commit all sectors of society, including the economy, to certain ecological standards and goals. Particularly since the beginning of the 1990s, so the proponents of this reformist agenda argue, the policies of ecological modernisation can 'no longer be interpreted as mere window-dressing' (Mol 1995: 2). In their view, the ongoing processes of institutional learning and reorganisation amount to a fundamental ecological restructuring of late modern society. In this respect, the contemporary policy of ecological modernisation is regarded as categorically different from earlier reformist approaches.

Ecological modernisation theory emerged in the early 1980s and has gained particular prominence amongst environmental sociologists in Germany, the Netherlands and, more recently, also in Britain. Its positive belief in the progressive ecologisation of modern society reflects the optimistic *Zeitgeist* to which I referred at various stages throughout this book. Martin Jänicke and Joseph Huber are widely considered as the founding fathers of this project to devise a theoretical model for late industrial society's attempt to respond to the undesirable side-effects of its own modernisation process (Prittwitz 1993b; Mol 1995, 1998; Spaargaren 1997). In a number of publications Huber has tried to demonstrate the compatibility of economy and ecology, and argued that technological progress and innovation, in particular, had finally made it possible to 'ecologise the economy' while 'economising ecology' (Huber 1982, 1985, 1989, 1991, 1993). Jänicke, on the other hand, mainly concentrated on the changing role of democratic institutions, particularly the role of the state (Jänicke 1978, 1984, 1986, 1988, 1990, 1993). Since the middle of the 1980s, he has been arguing for an 'innovative dual structure of the state' firstly, as a democratically legitimated 'bureaucratic mechanism of intervention' and, secondly, as 'initiator of processes of negotiation', which would take place at all societal levels and involve all sectors of society (Jänicke 1993: 15). In Jänicke's view, the ecological crisis necessitates and effectively promotes the transition towards 'a more decentralised and consensus oriented kind of politics which focuses the central state on strategic tasks and increasingly devolves the regulation of details to local actors' (ibid.: 24f.). A turning point for the development of ecological modernisation theory was Beck's concept of *reflexive modernisation* and his discussion of *the conflict of two modernities* (see Chapter 5). The theory of the risk society, and its capacity for its ecological self-critique, for the first time provided ecological modernisation theory with a sophisticated social theoretical framework. For contemporary proponents of ecological modernisation theory, the idea of modern society's reflexivity as it has been further developed by Beck himself, Giddens, Lash, and others, has become a central conceptual tool (Prittwitz 1993b; Mol 1995, 1998; Hajer 1995, 1996; Spaargaren 1997).

Today, ecological modernisation theory consists of a host of different strands, and there is substantial controversy between the respective proponents. Nevertheless, there is a set of assumptions which provide a common denominator for the various currents. These include, amongst others, the belief that the established economic and political order is, in principle, fully capable of incorporating ecological goals; that a sound physical environment is not irrelevant for the economy, but actually an important precondition for sustained economic growth and prosperity; that science and technology are not necessarily hostile to ecological principles, but can make a major contribution to environmental reform; that environmental policy can benefit substantially from using economic instruments and market forces; that bureaucratic top-down approaches have to be replaced by processes of consensus formation and the involvement of social movements and the wider public at the national and international level; and that anticipation, prevention and an integrated approach to environmental protection are both ecologically more effective and economically more viable than end-of-pipe solutions and attempts at *post hoc* damage limitation. In the contemporary academic debate, the two major competitors of ecological modernisation theory are neo-Marxist and postmodernist approaches. But as the intellectual climate of the 1990s is rather hostile to both these schools, ecological modernisation theory managed to established itself as the clearly dominant paradigm of thought. There is significant confidence that it will be successful in both the attempt to provide a model 'for analysing the way modern society reacts on and tries to cope with . . . the ecological crisis', and to provide 'a normative theory' on the basis of which 'the ecological crisis [can] be controlled and eventually solved' (Mol 1995: 49).

10.2   The ecologist critique of ecological modernisation

The ecological modernisation approach has attracted serious criticism from ecologically committed commentators in particular. To the extent that their objections centre around the main point that ecological modernisation is not sufficiently radical, that is that it is basically 'a moderate and conservative' approach 'confirming business as usual' (Blowers 1997: 853), these critical voices may cumulatively be described as the *ecologist* critique of the merely *reformist* (environmentalist) strategy of ecological modernisation. Ecologists welcome the fact that, with the emergence of the discourse of ecological modernisation, the existence of a comprehensive environmental problem is finally generally acknowledged, but they are concerned that this problem is framed exclusively in monetary terms and the terms of the natural sciences. On the one hand, this facilitates the incorporation of ecological concerns into social, political and economic decision-making processes. On the other hand, this conceptualisation of environmental problems 'explicitly avoids addressing basic social contradictions' (Hajer 1995: 32). As the proponents of this strategy themselves admit, ecological modernisation is 'first and foremost an economy and technology-oriented concept' (Jänicke 1993:18). As such it pre-empts any fundamental ideological conflict and neglects the set of emancipatory values and concerns which featured prominently in the more radical eco-political strands of the 1970s and early 1980s. As a matter of fact, ecological modernisation theorists have nothing much to say about questions of social justice and issues like the global North–South divide (Mol 1995; Blowers 1997). For these reasons, ecologists feel that ecological modernisation does not address their most fundamental concerns.

Furthermore, radical ecologists are critical of the fact that ecological modernisation regards the environmental problem as merely a '*design fault* of modernity' (Mol 1996: 305; my emphasis), or as Hajer puts it, an '*omission* in the workings of the institutions of modern society' (1995: 3; my emphasis) that can easily be put right. Ultimately, the emergence of environmental problems is considered as a management problem which can be solved by means of managerial fine tuning. This fundamentally managerial attitude demands 'an almost unprecedented degree of trust in experts and in our political elites' (Hajer 1995: 11) which directly contradicts the ecologist distrust in the expert culture and seems incompatible with the promise of grassroots involvement and bottom-up approaches. Beyond that, this managerialism also reflects a 'renewed belief in the possibility of mastery and control' of nature (ibid.: 53) which conflicts with the ecologist ideal of the liberation of, and reconciliation with, nature. Admittedly, the proponents of ecological modernisation are suggesting that their strategy, too, will 'restore the balance between nature and modern society' and achieve 'a kind of reembedding' of society into nature (Mol 1996: 306). But it is evident that their ideal of an *engineered balance* differs significantly from the ecologist vision of a *reconciliation* with nature. To some extent, the ecologist distrust in the managerialism of the ecological modernisation approach also gets support from the argument that 'subordinating the entire planet to human management' requires 'institutions of global governance and sources of cultural wisdom' which are simply not available (Gray 1997: 163). In order to be effective, the politics of ecological modernisation necessitates a degree of centralist regulation and intervention which is hardly compatible with the current agenda of devolution and deregulation (e.g. Gouldson and Murphy 1997).

Beyond this, ecologists are very sceptical about the fundamental belief that economic growth and the resolution of ecological problems can, in principle, be reconciled. As Mol points out, the ecological modernisation approach 'has little interest in changing the existing relations of production or altering the capitalist mode of production' (1995: 41). The proponents of ecological modernisation believe that such changes are not required because 'there is no principle or theoretical argument making a modern organization of production and consumption and its technology antithetical to sustainability' (Spaargaren 1997: 16). Whilst the earlier environmental movement was convinced that the principle of growth is unsustainable and has to be replaced by the principle of self-restriction, the proponents of ecological modernisation expect that internalising care for the environment will even initiate new rounds of technical innovation and economic growth. Hajer therefore fears that the strategy of ecological modernisation might not be more than 'eco-software', which 'will not save the planet if capitalist expansionism remains the name of the game' (1996: 255). As a matter of fact, even Jänicke concedes that, in the long term, ecological modernisation is likely to be unsuccessful as long as its achievements are 'neutralised by high industrial growth' (Jänicke 1993: 19). He believes that this strategy may enable modern societies to 'push the crisis back into latency' (ibid.: 25), but points out that unless we address 'eventually also the question of growth' (ibid.: 19), the crisis is unlikely to be 'solved in its causes' (ibid.: 25).

This leads to the more general criticism that ecological modernisation aims to solve the ecological crisis within the framework of the existing political, economic and social order. Admittedly, the proponents of this strategy do demand 'a reconstruction or rebuilding of some of the central institutions of modern industrial society' (Spaargaren 1997: 1). Nevertheless, they assume that, in principle, the existing social, political and economic institutions are thoroughly capable of internalising ecological concerns, and that 'the environmental issue can be remedied without having to completely redirect the course of social developments' (Hajer 1995: 66). Because of this fundamental confidence in the existing structures, Hajer describes ecological modernisation as 'basically a modernist and technocratic approach to the environment that suggests that there is a techno-institutional fix for the present problems' (ibid.: 32). It was, however, the lack of confidence in techno-institutional fixes, and the argument that the same institutions whose structural inadequacies gave rise to the ecological problem cannot be expected to function successfully as the main instruments of society's ecologisation, that made committed ecologists reject merely reformist approaches.

By and large, these ecologist points of criticism rehearse the argument we know from the so-called *Fundi/Realo* controversy. Ecologists insist that ecological modernisation is not – as ecological modernisation theorists prefer to believe – 'the product of the *maturation* of the social movements', but rather 'the repressive answer to radical environmental discourse' (Hajer 1996: 254). Once again, they see themselves confirmed in their view that 'the environmental movement is haunted by the dilemma of whether to argue on the terms set by the government or to insist on their own mode of expression' (Hajer 1995: 57), and thereby run the risk of alienating the politically more powerful negotiation partner. Being forced into this situation, they have no choice but to 'barter their expressive freedom for influence in concrete policy-making' (ibid.), unless, of course, they accept being completely marginalised politically. The common denominator of these basically *fundamentalist* arguments against the *realist* approach of ecological modernisation is the deep-seated doubt about the *appropriateness* of this strategy to the ecological problem. This doubt leads to the belief that although it might appear less attractive in the short term, the approach of radical ecologists is ultimately the ecologically more appropriate solution. But as I indicated above, the criterion of *ecological appropriateness* is a rather dubious normative standard, particularly if it is applied prior to a detailed analysis of what exactly the problem that is supposed to be solved actually consists in. And as there is a virtually unlimited number of possible environmental problem constructions (see Chapters 5 and 7), ecologists are wrong if they believe that their radical approach can categorically be regarded as *more appropriate*. For a society, for example, where the specifically ecologist concerns have, arguably, become a minority issue, and where the major challenge is to manage the transition to a post-ecologist politics of nature, ecological modernisation might actually represent a very suitable approach.

10.3   A post-ecologist reassessment of ecological modernisation

But to reject the *ecologist* criticism of ecological modernisation does not mean to say that there are no other doubts about the idea of the ecological restructuring of contemporary society. According to ecological modernisation theorists, this restructuring process is supposed to be guided by a new *ecological rationality*, which has, arguably, been established on the basis of 'the constant influx of new information about the ecological effects of [established] social practices and institutional arrangements' (Mol 1995: 394). This newly emerging rationality is expected to gradually catch up 'with the long standing dominance of the economic rationality' without implying 'the need for an abolition or abandoning of the economic rationality' (Spaargaren 1997: 24). Arthur Mol speaks of ecology's 'emancipation from the economic sphere' and the emergence of 'two (increasingly equal) interests and two rationalities' (1996: 307). But given the postmodern pluralisation and diversification of validity claims which societal discourse on the environment has to integrate, one may wonder whether such an independent ecological rationality will ever be available. Invariably, the project of an ecological rationality will get stuck in the same dilemma which was discussed in Chapter 5 (particularly Sections 5.4 and 5.5), where we critiqued Beck's metaphysics of risk.

If, amongst the multiple conceptualisations of the ecologically necessary and desirable something like an ecological rationality is really discernible, ecological modernisation theorists may be expected to tell us the ecological pendent to the unambiguous economic code of *payment or non-payment*. After all, ecological modernisation theorists regard economy and ecology as 'two equally valued domains' (Mol 1995: 30), and the unambiguous distinction between their two rationalities is indeed essential if the ecologisation of the economy is really meant to be more than a self-referential critique. But as we have seen in Chapter 7, such an ecological code is not easily available. Ever since Marx replaced Hegel's *world spirit* with the *world market*, social and political theorists have failed in their attempts to provide rationality with a substantive content other than economic profit, and ecologists are no exception from this general failure. As I argued in Chapter 8, their only point of reference is a flexible code of ecological correctness whose largely contingent and ever-changing content (*programme*) can be empirically identified by the instruments of the polling culture, but which – due to its empirical foundation – is more likely to stabilise and reproduce than radically change the established structures. So the so-called ecological modernisation of contemporary societies can, as I noted before, at best be a reformist process in which certain policies are being implemented and certain changes achieved, but which cannot be described as a directed and co-ordinated societal transformation towards an ecologically sound society, least of all to the ecologist utopias of the 1970s and 1980s. This leaves us with the question why contemporary societies should have adopted a strategy which seems so evidently *inappropriate* as their mainstream eco-political approach.

Irrespective of what individual concrete policies or even the whole process of ecological modernisation might achieve (or fail to achieve) *ecologically*, the societal discourse of ecological modernisation might be done more justice if it is judged by its success in a quite different function. In Chapters 8 and 9 we argued that in the process of cultural and societal modernisation, the specifically ecologist problem has actually dissolved, but that contemporary society still has to confront a problem that we described as the *simultaneity of the non-simultaneous* (see Section 9.3). At least to the fading modernist subject, not to mention the concrete human beings who are physically affected, the newly emerging post-ecologist patterns of thinking and policy making will appear as barbaric. But given the hyper-complex structure of contemporary society and the changing identity needs of the contemporary individual, there is no way that the development towards post-ecologism could be halted or even reversed, and so the question arises through what mechanisms late modern society can make this transition – which it cannot stop – at least bearable. In a way, this might be considered as the post-ecologist reformulation of the ecological problem. And whilst the strategy of ecological modernisation is evidently not able to secure the transition towards an ecological society, it is most certainly able to facilitate the transition towards a post-ecologist society. Arguably, the discourse and policy of ecological modernisation is fundamentally misinterpreted if it is expected (as both radical ecologists and EM-theorists do) to achieve ecological sustainability. Its important contribution can only be appreciated if the focus of attention is shifted to the *post-ecologist problem*.

The point here cannot be to deny that in certain areas – particularly at the micro level – ecological modernisation has already brought about concrete and substantial results, or to dispute that there is considerable potential for further improvement. But it remains a fact that 'any ecological modernisation that has occurred so far has not been on a sufficient scale to back up the claims of its advocates that it offers a genuine escape from the environmental problem' (Gouldson and Murphy 1997: 77). Furthermore, it also remains a fact that much of the structural change in advanced industrial societies that is described as ecological modernisation is actually not ecologically motivated, but driven by the restructuring of the global economy, whereby polluting industries, in particular, tend to be relocated into Third World countries. Certainly, the *dematerialisation* of the economy and the shift from resource- and energy-intensive industries towards knowledge and service industries – even though it might have ecologically positive side-effects – is not motivated by any *ecological* rationality. And the global competition for the lowest production costs is certainly not conducive to either social or ecological sustainability. Nevertheless, advanced industrial societies are extremely attached to their belief in ecological modernisation. And the theory of post-ecologism offers an explanation for this attachment.

With ecological modernisation, contemporary societies have found themselves an eco-political paradigm which combines elements of an ecologist and a post-ecologist politics of nature. On the one hand, ecological modernisation emulates the conditions of modernity, while, on the other hand, it does not obstruct the evolution and implementation of postmodernist patterns of self-construction and societal organisation. What ecological modernisation preserves or restores is not any physical state of nature, but the modernist, meaning-generating belief in the nature–society dualism, and the illusion of rational progress and control. In a post-ecologist context where binding ethical norms and standards of responsibility are not available, and the social distribution of opportunities in life is largely regulated by the principles of financial and political power, ecological modernisation simulates progress towards a more rational/ecological organisation of society for the benefit of universal human wealth and welfare. Environmental hyperactivity reassures us that progress and improvement are possible and reproduces the old Greenpeace belief according to which 'the optimism of action is better than the pessimism of thought'. At the same time, ecological modernisation secures the continuation of post-ecologist politics by avoiding a re-ideologisation of the environmental debate. As I have pointed out at various stages throughout this book, the reinstallation of (invariably ideological) concepts of nature as guiding principles of social organisation remains an attractive option. This could imply chances of development as well as threats; in any case, it would mean the abolition of postmodern plurality and re-entry into a new modernity. In both a positive and a negative sense, ecological modernisation is a protective device against such an emergence of new modernities, that is a device for securing development towards post-ecologist politics.

Ecological modernisation thus promotes and facilitates the continuation of the established socio-economic practice, while at the same time confirming the belief that society is performing the ecological U-turn. Taking up an expression coined by John Dryzek, ecological modernisation might be described as 'a discourse of reassurance' (1997: 146). In the cultural context which I labelled as a *denucleated modernity* (see Chapter 8), that is where the major structures and institutions of modernity remain in place, but no longer serve the purposes of the autonomous subject and are no longer controlled by its rationality, the discourse of ecological modernisation reassures us that we retain agency and control, that the ecological catastrophe is by no means inevitable, that there is no need to abandon the cherished principles of growth and profitability, that there is no need to reduce our standard of living, and that ideals of social justice and so on will not seriously challenge the principle of social differentiation and exclusion which provides the basis for our (new) patterns of self/identity-construction. In a pointed way, one might say that the strategy of ecological modernisation does not protect physical nature, but it protects what has become *natural* for us, particularly in the rich industrialised countries. Ecological modernisation does not respond to any threats emanating from particular conditions in the physical environment, but, first and foremost to the threats to our established patterns of social organisation and societal development emanating from the radical ecologist discourse of the 1970s and 1980s. Ecological modernization does not imply a radical transformation of late modern society, but in a seemingly paradoxical way, it promises and secures that, with minor amendments, everything can continue as before. Whilst change, in particular radical change as it had been demanded by the ecologists of the 1970s and 1980s, always implies uncertainty, the discourse of ecological modernisation reconfirms the old established certainties. The practice of ecological modernisation and the societal discourse about it may be disappointing from an ecologist point of view. However, we may, firstly, contest the normative validity of the ecologist problem perceptions and we, secondly, have to concede that ecological modernisation quite successfully addresses post-ecologist concerns, which weigh very heavily on advanced modern societies. This may be a rather heretical interpretation, but ecological modernisation has to be given credit for this.

Coming back, once again, to Niklas Luhmann, ecological modernisation may alternatively be described as the 'ecology of not-knowing'[1] (Luhmann 1998b: 75ff.). This expression may be understood in two different ways: firstly, it refers to a particular kind of ecological politics (one that cannot agree on its own goals and direction); secondly, in a more general sense, it refers to a cultural context where certainty (knowing) has been replaced by mere opinion (not-knowing), that is where we have to accommodate ourselves to the condition of not being able to know. As Luhmann points out, the most important requirement in a situation of fundamental uncertainty is the transition from the *communication of persuasion* to the *communication of agreement*. In Luhmann's view, this transition involves the introduction of 'a social style that practices discretion' and 'does not attempt to change the minds of those who have to get on with each other,[2] to convert them or to change them in any other way' (ibid.: 99). Under conditions of radical uncertainty, Luhmann argues, late modern societies have to develop a 'culture of unconvinced understanding' (ibid.: 103), which 'must be satisfied with messages that do not engage' and 'are interested only in a cease-fire' (ibid.: 99). Obviously, this Luhmannite notion of *understanding* is diametrically opposed to the Habermasian interpretation of the concept. Luhmann abandons Habermas's normative belief in communicative rationality and redesignates the concept of understanding to a

---

1 Official translation: 'ecology of ignorance'.
2 Official translation: 'who must understand each other'.

condition where the fundamental incompatibility between different opinions is *sufficiently invisible*, that is where communication partners have managed to find formulae which leave sufficient room for individual (contradictory) interpretation. This is exactly what the discourse of ecological modernisation achieves. Obviously, the main obstacle to communicative cease-fire in Luhmann's sense is any kind of ethics and ideology including all forms of rational fundamentalism. In Luhmann's words, they should be introduced into the ecological discourse 'only when the desired result is the breakdown of communication' (ibid.: 99). Ecological modernisation therefore strictly renounces eco-ethics, ecological fundamentalism and any kind of ideological leaning.

So we may conclude the theory of post-ecologist politics by suggesting that the currently dominant discourse of ecological modernisation – quite irrespective of its effects for the physical environment – has to be considered, first and foremost, as a peace-keeping strategy. And contrary to what ecologist criticism seems to imply, ecological modernisation has not been forced onto contemporary society or purposefully installed in order to serve only the interests of some social sectors. Instead, it has emerged by means of evolution as a societal practice that is *beneficial to all parties involved*. It offers an escape root for ecologists who failed to provide a theoretically convincing and politically effective ideology. It respects the needs of the fading subject by preserving modernist illusions. It respects the dilemma of a politics of nature that, for the lack of better criteria, takes refuge in economic criteria. And it respects the interests of those whose constantly growing wealth and ever more unsustainable lifestyle is possible only at the expense of radical social exclusion. What ecological modernisation achieves is the continuation of communication in a context that obstructs Habermasian understanding.

Most certainly, Hajer is fully correct with his suggestion that 'ecological modernisation will set the tone of environmental policy-making in the years to come' (1995: 262). But the reason for this is not, as ecological modernisation theorists would like to believe, that it paves the way to ecological sustainability. And it is equally erroneous to argue that this developmental practice will stay with us *although* it is utterly inappropriate. Ecological modernisation is here to stay because it is a highly appropriate lubricant for the smooth transition to a politics which (re-) distributes the opportunities of life according to the principles of wealth and power. The discourse of ecological modernisation demonstrates how, borrowing Luhmann's words, 'society develops figures of thought with which it can endure the unobservability of the world and allow intransparency to become productive' (Luhmann 1998b: 112).

Epilogue

This study was an intellectual experiment. It was intended to be an ecologist's enquiry into social theory, yet in the course of the investigations its ecologist foundations gradually melted away. The starting point for my explorations were the assumptions that, since the late 1980s, ecological thought, the eco-movement and ecological politics have gone through a phase of fundamental transformation, and that these changes have so far not been conceptualised and explained in any satisfactory way. So I undertook the attempt to provide a comprehensive theory for what Beck simply called 'the crisis of the ecological crisis' (see Epigraph). But contrary to many similar attempts (e.g. Hayward 1995; Jagtenberg and McKie 1997; Macnaghten and Urry 1998; Barry 1999), I decided 'to do just what Copernicus did in attempting to explain the celestial movements'. Because I found that ecological theory 'could make no progress by assuming' that ecological concern and activism revolve around the Other of society, I 'reversed the process, and tried the experiment of assuming' that the ecological discourse revolves around the idea of the human Self and the way it constructs its identity (compare Epigraph). This rearrangement of the basic parameters opened a new perspective on to ecological issues. It shifted the focus of attention from specific conditions in the physical environment which, according to ecologists, constitute objectively existing ecological problems, to certain cultural parameters which determine the way in which physical environmental conditions and their change are socially perceived and constructed as problematic or unproblematic. Where other theorists diagnose the beginning of the age of ecology, my experiment suggested that the contemporary eco-movement represents the last phase of a rearguard battle trying to defend a world-view that is irretrievably lost. Where the eco-sociological mainstream tries to theorise the protection of nature and the transition to ecological sustainability, my investigations centred around the abolition of nature and the dissolution of the ecologist problem. And whilst in the literature there is a widespread view that ecology has come to maturity and emerged as an ideological masterframe and independent rationality, I suggested that contemporary society's ecological discourse and politics of nature can only be interpreted within the framework of a theory of *post-ecologist* politics.

Ecologists will undoubtedly find this post-ecologist model and its implications completely unacceptable. Ecologically committed environmental sociologists will criticise the approach developed in this book for its 'rarefied level of abstraction'. They will ask for empirical evidence. They will want to know how one can argue that ecological thinking and activism are essentially about issues of identity, when it is so blatantly evident that they are about quite concrete physical issues in very real local life-worlds or habitats. Furthermore, they will wonder how one can seriously suggest that the ecological problem has dissolved, whilst at the same time forests are being cut down, species extinguished, genetic codes manipulated, whole human populations contaminated, etc., etc. They will say that they are 'sick and tired' of postmodernist theorists who confine themselves to deconstructing established patterns of thinking and policy making, and consistently fail to come up with concrete suggestions. They will reproduce all the well-known arguments, which have been constantly repeated for well over two decades. Time and again, contemporary sociology has had to confront the criticism that, instead of generating concrete knowledge about society on the basis of which actual problems may then be addressed in a pragmatic way, it has retreated to the discussion of irresolvable philosophical problems, with the question of truth being a particularly popular hobby horse. But, especially, this issue of absolute truth, so the argument runs, is really completely irrelevant, for in order to cope with our concrete life-world problems, we factually only require common-sense truths and firmly established beliefs, both of which are readily available. These arguments are anything but new. In a way, they are all perfectly justified, and I might even add that I fully share them myself – but only, and this is a most important qualification, only from an ecologist point of view, that is only as long as the ecologist beliefs and problem perceptions are regarded as sacrosanct.

But within the academic debate, it must be allowed to think the (ecologically) impossible, that is to discard all rules of ecological correctness. There is no other way of revealing the unquestioned assumptions underlying the established societal patterns of constructing and processing so-called *environmental* problems. It is true that the theory of post-ecologism does not make political prescriptions. But it is not true that it denies that there is considerable human-induced change in the physical environment which leads to the extinction of species, rising sea-levels, desertification, contamination, and so on. Also, the theory of post-ecologism does not deny that individuals, communities and whole societies have to deal with concrete life-world issues, and that physical environmental change may represent unprecedented challenges which will have to be confronted. The message of this book is not that there are no problems, that nothing needs to be done, or that nothing can be done. But from its second-order perspective, the theory of post-ecologism does not ask how these problems (for ecological or whatever other reasons) *ought to be addressed*. Instead, it asks how and why contemporary societies frame certain issues as ecological problems, and how they then *factually* process them.

As regards the question of empirical evidence, it may be repeated once again that is not possible to provide empirical evidence for a theory of how contemporary society constructs its empirical issues. It is the nature of a theory that it is theoretical, and the results it produces are not absolute truths but offers of plausibility, which have to compete with other such offers. Their validity depends on the cultural parameters of their construction, and it expires at the same time as these parameters themselves do. With regard to the demand for concrete political prescriptions, it might be pointed out once again that it is wrong to assume that society in any way depends on such prescriptions. Well-meaning social and political theorists tend to overestimate their societal importance. Whilst their recommendations have (perhaps fortunately) in most cases been ignored, societal development has so far never come to a halt, or reached a point where it could not continue without taking advice from political theorists. Factually, there has never been a normative vacuum. Action and development have always taken place, everywhere and under all circumstances. Against this background it seems perfectly legitimate to interrupt the constant flow of concrete political prescriptions and lean back for a while in order to observe and theorise. Whilst observation and interpretation can certainly not be a substitute for concrete policy making, it is equally impossible for the latter to substitute for the former.

On the basis of the theory of post-ecologist politics, we can analyse the ideological foundations of ecological thought and convincingly explain the relative failure of traditional eco-politics. We can interpret the past and the present of the ecological issue, and the 'crisis of the ecological crisis'. We can, furthermore, use this interpretation as a basis for speculations about both the future of the ecological issue and the further development of the politics of nature. A theory of post-ecologist politics provides the theoretical tools (though not normative standards) for the analysis and the critique (in the Kantian sense) of ecological prescriptions. Well-meaning ecologists and less well-meaning fundamentalists of all thinkable ideological provenance (including neo-conservatives and neo-liberals) will use concepts of naturalness to legitimate their political interests. A theory of post-ecologist politics can reveal that in the post-natural condition, no concept of nature and no eco-ethics, however rational and legitimate they may present themselves as, can represent a truly common good or interest. On the contrary, such concepts always seek to secure opportunities in life for some at the cost of taking them away from others. In the age of post-ecologism this is, of course, no longer to be criticised as immoral, and Horkheimer and Adorno's talk of the 'new barbarism' therefore cannot be sustained.

So, beyond its specifically ecologist point of reference, the theory of post-ecologist politics may be considered as a critical tool applicable to any kind of ideology which bases its political demands on allegedly irreducible concepts of nature. But it can never provide a normative critique in the first-order, moral or political sense. Only in one respect, and then only indirectly, can this theory be said to transcend its self-limitation to analysis and description: by exposing the implications of a post-ecologist politics of nature, a theory of post-ecologist politics can indirectly appeal to the remains of the humanist and ecologist belief systems and tradition of thought. It does not have the resources itself to describe the post-ecologist condition as barbaric, but as long as its predecessor or counterpart survives, it can try to imply such a judgement. To the extent that a theory of post-ecologist politics appeals to normative criteria which it cannot generate itself and which it actually describes as contingent, it is parasitic on ecologism. *Vive l'écologisme!*

References

Achterberg, Wouter (1993) 'Can Liberal Democracy Survive the Environmental Crisis? Sustainability, Liberal Neutrality and Overlapping Consensus', in Dobson and Lucardie 1993, pp. 81–101.

Adorno, Theodor W. (1973) *Negative Dialectics* (trans. E. B.Ashton), London: Routledge.

Adorno, Theodor W., Albert, Hans, Dahrendorf, Ralf, Habermas, Jürgen, Pilot, Harald and Popper, Karl R. (1969) *Der Positivismusstreit in der deutschen Soziologie*, Hamburg: Luchterhand.

Albrow, Martin (1996) *The Global Age*, Cambridge: Polity.

Atkinson, Adrian (1991) *Principles of Political Ecology*, London: Belhaven Press.

Bahro, Rudolf (1986) *Building the Green Movement*, London: GMP.

Baker, Susan (ed.) (1997) *The Politics of Sustainable Development*, London and New York: Routledge.

Baringhorst, Sigrid (1996) 'Das Spektakel als Politikon. Massenmediale Inszenierungen von Protest- und Hilfsaktionen', *Forschungsjournal Neue Soziale Bewegungen*, vol. 9, no. 1, pp. 15–25.

Baringhorst, Sigrid (1997) 'Flucht in den symbolischen Inszenierungszauber', *Frankfurter Rundschau*, 16 August 1997, p. 14.

Barry, John (1999) *Rethinking Green Politics: Nature, Virtue and Progress*, London, Thousand Oaks, CA and New Delhi: Sage.

Bauman, Zygmunt (1993) *Postmodern Ethics*, Oxford and Cambridge, MA: Basil Blackwell.

Bauman, Zygmunt (1999) *In Search of Politics*, Cambridge: Polity.

Beck, Ulrich (1986) *Risikogesellschaft. Auf dem Weg in eine andere Moderne*, Frankfurt: Suhrkamp.

Beck, Ulrich (1988) *Gegengifte. Die Organisierte Unverantwortlichkeit*, Frankfurt: Suhrkamp.

Beck, Ulrich (1992) *Risk Society: Towards a New Modernity* (trans. Mark Ritter), London, Newbury Park, MA and New Delhi: Sage.

Beck, Ulrich (1993) *Die Erfindung des Politischen*, Frankfurt: Suhrkamp.

Beck, Ulrich (1995a) *Ecological Politics in an Age of Risk* (trans. Amos Weisz), Cambridge: Polity.

Beck, Ulrich (1995b) *Ecological Enlightenment: Essays on the Politics of the Risk Society* (trans. Mark Ritter), New Jersey: Humanities Press.

Beck, Ulrich (1996) 'Risk Society and the Provident State', in Scott Lash *et al.* 1996, pp. 27–43.

Beck, Ulrich (1997a) *The Reinvention of Politics: Rethinking Modernity in the Global Social Order* (trans. Mark Ritter), Cambridge: Polity.

Beck, Ulrich (ed.) (1997b) *Kinder der Freiheit*, Frankfurt: Suhrkamp.

Beck, Ulrich (1997c) 'Global Risk Politics', in Jacobs 1997a, pp. 18–33.

Beck, Ulrich (1998a) *Democracy without Enemies* (trans. Mark Ritter), Cambridge: Polity.

Beck, Ulrich (ed.) (1998b) *Politik der Globalisierung*, Frankfurt: Suhrkamp.

Beck, Ulrich (1999) *What is Globalization?* (trans. Patrick Camiller), Cambridge: Polity.

Beck, Ulrich (ed.) (2000a) *Die Zukunft von Arbeit und Demokratie*, Frankfurt: Suhrkamp.

Beck, Ulrich (2000b) *The Brave New World of Work*, Cambridge: Polity.

Beck, Ulrich, Giddens, Anthony and Lash, Scott (1994) *Reflexive Modernization: Politics, Tradition and Aesthetics in the Modern Social Order*, Cambridge: Polity.

Beck, Ulrich, Hajer, Maarten and Kesselring, Sven (eds.) (1999) *Der unscharfe Ort der Politik. Empirische Fallstudien zur Theorie der reflexiven Modernisierung*, Opladen: Leske and Budrich.

Benton, Ted (1993) *Natural Relations: Ecology, Animal Rights and Social Justice*, London: Verso.

Benton, Ted (1994) 'Biology and Social Theory in the Environmental Debate', in Redclift and Benton 1994, pp. 28–50.

Benton, Ted (1997) 'Beyond Left and Right? Ecological Politics, Capitalism and Modernity', in Jacobs 1997a, pp. 34–46.

Blowers, Andrew (1997) 'Environmental Policy: Ecological Modernisation or the Risk Society?', in *Urban Studies*, vol. 34, nos 5–6, pp. 845–71.

Blühdorn, Ingolfur (1995) 'Campaigning for Nature: Environmental Pressure Groups in Germany and Generational Change in the Ecology Movement', in Blühdorn et al. 1995, pp. 167–220.

Blühdorn, Ingolfur (1997) 'A Theory of Post-Ecologist Politics', *Environmental Politics*, vol. 6, no. 3, Autumn 1997, pp. 125–47.

Blühdorn, Ingolfur (2000) 'The Silent Counter-Revolution. Political Ecology and the Neo-Materialist Agenda', in *Social Science Forum Journal*, http://www.social-science-forum.org

Blühdorn, Ingolfur (2001) 'Green Futures? A Future for the Greens?', in Goodbody 2001 (forthcoming).

Blühdorn, Ingolfur, Krause, Frank and Scharf, Thomas (eds.) (1995) *The Green Agenda: Environmental Politics and Policies in Germany*, Keele: Keele University Press.

Böhme, Gernot (1992) *Natürlich Natur. Über Natur im Zeitalter ihrer technischen Reproduzierbarkeit*, Frankfurt: Suhrkamp.

Bohnke, Ben-Alexander (1997) *Abschied von der Natur. Die Zukunft des Lebens ist Technik*, Düsseldorf and Munich: Metropolitan Verlag.

Bramwell, Anna (1989) *Ecology in the 20th Century*, New Haven, CT and London: Yale University Press.

Bramwell, Anna (1994) *The Fading of the Greens*, New Haven, CT and London: Yale University Press.

Brand, Karl-Werner (ed.) (1997) *Nachhaltige Entwicklung. Eine Herausforderung an die Soziologie*, Opladen: Leske and Budrich.

Brand, Karl-Werner (1999a) 'Transformation der Ökologiebewegung', in Klein et al. 1999, pp. 237–56.

Brand, Karl-Werner (1999b) 'Dialectics of Institutionalisation: The Transformation of the Environmental Movement in Germany', in Rootes 1999, pp. 35–58.

Braun, Bruce and Castree, Noel (eds.) (1998) *Remaking Reality: Nature at the Millenium*, London and New York: Routledge.

Breuer, Stefan (1995) *Die Gesellschaft des Verschwindens: von der Selbstzerstörung der technischen Zivilisation*, Hamburg: Rotbuch Verlag.

Bruckmeier, Karl (1997) 'NGO-Netzwerke als globale Umweltakteure', in Brand (ed.) 1997, pp. 131–48.

Bruntland, Gro Harlem (1987) *Our Common Future. World Commission on Environment and Development*, Oxford and New York: Oxford University Press.

Byrne, David (1999) *Social Exclusion*, Buckingham: Open University Press.

Carson, Rachel (1962) *Silent Spring*, London: Penguin.

Carter, Neil (1997) 'Prospects: The Parties and the Environment in the UK', in Jacobs 1997a, pp. 192–205.

Christoff, Peter (1996) 'Ecological Modernisation, Ecological Modernities', *Environmental Politics*, vol. 5, no. 3, Autumn 1996, pp. 476–500.

Conley, Verena A. (1997) *Ecopolitics: The Environment in Poststructuralist Thought*, London and New York: Routledge.

Cronon, William (ed.) (1995) *Uncommon Ground: Toward Reinventing Nature*, New York: W. W. Norton.

Dalton, Russell (1994) *The Green Rainbow: Environmental Groups in Western Europe*, New Haven, CT and London: Yale University Press.

Daly, Herman (1995) 'On Wilfried Beckerman's Critique of Sustainable Development', *Environmental Values*, vol. 4, no. 1, pp. 49–55.

Darier, Éric (ed.) (1999) *Discourses of the Environment*, Oxford and Massachusetts: Blackwell.

Demeritt, David (1998) 'Science, Social Constructivism and Nature', in Braun and Castree 1998, pp. 173–93.

Dickens, Peter (1992) *Society and Nature: Towards a Green Social Theory*, New York, London, Toronto, Sydney, Tokyo and Signapore: Harvester Wheatsheaf.

Dickens, Peter (1996) *Reconstructing Nature: Alienation, Emancipation and the Division of Labour*, London and New York: Routledge.

Dobson, Andrew (1990) *Green Political Thought*, London: Unwin Hyman.

Dobson, Andrew (1993) 'Critical Theory and Green Politics', in Dobson and Lucardie, pp. 190–209.

Dobson, Andrew (1995) *Green Political Thought*, (2nd edn), London and New York: Routledge.

Dobson, Andrew (1996) 'Environmental Sustainabilities: An Analysis and a Typology, *Environmental Politics*, vol. 5, no. 3, Autumn 1996, pp. 401–28.

Dobson, Andrew (1998) *Justice and the Environment: Conceptions of Environmental Sustainability and dimensions of Social Justice*, Oxford University Press.

Dobson, Andrew (ed.) (1999) *Fairness and Futurity: Essays on Environmental Sustainability and Social Justice*, Oxford 1999, Oxford University Press.

Dobson, Andrew and Lucardie, Paul (eds.) (1993) *The Politics of Nature: Explorations in Green Political Thought*, London and New York: Routledge.

Doherty, Brian (1999) 'Paving the Way: The Rise of Direct Action against Road-Building and the Changing Character of British Environmentalism', *Political Studies*, vol. 47, no. 2, pp. 275–91.

Dryzek, John (1987) *Rational Ecology: Environment and Political Economy*, Oxford: Basil Blackwell.

Dryzek, John (1990) 'Green Reason: Communicative Ethics for the Biosphere' *Environmental Ethics*, vol. 12, pp. 195–210.

Dryzek, John (1995) 'Political and Ecological Communication', *Environmental Politics*, vol. 4, no. 4, Winter 1995, pp. 13–30.

Dryzek, John (1996) 'Strategies of Ecological Democratization', in Lafferty and Meadowcroft 1996, pp. 108–23.

Dryzek, John (1997) *The Politics of the Earth: Environmental Discourses*, Oxford: Oxford University Press.

Dunlap, Riley and Catton, William (1994) 'Struggling with Human Exemptionalism: The Rise, Decline and Revitalization of Environmental Sociology', *The American Sociologist*, Spring 1994, pp. 5–30.

Eckersley, Robyn (1990) 'Habermas and Green Political Thought: Two Roads Diverging', *Theory and Society*, vol. 19, pp. 739–76.

Eckersley, Robyn (1992) *Environmentalism and Political Theory: Towards an Ecocentric Approach*,

London: University College London Press.

Eder, Klaus (1996a) *The Social Construction of Nature*, London: Sage.

Eder, Klaus (1996b) 'The Institutionalisation of Environmentalism: Ecological Discourse and the Second Transformation of the Public Sphere', in Lash *et al.* 1996, pp. 203–23.

Elliot, Robert (1997) *Faking Nature: The Ethics of Environmental Restauration*, London and New York: Routledge.

Foster, John (ed.) (1997) *Valuing Nature? Ethics, Economics and the Environment*, London and New York: Routledge.

Frankland, Gene and Schoonmaker, Donald (1992) *Between Protest and Power: The Green Party in Germany*, Boulder, CO, San Francisco and Oxford: Westview Press.

Gare, Arran E. (1995) *Postmodernism and the Environmental Crisis*, London and New York: Routledge.

Gerhards, Jürgen (1984) *Wahrheit und Ideologie. Eine kritische Einführung in die Systemtheorie von Niklas Luhmann*, Cologne: Janus Presse.

Giddens, Anthony (1990) *The Consequences of Modernity*, Cambridge: Polity.

Giddens, Anthony (1994) *Beyond Left and Right: The Future of Radical Politics*, Cambridge: Polity.

Giddens, Anthony (1998) *The Third Way: The Renewal of Social Democracy*, Cambridge: Polity.

Giddens, Anthony (1999) *Runaway World: How Globalisation is Reshaping our Lives*, London: Profile Books.

Goldblatt, David (1996) *Social Theory and the Environment*, Cambridge: Polity.

Goldsmith, Edward (1988) *The Great U-Turn: De-industrializing Society*, Bideford: Green Books.

Goodbody, Axel (ed.) (2001) *Visions, Dreams, Realities. Environmentalism in Contemporary German Culture*, Oxford: Berghahn (forthcoming).

Goodin, Robert E. (1992) *Green Political Theory*, Cambridge: Polity.

Gouldson, Andrew and Murphy, Joseph (1997) 'Ecological Modernisation: Restructuring Industrial Economies', in Jacobs 1997a, pp. 74–86.

Görg, Christoff (1992) *Neue Soziale Bewegungen und Kritische Theorie. Eine Aufarbeitung gesellschaftstheoretischer Erklärungsansätze*, Wiesbaden: Deutscher Universitäts Verlag.

Gorz, André (1994) *Capitalism, Socialism, Ecology*, London: Verso.

Gray, John (1997) *Endgames: Questions in Late Modern Political Thought*, Cambridge: Polity.

Gregg, Paul and Wadsworth, Jonathan (eds.) (1999) *The State of Working Britain*, Manchester and New York: Manchester University Press.

Grove-White, Robin (1997) 'Environment, Risk and Democracy', in Jacobs 1997, pp. 109–22.

Gruhl, Herbert (1997) *Ein Planet wird geplündert. Die Schreckensbilanz unserer Politik*, Frankfurt: Fischer.

Grundmann, Reiner (1990) 'Luhmann Conservative, Luhmann Progressive', European University Institute Florence, Dept. of Law, Working Paper Law 1990/7.

Gumbrecht, Hans-Ulrich and Pfeiffer, K. Ludwig (eds.) (1988) *Materialität der Kommunikation*, Frankfurt: Suhrkamp.

Habermas, Jürgen (1971) 'Theorie der Gesellschaft oder Sozialtechnologie? Eine Auseinandersetzung mit Niklas Luhmann', in J. Habermas and N. Luhmann 1971, pp. 142–290.

Habermas, Jürgen (1981) 'New Social Movements', *Telos*, vol. 49, pp. 33–7.

Habermas, Jürgen (1984) *The Theory of Communicative Action. Volume 1: Reason and the Rationalization of Society* (trans. Thomas McCarthy), Boston: Beacon Press.

Habermas, Jürgen (1987a) *The Theory of Communicative Action. Volume 2: Lifeworld and System: A Critique of Functionalist Reason* (trans. Thomas McCarthy), Cambridge: Polity.

Habermas, Jürgen (1987b) *The Philosophical Discourse of Modernity: Twelve Lectures* (trans. Frederick Lawrence), Cambridge: Polity.

Habermas, Jürgen (1996) *Die Einbeziehung des Anderen. Studien zur Politischen Theorie*, Frankfurt: Suhrkamp.

Habermas, Jürgen (1998) *Die Postnationale Konstellation. Politische Essays*, Frankfurt: Suhrkamp.

Habermas, Jürgen and Luhmann, Niklas (1971) *Theorie der Gesellschaft oder Sozialtechnologie – Was leistet die Systemforschung?*, Frankfurt: Suhrkamp.

Hajer, Maarten A. (1995) *The Politics of Environmental Discourse: Ecological Modernisation and the Policy Process*, Oxford: Clarendon Press.

Hajer, Maarten A. (1996) 'Ecological Modernisation as Cultural Politics', in Lash *et al.* 1996, pp. 246–68.

Hamm, Bernd (1996) *Struktur moderner Gesellschaften*, Opladen: Leske and Budrich.

Hannigan, John (1995) *Environmental Sociology: A Social Constructionist Perspective*, London and New York: Routledge.

Haraway, Donna (1994) 'A Game of Cat's Cradle: Science Studies, Feminist Theory, Cultural Studies', *Configurations*, vol. 1, p. 59–71.

Hayward, Tim (1995) *Ecological Thought: An Introduction*, Cambridge: Polity.

Hellmann, Kai-Uwe (1996a) editor's introduction to Luhmann 1996a, pp. 7–45.

Hellmann, Kai-Uwe (1996b) *Systemtheorie und neue soziale Bewegungen. Identitätsprobleme in der Risikogesellschaft*, Opladen: Westdeutscher Verlag.

Hinterberger, Friedrich, Luks, F. and Stewen, M. (1996) *Ökologische Wirtschaftspolitik. Zwischen Ökodiktatur und Umweltkatastrophe*, Berlin, Basel and Boston, MA: Birkhäuser Verlag.

Hjelmar, Ulf (1996) *The Political Practice of Environmental Organizations*, Aldershot, Brookfield, IL, Hong Kong, Singapore and Sydney: Avebury.

Holland, Alan (1997) 'Substitutability: Or, Why Strong Sustainability is Weak and Absurdly Strong Sustainability is not Absurd', in Foster 1997, pp. 119–34.

Horkheimer, Max and Adorno, Theodor W. (1972) *Dialectic of Enlightenment* (trans. John Cumming), New York: Herder and Herder.

Horkheimer, Max (1947) *Eclipse of Reason*, New York: Oxford University Press.

Huber, Joseph (1982) *Die verlorene Unschuld der Ökologie. Neue Technologien und superindustrielle Entwicklung*, Frankfurt: Fischer.

Huber, Joseph (1985) *Die Regenbogengesellschaft. Ökologie und Sozialpolitik*, Frankfurt: Fischer.

Huber, Joseph (1989) *Technikbilder. Weltanschauliche Weichenstellungen der Technik- und Umweltpolitik*, Opladen: Westdeutscher Verlag.

Huber, Joseph (1991) *Umwelt Unternehmen. Weichenstellungen für eine ökologische Marktwirtschaft*, Frankfurt: Fischer.

Huber, Joseph (1993) 'Ökologische Modernisierung: Zwischen bürokratischem und zivilge-sellschaftli-chem Handeln', in Prittwitz 1993a, pp. 51–69.

Hülsberg, Werner (1988) *The German Greens: A Social and Political Profile*, London and New York: Verso.

Inglehart, Ronald (1977) *The Silent Revolution: Changing Values and Political Styles Among Western Publics*, Princeton, NJ: Princeton University Press.

Inglehart, Ronald (1990) *Culture Shift in Advanced Industrial Society*, Princeton, NJ: Princeton University Press.

Inglehart, Ronald (1997) *Modernization and Postmodernization. Cultural, Economic, and Poiltical Change in 43 Societies*, Princeton, NJ: Princeton University Press.

Jacobs, Michael (ed.) (1997a) *Greening the Millennium? The New Politics of the Environment*, Oxford: Blackwell.

Jacobs, Michael (1997b) 'Environmental Valuation, Deliberative Democracy and Public

Decision-making Institutions', in Foster 1997, pp. 211–31.

Jagtenberg, Tom and McKie, D. (1997) *Eco-Impacts and the Greening of Postmodernity*, London, Thousand Oaks, CA and New Delhi: Sage.

Jahn, Detlef (1997) 'Green Politics and Parties in Germany', in Jacobs 1997a, pp. 174–82.

Jahn, Thomas and Wehling, Peter (eds.) (1990) *Ökologie von Rechts. Nationalismus und Umweltschutz bei der Neuen Rechten und den 'Republikanern'*, Frankfurt: Campus.

Jamison, Andrew (1996) 'The Shaping of the Global Environmental Agenda: The Role of Non-Governmental Organisations', in Lash *et al.* 1996, pp. 224–45.

Jänicke, Martin (ed.) (1978) *Umweltpolitik. Beiträge zur Politologie des Umweltschutzes*, Opladen: Westdeutscher Verlag.

Jänicke, Martin (1984) 'Umweltpolitische Prävention als ökologische Modernisierung und Strukturpolitik', Wissenschaftszentrum Berlin (IIUG dp 84–1).

Jänicke, Martin (1986) *Staatsversagen. Die Ohnmacht der Politik in der Industriegesellschaft*, Munich: Piper.

Jänicke, Martin (1988) 'Ökologische Modernisierung. Optionen und Restriktionen präventiver Umweltpolitik', in Simonis 1988, pp. 12–26.

Jänicke, Martin (1990) 'Erfolgsbedingungen von Umweltpolitik im internationalen Vergleich', *Zeitschrift für Umweltpolitik und Umweltrecht*, no. 13, pp. 213–32.

Jänicke, Martin (1993) 'Ökologische und politische Modernisierung in entwickelten Industriegesellschaften', in Prittwitz 1993a, pp. 15–30.

Jesinghausen, Martin (1995) 'General Election to the German Bundestag on 16 October 1994: German Pragmatists in Conservative Embrace Or a New Era for German Parliamentary Democracy', *Environmental Politics*, vol. 4, no. 1, Spring 1995, pp. 108–35.

Kant, Immanuel (1787) *Critique of Pure Reason*, (trans. J. M. D. Meiklejohn), London: Dent and Sons, Everyman's Library.

Kant, Immanuel (1793) 'On the Common Saying: This may be True in Theory, but it does Not Apply in Practice!', in *Kant: Political Writings*, ed. Hans Reiss, trans. H. B. Nisbet, Cambridge: Cambridge University Press.

Kelly, Petra (1984) *Fighting for Hope*, London: Chatto and Windus, Hogarth Press.

Kitsuse, J. and Spector, M. (1981) 'The Labeling of Social Problems' in Rubington and Weinberg 1981, pp. 198–206.

Klandermans, Bert (ed.) (1989) *Organizing for Change*, Greenwich, CT: JAI Press.

Klein, Ansgar, Legrand, Hans-Josef and Leif, Thomas (eds.) (1999) *Neue Soziale Bwegegungen. Impulse, Bilanzen und Perspektiven*, Opladen: Westdeutscher Verlag.

Kneer, Georg (1996) *Rationalisierung, Disziplinierung und Differenzierung. Sozialtheorie und Zeitdiagnose bei Habermas, Foucault und Luhmann*, Opladen: Westdeutscher Verlag.

Krieger, David J. (1996) *Einführung in die allgemeine Systemtheorie*, Munich: Wilhelm Fink.

Krohn, Wolfgang and Küppers, Günther (1989) *Die Selbstorganisation der Wissenschaft*, Frankfurt: Suhrkamp.

Lafferty, William and Meadowcroft, James (eds.) (1996) *Democracy and the Environment: Problems and Prospects*, Cheltenham and Brookfield, IL :Edward Elgar.

Latour, Bruno (1993) *We Have Never Been Modern* (trans. Catherine Porter), New York, London, Toronto, Sydney, Tokyo and Signapore: Hervester Wheatsheaf.

Lash, Scott (1993) 'Reflexive Modernization: The Aesthetic Dimension', *Theory, Culture & Society* no. 10, pp. 1–23.

Lash, Scott, Szerszynski, Bronislaw and Wynne, Brian (eds.) (1996) *Risk, Environment and Modernity. Towards a New Ecology*, London, Thousand Oaks, CA and New Delhi: Sage.

Levitas, Ruth (1998) *The Inclusive Society? Social Exclusion and New Labour*, Basingstoke: Macmillan.

Link, Thomas (1986) *Zum Begriff der Natur in der Gesellschaftstheorie Theodor W. Adornos*, Cologne and Vienna: Böhlau Verlag.

Lucardie, Paul (1997) 'Greening and Un-Greening the Netherlands', in Jacobs 1997a, pp. 183–91.

Luhmann, Niklas (1985) 'Die Autopoiesis des Bewußtseins', *Soziale Welt*, vol. 36, pp. 402–46.

Luhmann, Niklas (1986) *Ökologische Kommunikation. Kann die moderne Gesellschaft sich auf ökologische Gefährdungen einstellen?* Opladen: Westdeutscher Verlag.

Luhmann, Niklas (1987) *Soziologische Aufklärung. vol. 4: Beiträge zur funktionalen Differenzierung der Gesellschaft*, Opladen: Westdeutscher Verlag.

Luhmann, Niklas (1988a) *Die Wirtschaft der Gesellschaft*, Frankfurt: Suhrkamp.

Luhmann, Niklas (1988b) 'Wie ist das Bewußtsein an Kommunikation beteiligt?', in Gumbrecht *et al.* 1988, pp. 884–905.

Luhmann, Niklas (1989) *Ecological Communication* (trans. and introduced by John Bednarz), Cambridge: Polity.

Luhmann, Niklas (1990) *Die Wissenschaft der Gesellschaft*, Frankfurt: Suhrkamp.

Luhmann, Niklas (1991) 'Am Ende der kritischen Soziologie', *Zeitschrift für Soziologie*, vol. 20, pp. 147–52.

Luhmann, Niklas (1993a) *Das Recht der Gesellschaft*, Frankfurt: Suhrkamp.

Luhmann, Niklas (1993b) *Risk: A Sociological Theory* (trans. Rhodes Barrett), Berlin and New York: Walter de Gruyter.

Luhmann, Niklas (1995) *Social Systems* (trans. John Bednarz and Dirk Baecker), Stamford, CA: Stamford University Press.

Luhmann, Niklas (1996a) *Protest: Systemtheorie und soziale Bewegungen* (ed. and introduced by Kai-Uwe Hellmann) Frankfurt: Suhrkamp.

Luhmann, Niklas (1996b) *Die Realität der Massenmedien*, Opladen: Westdeutscher Verlag.

Luhmann, Niklas (1998a) *Die Gesellschaft der Gesellschaft*, Frankfurt: Suhrkamp.

Luhmann, Niklas (1998b) *Observations on Modernity* (trans. William Whobrey), Stamford, CA: Stamford University Press.

Macnaghten, Phil and Urry, John (1998) *Contested Natures*, London, Thousand Oaks, CA and New Delhi: Sage.

Maffesoli, Michel (1995) *The Time of the Tribes: The Decline of Individualism in Mass Society*, London, Thousand Oaks, CA and New Delhi: Sage.

Marcuse, Herbert (1941) *Reason and Revolution*, Oxford: Oxford University Press.

Markovits, Andrei S. and Silvia, S. J. (1997) 'Changing Shades of Green: Political Identity and Alternative Politics in United Germany', *Debatte*, vol. 5, no. 1, pp. 49–66.

Martell, Luke (1994) *Ecology and Society. An Introduction*, Cambridge: Polity.

Marx, Karl (1977) *Selected Writings*, ed. David McLellan, Oxford: Oxford University Press.

Mathews, Freya (1991) *The Ecological Self*, London: Routledge.

Mathews, Freya (ed.) (1996) *Ecology and Democracy*, special issue of *Environmental Politics*, vol. 4, no. 4, Winter 1995.

Maxeiner, Dirk and Miersch, Michael (1996) *Öko-Optimismus*, Düsseldorf and Munich: Metropolitan Verlag.

McCarthy, James (1998) 'Environmentalism, Wise Use and the Nature of Accumulation in the rural West', in Braun and Castree 1998, pp. 126–49.

McKibben, Bill (1990) *The End of Nature*, London: Penguin.

McMichael, Philip (1996) *Development and Social Change: A Global Perspective*, Thousand Oaks, CA, London and New Delhi: Pine Forge.

Meadows, Donella, Meadows, Dennis, Randers, Jørgen and Behrens, William (1974) *The Limits to Growth. A Report for the Club of Rome's Project on the Predicament of Mankind*, London: Pan.

Melucci, Alberto (1989) *Nomads of the Present: Social Movements and Individual Needs in Contemporary Society*, London: Hutchinson.

Melucci, Alberto (1996) *The Playing Self: Person and Meaning in the Planetary Society*, Cambridge: Cambridge University Press.

Merchant, Carolyn (1980) *The Death of Nature: Women, Ecology and the Scientific Revolution*, San Francisco: Harper and Row.

Metzner, Andreas (1993) *Probleme sozio-ökologischer Systemtheorie. Natur und Gesellschaft in der Soziologie Luhmanns*, Opladen: Westdeutscher Verlag.

Miller, Max (1994) 'Intersystemic Discourse and Co-ordinated Dissent: A Critique of Luhmann's Concept of Ecological Communication', *Theory, Culture & Society*, vol. 11, pp. 101–21.

Mol, Arthur (1995) *The Refinement of Production: Ecological Modernization Theory and the Chemical Industry*, Utrecht: van Arkel.

Mol, Arthur (1996) 'Ecological Modernisation and Institutional Reflexivity: Environmental Reform in the Late Modern Age', *Environmental Politics*, vol. 5, no. 2, Summer 1996, pp. 302–23.

Mol, Arthur (1998) 'Ecological Modernization Theory in Debate: A Review', paper presented at the 14th World Congress of Sociology, Montreal, July 1998.

Müller-Brandeck-Boquet, Gisela (1993) 'Von der Fähigkeit des deutschen Föderalismus zur Umweltpolitik', in Prittwitz 1993, pp. 103–12.

Murphy, Raymond (1994) *Rationality and Nature: A Sociological Inquiry into a Changing Relationship*, Boulder, CO: Westview.

Murphy, Raymond (1997) *Sociology and Nature: Social Action in Context*, Boulder, CO: Westview.

Neale, Alan (1997) 'Organising Environmental Self-Regulation: Liberal Governmentality and the Persuit of Ecological Modernisation in Europe', *Environmental Politics*, vol. 6, no. 4, pp. 1–24.

Neckel, Sighard and Wolf, Jürgen (1994) 'The Fascination of Amorality: Luhmann's Theory of Morality and its Resonances among German Intellectuals', *Theory, Culture & Society*, vol. 11, pp. 69–99.

O'Neill, Michael (1997) *Green Parties and Political Change in Contemporary Europe: New Politics, Old Predicaments*, Aldershot: Ashgate.

Papadakis, Elim (1996) *Environmental Politics and Institutional Change*, Cambridge: Cambridge University Press.

Pepper, David (1993) *Eco-Socialism: From Deep Ecology to Social Justice*, London and New York: Routledge.

Poguntke, Thomas (1993) 'Goodbye to Movement Politics? Organisational Adaptation of the German Green Party', *Environmental Politics*, vol. 2, no. 3, Autumn 1993, pp. 379–404.

Porritt, Jonathon (1997) 'Environmental Politics: The Old and the New', in Jacobs 1997a, pp. 47–73.

Princen, Thomas and Finger, Matthias (1994) *Environmental NGOs in World Politics: Linking the Local and the Global*, London and New York: Routledge.

Prittwitz, Volker v. (ed.) (1993a) *Umweltpolitik als Modernisierungsprozeß. Politikwissenschaftliche Umwelt-forschung und -lehre in der Bundesrepublik*, Opladen: Leske and Budrich.

Prittwitz, Volker v. (1993b) 'Reflexive Modernisierung und öffentliches Handeln', in Prittwitz 1993a, pp. 31–49.

Raschke, Joachim (1993) *Die Grünen. Wie sie wurden, was sie sind*, Cologne: bund.

Raschke, Joachim (1996) 'Versauern in der Nische', *Der Spiegel*, 38 1996, p. 41–3.

Raschke, Joachim (1999) 'Machtwechsel und soziale Bewegungen', in Klein *et al.* 1999, pp. 64–88.

Rawcliffe, Peter (1998) *Environmental Pressure Groups in Transition*, Manchester: Manchester University Press.

Redclift, Michael and Benton, Ted (eds.) (1994) *Social Theory and the Global Environment*, London and New York: Routledge.

Redclift, Michael and Woodgate, Graham (eds.) (1997) *The International Handbook of Environmental Sociology*, Cheltenham and Northampton, MA, USA: Edward Elgar.

Reitan, Marit (1998) 'Ecological Modernisation and *Realpolitik*: Ideas, Interests and Institutions', *Environmental Politics*, vol. 7, no. 2, pp. 1–26.

Richardson, Dick and Rootes, Chris (1995) *The Green Challenge. The Development of Green Parties in Europe*, London and New York: Routledge.

Riordan, Colin (ed.) (1997) *Green Thought in German Culture*, University of Wales Press.

Robert, Rüdiger (1993) 'Modernisierung der Demokratie. Umweltschutz und Grundgesetz', in Prittwitz 1993, pp. 93–101.

Robertson, George, Mash, Melinda, Tickner, Lisa, Bird, Jon, Curtis, Barry and Putnam, Tim (eds.) (1996) *Future Natural: Nature, Sience, Culture*, London and New York: Routledge.

Rootes, Christopher (1997) 'Environmental Movements and Green Parties in Western and Eastern Europe', in Redclift and Woodgate 1997, pp. 319–47.

Rootes, Christopher (ed.) (1999) *Environmental Movements: Local, National and Global*, special issue of *Environmental Politics*, vol. 8, no. 1.

Rose, Nikolas (1996) *Inventing our Selves: Psychology, Power and Personhood*, Cambridge: Cambridge University Press.

Roth, Roland (1994) *Demokratie von Unten. Neue Soziale Bewegungen auf dem Wege zur politischen Institution*, Cologne: Bund.

Roth, Roland (1999) 'Neue soziale Bewegungen und liberale Demokratie. Herausforderungen, Innovationen und paradoxe Konsequenzen', in Klein *et al.* 1999, pp. 47–63.

Rowell, Andrew (1996) Green Backlash. Global Subversion of the Environmental Movement, London and New York: Routledge.

Rubington, E. and Weinberg, M. (eds.) (1981) *The Study of Social Problems*, New York: Oxford University Press.

Rucht, Dieter (1989) 'Environmental Movement Organizations in West Germany and France: Structures and Interorganizational Relations', in Klandermans 1989, pp. 61–94.

Rucht, Dieter and Roth, Roland (1992) 'Über den Wolken . . .', *Forschungsjournal Neue Soziale Bewegungen*, no. 2, pp. 22–33.

Rucht, Dieter, Blattert, Barbara and Rink, Dieter (1997) *Soziale Bewegungen auf dem Weg zur Institutionalisierung. Zum Strukturwandel alternativer Gruppen in beiden Teilen Deutschlands*, Frankfurt: Campus.

Rutherford, Paul (1999) 'Ecological Modernization and Environmental Risk', in Darier 1999, pp. 95–118.

Sachs, Wolfgang (1997) 'Sustainable Development. Zur politischen Anatomie eines internationalen Leitbilds', in Brand (ed.) 1997, pp. 93–110.

Saward, Michael (1993) 'Green Democracy?', in Dobson/Lucardie 1993, pp. 63–80.

Scharf, Thomas (1994) *The German Greens: Challenging the Consensus*, Oxford: Berg.

Schulze, Gerhard (1993) *Die Erlebnisgesellschaft. Kultursoziologie der Gegenwart*, Frankfurt: Campus.

Shepard, Paul (1995) 'Virtually Hunting Reality in the Forests of Simulacra', in Soulé and Lease 1995, pp. 17–29.

Simonis, Udo E. (ed.) (1988) *Präventive Umweltpolitik*, Frankfurt: Campus.

Soulé, Michael E. (1995) 'The Social Siege of Nature', in Soulé and Lease 1995, pp. 137–70.

Soulé, Michael E. and Lease, G. (eds.) (1995) *Reinventing Nature? Responses to Postmodern Deconstrucionism*, Washington, DD and Covelo, CA: Island Press.

Spaargaren, Gert (1996) 'Ecological Modernization Theory and the changing discourse on Environment and Modernity', unpubl. paper presented at the Euroconference on 'Environment and Innovation', Vienna, Oct. 23–6, 1996.

Spaargaren, Gert (1997) *The Ecological Modernization of Production and Consumption: Essays in Environmental Sociology*, Wageningen, NL: Wageningen Agricultural University (dissertation).

Taylor, Charles (1989) *Sources of the Self: The Making of Modern Identity*, Cambridge: Cambridge University Press.

Weale, Albert (1992) *The New Politics of Pollution*, Manchester: Manchester University Press.

Weidner, Helmut and Jänicke, Martin (1998) 'Vom Aufstieg und Niedergang eines Vorreiters. Eine umweltpolitische Bilanz der Ära Kohl', in Wever 1998, pp. 201–28.

Weizsäcker, Ernst Ulrich v. (1994) *Earth Politics*, London and New Jersey: Zed Books.

Weizsäcker, Ernst Ulrich v. (1999) *Das Jahrhundert der Umwelt. Vision: Öko-effizient leben und arbeiten*, Frankfurt and New York: Campus.

Wewer, Göttrik (ed.) (1998) *Bilanz der Ära Kohl*, Opladen: Leske and Budrich.

Wellmer, Albrecht (1985) *Zur Dialektik von Moderne und Postmoderne. Vernunftkritik nach Adorno*, Frankfurt: Suhrkamp.

Welsch, Wolfgang (1987) *Unsere postmoderne Moderne*, Weinheim: VCH, Acta Humaniora.

Welsh, Ian (1999) 'New Social Movements Yesterday, Today and Tomorrow', review article in *Anarchist Studies*, vol. 7, no. 3, pp. 75–81.

Wiesenthal, Helmut (1993) *Realism in Green Politics: Social Movements and Ecological Reform in Germany*, ed. John Ferris, Mancheser: Manchester University Press.

Worster, Donald (1995) 'Nature and the Disorder of History', in Soulé and Lease 1995, pp. 65–85.

Yearley, Steven (1991) *The Green Case: A Sociology of Environmental Issues, Arguments and Politics*, London: Harper Collins.

Young, Jock (1999) *The Exclusive Society*, London, Thousand Oaks, CA and New Delhi: Sage.

Young, John (1990) *Post Environmentalism*, London: Belhaven Press.

Zilleßen, Horst (1993) 'Die Modernisierung der Demokratie im Zeichen der Umweltproblematik', in Prittwitz 1993, pp. 81–91.

Index